HARRY HOOPER

Sport and Society

Series Editors
Benjamin G. Rader
Randy Roberts

*A list of books in the series
appears at the end of this volume.*

HARRY HOOPER

An American Baseball Life

Paul J. Zingg

UNIVERSITY OF ILLINOIS PRESS
Urbana and Chicago

First paperback edition, 2004
© 1993 by the Board of Trustees
of the University of Illinois
All rights reserved
Manufactured in the United States of America
P 5 4 3 2 1

∞ This book is printed on acid-free paper.

The title page photograph appears courtesy of Bob Wood.

The Library of Congress has cataloged the hardcover edition as follows:
Zingg, Paul J., 1947–
Harry Hooper : an American baseball life / Paul J. Zingg.
p.   cm. – (Sport and society)
Includes bibliographical references (p.) and index.
ISBN 0-252-02006-5 (alk. paper)
1. Hooper, Harry. 2. Baseball players–United States–Biography.
I. Title. II. Series.
GV 865.H58Z56   1993
796.323'.092–dc20   92-33878
[B]

Paperback ISBN 0-252-07170-0

To Harry, John, and Marie

Contents

Illustrations follow pages 106 and 156

Acknowledgments

As a longtime fan of the Boston Red Sox, I initially linked Harry Hooper with the club's rich history before the famine—the triumphant years of Tris Speaker, Bill Carrigan, Larry Gardner, Carl Mays, Duffy Lewis, Smoky Joe Wood and Babe Ruth, when the team won four World Series from 1912 to 1918. As the followers of the Red Sox know so well, the championship won in the final throes of the First World War seventy-five years ago was the last time Boston prevailed in the Fall Classic. The years of agony and near glory since have been attributed to everything from the curse of the Bambino to the unrepentant sins of the Puritans. They have been chronicled in the prose of Roger Angell, Thomas Boswell, Peter Gammons, Bart Giamatti, David Halberstam, Dan Riley, John Updike, George Will, and a host of others who have perpetuated a Red Sox literary tradition—a virtual subgenre of American baseball writing. I owe all of these authors an appreciation for noting something significant and transcendent in the play of men at a park in the Fens.

I owe the choice of Hooper as the biographical subject through whom I would examine the rising role and respectability of baseball in American society to more intimate influences and fortuitous circumstances. Soon after my arrival at Saint Mary's College as dean of the School of Liberal Arts in the summer of 1986, I wandered out to the varsity ball field to watch a game between two youth league teams. At the entrance to the field was a granite rock to which was attached a bronze plaque. It read:

> Dedicated to Harry B. Hooper, Class of 1907, the first Saint Mary's graduate to be elected to the National Baseball Hall of Fame at Cooperstown, New York.

> A member of the Saint Mary's Phoenix team of 1905–1907, Harry Hooper starred for twelve years with the Boston Red Sox and played a total of seventeen years in the American League.

A fine student-athlete, a defensive giant and one of the greatest lead-off hitters of all time, his professional and personal career stands exemplary for players of all ages.

Although the project that would become this book was not yet formulated in my mind, Hooper's existence was. There was nothing inevitable in the two coming together (not even words written in stone), but, as I explain in the introduction that follows, the fruitful exploration of Hooper's life with his three children made the linkage irresistible. The dedication of this book to them underscores the depth of my gratitude for their kindness and openness.

Saint Mary's College provided more than just a reference point for Hooper. Grants from the Faculty Development Fund and the alumni helped meet my research and travel expenses. Most important, though, were the advice and encouragement of my colleagues in the history department and throughout the college who read the manuscript at various stages and helped shape it. I particularly wish to thank Chester Aaron, Glenna Breslin, Ben Frankel, Carl Guarneri, Bob Hass, Brother Ron Isetti, Kathy Roper, and Mike Russo for their kind attention to my scholarship and insistence that I escape the dean's office enough to pursue it. With respect to the latter, no one has been more important than my administrative assistant, Nobi Stienecker. Whether protecting my time, preparing the manuscript (a grateful nod in this respect to Joanarden Clark as well), or keeping distractions to a minimum, Nobi has been an indispensable partner throughout the duration of this project. *Watakushi no yujin, kokorokara kansha itashimasu.*

Beyond Saint Mary's there are several folks who deserve special thanks for their assistance and support. Bill Deane and Tom Heitz of the National Baseball Library made my work in Cooperstown, as they have for so many others, the most enjoyable of any archival research; Jack Moore, Carl Prince, Benjamin Rader, Bob Wood and, especially, Larry Ritter read drafts of the manuscript and provided useful suggestions and timely encouragement; Betsy Reed took me to my first game at Fenway and actually knew who Harry Hooper was before I started writing about him; the UCGC provided escape to another kind of ballpark; Benjamin demonstrated some of Harry's catching ability, and Belle stayed true as his biggest fan. My own is Candace, who secretly likes baseball, although she can't understand why I remain faithful to the Giants and the Red Sox. Like the pilgrims and believers she writes about in her own books, it must be the required penance of unrequited desire.

Introduction

HARRY BARTHOLOMEW HOOPER
Boston A.L. 1909–1920
Chicago A.L. 1921–1925

Leadoff hitter and right fielder of 1912–15–16–18 World Champion
Red Sox. Noted for speed and strong arm. Collected 2,466 hits for .281
career average. Had 3,981 put outs and 344 assists. Lifetime fielding
average .966.
                —Baseball Hall of Fame plaque, Cooperstown, N.Y.

It's very hard to explain the feelings, my feelings, to be on this stand
today. It's the culmination of many years of dreams and hopes, often
very faint.
                —Harry Hooper, August 9, 1971

More than any other sport, baseball measures the performances of
its players and teams in statistics. Their seemingly infinite variety
and numbing complexity suggest that the game can be understood in
terms of complicated equations and comparative calculations. Indeed, some numbers are woven into the very fabric of baseball's
history: 56, .406, 755, and 511—Joe DiMaggio's consecutive game
hitting streak, Ted Williams's batting average in 1941, Hank Aaron's
lifetime home run total, and Cy Young's career wins, for example,
are benchmarks of the game, as essential to its appreciation as the
Green Monster in Fenway, the ivy in Wrigley, or a Nolan Ryan fastball. The raised bronze inscriptions on the plaques of the inductees
into baseball's Hall of Fame celebrate the numbers and compel us to
consider their significance. Harry Hooper's plaque is no exception.

At first glance, however, his seventeen-year career seems more
noted for endurance than outstanding performance. Although his
hits and the 8,785 at bats in which they occurred place him sixty-
seventh and forty-ninth, respectively, on the all-time lists in these
categories, he does not rank particularly high in many of the glam-

our areas for hitters. He falls well short of the top one hundred in batting average, runs batted in, and home runs. He fares better in certain categories, triples (160) and walks (1,136), for example, where his output places him thirty-ninth and thirty-seventh, respectively, among the all-time leaders. But on these record lists, like the others above, more than a third of the players who have better numbers than he have not enjoyed the kind of day Harry did on August 9, 1971. For here, in the postcard village of Cooperstown on the southern edge of New York State's Otsego Lake, the eighty-three-year-old Hooper acknowledged his enshrinement in the Baseball Hall of Fame among 103 other men as the best his sporting profession has ever seen.

What accounts for Hooper's presence on the platform with his fellow inductees Chick Hafey, Rube Marquard, and Satchel Paige?[1] A closer look at the statistical record provides some clues. When he retired after the 1925 season, Hooper held every major fielding record for an American League right fielder, including most games (2,153), putouts (3,718), assists (322), double plays (79), and total chances (4,180). Two of his league records—assists and double plays—have never been equaled and the latter still stands as the all-time Major League mark. It is clear that Hooper more than held his own with Tris Speaker and Duffy Lewis, his Boston teammates for six years, in setting "the standard by which great fielding outfields are judged."[2]

Fielding alone, however, or even predominantly, has never warranted an invitation to Cooperstown. If Hooper is more than an "idiosyncratic selection of the Hall of Fame," there must be something more to the record.[3] His plaque provides further evidence of his honored status in referring to baseball's most competitive showcase, the World Series, where he appeared four times. His performance in these championships, all won by his Red Sox teams, particularly underscored the strength of his skills and the quality of his play. Harry still holds both single game and entire Series assists records for a right fielder. Only one error mars an otherwise perfect fielding performance in twenty-four World Series games. Moreover, his lifetime batting and slugging averages in World Series competition, .293 and .435, respectively, include two home runs in a five-game Series, a record that stood for fifty-four years until Donn Clendenon hit three for the New York Mets in 1969, and a thirteen-game consecutive hitting streak set in 1918, not surpassed until 1957 by Hank Bauer of the Yankees.

The numbers, no matter how impressive, only suggest the story behind them. That his hitting in the World Series was significantly stronger than his regular season averages intimated as much about his play under pressure as his captaincy of the last two Boston championship teams inferred the effectiveness of his leadership. The dimensions of his fame are revealed somewhat further in the observations of his contemporaries. Walter Johnson, the pitcher with the most wins in the history of the American League and against whom Hooper batted over .300 lifetime, praised Harry as "the toughest of them all in a pinch."[4] Both John McGraw and Babe Ruth echoed this assessment in placing Hooper in right field on their all-time all-star teams.[5] McGraw, in particular, undoubtedly remembered how Harry batted .357 against his ace, Christy Mathewson, in the 1912 Series.

Johnson, McGraw, Ruth, Mathewson. The list of the greats from Hooper's era with and against whom he played is a who's who of the game—Grover Cleveland Alexander, Home Run Baker, Chief Bender, Frank Chance, Ty Cobb, Eddie Collins, Stan Coveleski, Sam Crawford, Red Faber, Elmer Flick, Harry Heilmann, Waite Hoyt, Joe Jackson, Napoleon Lajoie, Herb Pennock, Eddie Plank, Sam Rice, Eppa Rixey, Joe Sewell, George Sisler, Tris Speaker, Casey Stengel, Rube Waddell, Ed Walsh, Smoky Joe Wood, Cy Young. Similarly, the period 1909–25 witnessed events both on and off the Major League playing fields that forever affected the conduct and character of the game—the Black Sox scandal of 1919, the transition from the "scientific" strategy of the "dead ball" age to the run-scoring frenzy of the "lively ball" era, the failure of the Federal League, the death of Ray Chapman on a pitched ball by Carl Mays, the rising power of the owners, and everywhere, in the construction of new ballparks, the attention of the sporting press and the patronage of the public, signs that baseball truly was the national game and that its players had assumed a special place in the cultural life of the country.

That Harry Hooper played baseball with these men, in these times of change and controversy, seems at first, like his records, little more than an interesting, if not noteworthy, happenstance of a professional sporting career. The histories of baseball in the early twentieth century, including the biographies of Cobb, Ruth, and McGraw, only mention Hooper in passing, if at all.[6] He stands on the periphery—Speaker's junior partner in the Boston outfield, a soft-spoken advocate for playing Ruth on days when he did not pitch, a respected veteran picked up by Chicago after the banishment of the Black Sox, a rare collegian in the Major Leagues, an occasional hero in a World Series game, a spokesman for the players in an abortive strike threat.

Yet there is something odd here. Barely acknowledged, rarely celebrated, Hooper is constantly on the scene. Like his performance on the field, the beat of his presence is steady, solid, and studied. Although his play at times achieved the spectacular, he eschewed flamboyance for simplicity, exaggeration for modesty. Possessing neither the crafted appeal of Mathewson nor the raw excitement of Ruth, Hooper practiced his profession quietly, skillfully, and confidently. More Everyman than Superman, he is a mirror of the game and its human touches in ways that his myth-encrusted contemporaries can never be.

Several aspects of Hooper's reflections on the game and his times particularly mark their value. More than a circumstantial presence, he was both an active participant in many of the key events that shaped Major League baseball in his era and an agent to the rising role and respectability of the game in American society. His leadership of his Boston teams, for example, manifested itself in strategic decisions affecting the play of the outfield, the use of Ruth, the alignment of fielders, and the establishment of the batting order. Yet, in more profound ways, his approach to his profession, both physically and mentally, influenced and impressed teammates and rival ballplayers alike and earned him deep respect among fans, the sporting press, and management. Moreover, as a college graduate and a Californian with rural roots, Hooper ran counter to the urban, eastern origins and illiterate reputations of the Major Leaguers of his era but suggested the broadened and more reputable social base upon which the game was beginning to rely for its players.[7]

Underscoring the strength of Hooper's representation as both mirror and nexus is his accessibility. Although he has his admirers, some, like Ellery Clark and Donald Honig, who have showered him with praise in their team histories of the Red Sox, he has not been burdened with a fictionalized persona.[8] With neither press agency nor hagiographic fantasy playing a part in shaping his reputation, his is a remarkably open book to examine. There are no marble images to polish or patch, only the fundamental questions of whether his is a life worth telling and if the evidence exists to tell it.

When I first asked these questions, I was considering a study on the relationship between collegiate and professional baseball in the late nineteenth and early twentieth centuries. I was interested in the place and role of both levels of the game in American society and particularly intrigued with the motivations of collegiate ballplayers to explore the professional route, especially at a time when the respectability of the professional game was very much in doubt. On a trip to the National Baseball Library in Cooperstown in June 1988, I began to draw up a short list of former collegians who had enjoyed successful Major League careers as possible subjects for this study. The list included Dave Fultz, Christy Mathewson, Eddie Plank, Ed Reulbach, John Montgomery Ward, and Harry Hooper.

Several developments crystallized my focus on Hooper. Although I knew at the time that Hooper was an alumnus of Saint Mary's College of California, where I served as dean of the School of Liberal Arts, I had very little knowledge about the rich athletic history of the college or Hooper's life beyond *The Baseball Encyclopedia*. The archives at Saint Mary's helped with the former, the files at Cooperstown with the latter. The key to the project, however, was a single line in a 1971 newspaper clipping about Harry Hooper Day at Saint Mary's that referred to his children. It reported that his two sons, Harry, Jr., and John, were also alumni of the college and that they had played a major role in assembling the data to build the case for their father's consideration for the Hall of Fame. The alumni directory of the college provided their addresses, and I immediately wrote to introduce myself and my interest in their father.

I could not have imagined the kindness of their reception or the extent of their assistance. I contacted Harry, Jr., first, for he lived only a two-hour drive away in Capitola, California. A retired army colonel, the elder Hooper son lived in a house on a cliff overlooking the Pacific within sight of his father's home for over forty years. During the course of an afternoon's visit, he shared his reminiscences and several scrapbooks of clippings and photographs with me and played an old reel-to-reel tape recording of his father's induction speech into the Hall of Fame. We were joined later in the day by his older sister, Marie, who had driven down from Burlingame. As I was leaving, Harry particularly urged me to visit his brother in Baytown, Texas. "After all," he said, "John's really the one you need to see."

I paid my first visit to John in September 1989. His home in this Houston suburb just east of the San Jacinto River was only a few miles from the great complex of oil refineries where he had worked as an engineer for forty years before his recent retirement. Initially, our conversation was very much like that which I had had with his brother. It covered the same ground and even focused on the same materials, copies of which John had. I was somewhat disappointed, for Harry had led me to believe that John's holdings were both more extensive and valuable than his own. All I had seen so far, though, were clippings of old interviews of his father about the time of his induction into the Hall of Fame and some of the papers that John had assembled to promote Harry's selection. It was becoming clear to me that John saw my interest in his father as focused only on his playing record and that he himself had not given much thought to any larger meanings of Harry's baseball life and times. While I was leafing through the pages of one of his scrapbooks, though, John reached to the top shelf of a bookcase in his study and retrieved a small and obviously old and worn book. "Here," he offered casually, "perhaps this will be of some interest to you." It was his father's diary of his 1909 rookie season in the Major Leagues.

"Left Capitola on the 11:20 A.M. train," read the first entry for Saturday, February 27, 1909. Twenty-one-year-old Harry Hooper had started his trip to join the Boston Red Sox for spring training in Hot Springs, Arkansas. He was also beginning the chronicle of his career, his words bringing to life the distant world of his profession. Hal Chase and Tris Speaker, Ty Cobb and Jake Stahl, yannigans and cardigans, billiards and checkers, Saturday burlesque and Sunday Mass, slumps and streaks. "President Taft sees game," he noted for Monday, April 19. "Doc Powers who took sick at the finish of the opening game died today. We sent $25 for a wreath," he reported on April 26. "Got hit off Johnson which scored winning run," he recorded his first game-winning RBI against the great Washington pitcher on June 28.

I turned to John and asked, somewhat hesitantly, "Do you have anything more like this? Letters, maybe, or other writings of your father's?"

It was all the cue he needed. From a trunk he retrieved several packets of letters. A few contained the rich and intimate correspondence between his father and mother during the early years of their marriage and in the latter part of Harry's Major League career. Another bundle of letters offered the collected exchanges between John and his father when John briefly pursued a professional baseball career of his own in the late 1940s. An entire scrapbook held scores of letters and cards to Harry from a galaxy of the game's stars. Many were congratulatory wishes upon his election to the Hall of Fame, but others revealed the company Harry had kept and the respect he had earned. I was particularly struck by a letter to Harry from Babe Ruth, written only weeks before the Babe's death and thanking Harry for inquiring about his health.

The more I expressed my delight in what I was seeing, the more John delivered. I felt like Charlie in Willy Wonka's chocolate factory, each revelation more tantalizing than the one before, each appreciative comment of my own matched with another delicious serving from the Hooper archive. John kept scurrying around the room, producing items from every drawer and corner. Tape recordings of Harry reminiscing about his career, some of them conversations with old friends and teammates like Larry Gardner. A series of first-person written narratives, six by Harry and one by his father, Joseph, on the family's early history in California and Harry's youth. World Series programs, contracts, telegrams, even Harry's grammar school report card and diploma.

Something wonderful was happening. With each new item that John brought to my attention, I developed a deeper appreciation for the value of the collection and the importance of his father. The diary, the letters, and the narratives underscored Harry's role not merely as a participant in the events of his era but as a chronicler of them. Candid, ingenuous, and fresh, Harry's words reflected thoughtful observation and engaged perspective.

My enthusiasm for these materials affected John as well. He understood more clearly the nature of my interest in his father and appreciated more profoundly the value of his efforts to preserve the family records. For not only do the Hooper papers tell Harry's story and constitute a unique source, they also provide a true rendition of the American dream. The promise of that dream, its pull on his father, is where Harry's story begins.

There are few, if any, elements of the American experience more compelling and fundamental than the notion of the American dream. Yet, like the attempt to identify the national character, with which it is inseparably linked, those who seek to define the dream, no less than those who chase it, often resemble the blind man in a dark room looking for a black cat that is not necessarily there.[9] Its elusiveness, however, has neither dampened the quest nor dimmed its appeal. After the Civil War, no place in the United States offered greater prospect of the dream fulfilled than California, the "final frontier of geography and of expectation."[10]

The passage to California of Hooper's immigrant parents held all the drama of so many other tens of thousands who staked their futures on promises of fulfillment and renewal. They found in the trains that took them across the country a metaphor for their gamble. Connecting them to their past, yet carrying them beyond it, the rails beckoned hopes even as they provided retreat. For Joe Hooper and Mary Keller, the trip was strictly one way—west—but their route was already an agent of commerce and culture by the time they arrived in California in 1876 and 1878, respectively. Baseball, too, had come their way before in the leisure experiences of the transplanted Forty-niners and the triumphant transcontinental tour of the Cincinnati Red Stockings in 1869. For the next eighty years, the railroad linked the principal business sites of the ballplaying professionals until the lure of the West once again proved irresistible to new fortune seekers. Only then, with Major League franchises established on both sides of the continent, did the railroad give way to a faster form of transportation.

Both Harry's parents and his future profession struggled to establish themselves in the 1880s and 1890s. Like a single set of tracks running parallel, seeming only to intersect in the distance, they contended in their separate ways with the natural forces of their respective environments. Chapters 1 and 2 explore these and the formative contexts they provided for Harry's life and career. The family farms of his childhood in the Santa Clara and San Joaquin valleys introduced him to hard work, underscored his respect for it, and influenced the modest perspective he would have about his later achievements in a world of professional play. Although too young to understand the exact effects that weather, soil quality, and market conditions had on the operations of the farm, he learned that a narrow margin existed between success and failure and that the difference often depended upon the thoroughness of preparation for the recurring seasons. That thin differential also characterized the business of baseball. Franchises—indeed, whole leagues—formed and fell amid owner-player disputes, ruthless competitive practices, rising operational costs, and wavering patronage. However, there was no denying the appeal of the game. As Harry approached adolescence, the separate lines of his early life and baseball began to converge.

Accorded the opportunity to pursue his education beyond a few grade school years, Harry joined the children of other first-generation immigrants in widening the dimensions of their parents' hopes. Chapter 3 examines the significant developments affecting American higher education in the last quarter of the nineteenth century that provided access for young Hooper and others like him. Serving different student groups in different ways, the collegiate experience particularly offered Hooper and his classmates at Saint Mary's middle-class respectability and mobility. Harry found these rewards stemming from success both in the classroom and on the playing field. The Christian Brothers who ran Saint Mary's appreciated the value of athletics in the development of the whole person and encouraged Harry's enjoyment of baseball. His outstanding play for the college's championship team in 1907 influenced his immediate postbaccalaureate plans. Seeking to put his degree in civil engineering to work, yet also wishing to continue to play ball, Harry managed to do both in Sacramento. He accepted a surveyor's position with the Western Pacific Railroad and also signed a contract to play on weekends and holidays for the local entry in the California League. The arrangement moved him a step closer to a complete merger of his sporting passion and career direction. That he would even consider this possibility reflected the extent of his talents and the appeal of the professional arena.

Tracks and hopes had brought his parents to California thirty years earlier. In 1909 they carried Harry Hooper to a situation and setting as uncertain and unfamiliar as anything they had encountered. Relying largely on his diary, chapter 4 covers Harry's initial season in the Major Leagues. From Majestic Park in Hot Springs, Arkansas, to the Huntington Avenue Grounds in Boston, from rookie to regular, from a porkpie hat and cardboard grip to a felt fedora and leather luggage, Hooper provides a vivid account of his first year with the Red Sox. No less than his own transition during the season, the club revamped its roster, displacing the fading veterans of recent years with talented newcomers. Two of these players, the Texan Tris Speaker and a hard-throwing right-hander two years younger than he, Joe Wood, particularly impressed Harry. They also impressed the league as Boston vaulted to third place in the standings for its strongest finish and best record since 1904. Both Hooper and the Red Sox confidently looked to the future.

The emergence of the Red Sox as the most successful team in the American League over the next decade and the development of Hooper as his circuit's premier right fielder and leadoff hitter are the central themes of chapter 5. Boston capped its steady move to the top of the standings with a World Series triumph over the New York Giants in 1912. The eight-game championship (necessitated by a tie in game 2) is still regarded by some as the greatest in the history of the Series. McGraw, Mathewson, Marquard, Merkle, and Meyers of the Giants against the less alliterative but no less talented Boston stars Stahl, Wood, Bedient, Speaker, and Hooper. Having batted .311 during the 1912 regular season, Harry enhanced the solid reputation he was beginning to develop with an outstanding Series. Winning games with his hitting, saving them with his fielding, Hooper earned accolades from both benches and the sporting press. His clutch play in this and several Series to come made the most lasting impression among his admirers.

Surely Harry's most ardent fan was Esther Henchy, his nineteen-year-old Capitola sweetheart, whom he married in November 1912. The correspondence between them, especially during their first year of marriage, provides an intimate portrait of the life of a Major Leaguer away from the ballpark. Chapter 6 builds on their letters to explore such topics as the place and role of a baseball wife, the trials of the season's separations, and the rising respectability of the game itself in the years just before the outbreak of the First World War. The responsibilities of Hooper's new marital status added another dimension to his maturation as a ballplayer. The teammates with whom he associated, the care he took to stay in shape, and the manner with which he conducted himself reflected his personal preferences and habits as much as they signaled the nascence of a positive professional image for his occupation. The arrival of a new owner in Boston, the challenge of the Federal League, and the birth of his first child complicated Hooper's life in 1914. The year also marked the midpoint of his career with the Red Sox and the eve of a period of sustained crisis for the Major Leagues.

Hooper considered the 1915 Red Sox to be the best team on which he had played. It is a view that is hard to dispute. Surviving the attempted raids of the Federals on their roster, the Red Sox fielded a veteran cast, bolstered by a young left-hander named Babe Ruth, and drove to the pennant and a successful World Series date with the Philadelphia Phils. Chapter 7 assesses Hooper's role on the club and reputation in the league at this stage of his career. His defensive prowess and "scientific" work at bat and on the base paths characterized the way Major League ball continued to be played in this era. Success accompanied those teams that best executed the established formula and none did it better than Harry's teams of the teens.

Hooper's importance to the Red Sox increased significantly with the departure of Speaker and Wood before the 1916 season. Appointed team captain, he proved equal to the task and led Boston to a second consecutive pennant and World Series triumph. Yet, as chapters 8 and 9 examine, the aftermath of the Federal League challenge and the raging storm of the European war threatened player interests and the fragile stability of the Major Leagues. The uncertainties of these matters were particularly felt during 1918. The draft, a curtailed regular season, reduced attendance, and questions about the place of baseball in a nation at war created the most serious crises for the game since the 1903 National Agreement. The World Series of 1918, less a celebration than an awkward finale to a troubled season, reflected all of these problems. In his fourth Series appearance—and Boston's last triumph in the Fall Classic—Harry failed to achieve the heroic standards of play he had set in the previous championships. Nevertheless, as the principal spokesman for the players in a threatened strike midway through the Series, he marked his presence in a way that continued to strengthen his reputation as a skilled and respected professional. Like his role earlier in the season in converting Ruth to an everyday player in the Boston lineup, Hooper's mediation between the players and commissioners reflected common sense and keen judgment.

As the nation struggled to return to normalcy after the Great War, Major League baseball anticipated its most successful season in years. Released from military service, players rejoined their former teams and rosters strengthened significantly. The pennant races promised to be tight and exciting. Disillusioned with the widespread social and political unrest that accompanied a postwar economic recession, seeking relief from their troubles and reassurance in familiar rituals, fans filled the ballparks once again in record numbers. The game failed the public trust, however, in two dramatic ways— the "Black Sox" threw the 1919 World Series and Boston sold Babe Ruth to the New York Yankees. Both events directly affected the shape of Harry Hooper's remaining Major League career. As chapter 10 relates, Ruth's departure deepened Hooper's disgust with the way his club was being run. He considered retirement or a change of uniform. Wooed by Chicago's Charlie Comiskey, who was anxious to rebuild his team with a clean cast, Harry opted to stay in the Majors a while longer. Enjoying some of the best individual years of his career, although the White Sox never finished higher than fifth place while he was with them, Hooper played right field for Chicago long enough—five years—and well enough– .302 batting average—to earn a spot on the team's all-time all-star team in a 1969 poll.[11]

Closing his Major League career after the 1925 season, Hooper found the pull of the game strong enough not to step away from it completely. He became the player-manager of the San Francisco Mission Bells of the Pacific Coast League for one season in 1927 and then, like his former teammates Joe Wood, Larry Gardner, and Stuffy McInnis, gravitated to the collegiate ranks, where he coached the Princeton University baseball team for two years in 1931–32. These positions and other aspects of his life after "the show" are treated in the epilogue. Like his fellow former ballplayers, Harry missed the excitement and reassuring routine of his previous professional arena. Yet, unlike many of them, he had prepared for his retirement from the game. The operations of a small real estate agency and some agricultural interests promised a modest livelihood for him and Esther. Persuaded by his wife to accept an appointment as Capitola's postmaster in 1933, though, Harry spent twenty-four years in his second career before retirement at age seventy in 1957.

Reminiscing about his life and baseball career in his induction ceremony remarks at Cooperstown fourteen years later, Hooper remembered his parents' sacrifice in sending him to Saint Mary's College. If that had not happened, Harry explained, "I'd have turned out to be a dry farmer over in the San Joaquin Valley and nobody would ever have heard of me." Perhaps. We do know, though, what the happy consequences of his parents' decision were for Harry and the game he loved. Attracted to baseball for its fundamental appeal as a sporting activity, test of skill, and matter of fun, he played a significant role in elevating the status of professional ballplayers and underscoring the respectability and legitimacy of their career path. The character and conduct of his play earned him the game's highest honor. If Harry had a hard time explaining his feelings at his induction ceremony, it was the awkward circumstance of a modest man acknowledging the just reward of his deeds. The uncommon moment recognized a worthy career and affirmed a place for Everyman within the pantheon.

1

Passage to California

I got to thank most of all my parents, who were poor.
—Harry Hooper, August 9, 1971

The first time Joe Hooper left home he did not roam very far or remain away very long.[1] It was the fall of 1865 and the remote northern shore of Prince Edward Island offered few prospects for a fourteen-year-old on his own. His venture took him only ten miles and lasted less than a year. But it set him on a course for the distant coast of another land where his own son would begin the odyssey of his lifetime at almost the same age.

Born the fourth child, and second son, of William Hooper and his Portuguese wife, Louisa, Joe saw seven more brothers and sisters after him swell the family's size and stretch its modest resources. The family properties in Morell, overlooking the white sand dunes of St. Peter's Bay, consisted of a small inn and tannery and adjacent fields which yielded their fair share of potatoes, berries, and grains, enough to feed Hooper's livestock and provide an occasional surplus for the markets of Charlottetown. But the local market and the trade it represented with the United States, spurred by the Canadian-American reciprocity treaty of 1854 and the demands of the Union army during the Civil War, showed signs of slowing.[2]

If Joe was concerned about his family's economic situation, he was also aware of a wanderlust that characterized the Hooper clan. His father was only eighteen when he left Northleigh Parish in Devonshire, England, in 1842 for the Crown colony of Bermuda. The son of a shoemaker, William found employment in the household of the governor-general of the island. He also found his future wife. Her name as impressive as its bearer, Louisa Maria Esperansa Dorasarie Antone Rosario had arrived at Bermuda aboard the ship of her sea-captain father. She remained on the island, also in the employ of the governor-general, to tutor English in the British consulate at Hamilton while her father embarked on another voyage. Fluent in six languages, widely traveled, fiercely independent, and only nineteen when she and William first met, the beautiful *jovem* had many suitors. Despite her father's concerns that she marry a Catholic, Louisa wed the Methodist William in 1845. Five years later, with three children already in the family and Louisa pregnant with Joseph, the couple sailed for Prince Edward Island and the new opportunities which William was sure awaited. His savings from three years' service in the Queen's Commissariat in Bermuda provided the means for the move and the start in Morell.

The Hoopers did well in their new home and shared in the general prosperity of the island throughout the 1850s. Although the dunes along the northern shore blocked the sea inlets, preventing all but small boats from using them as harbors, William transported his leathers and crops overland in his own stage line to the northern tip of Hillsborough Bay for delivery to the Charlottetown market and to the port village of Souris at Rollo Bay on the island's eastern coast. The commercial aspects of William's tanning and farming brought him to Charlottetown several times a year and increased both his visibility in the community and his interest in colonial politics. In early September 1864 he joined other prominent islanders who had assembled there with delegates from Nova Scotia and New Brunswick to consider a confederation of the Maritime Colonies.

Joseph's decision to strike out on his own reflected family patterns, not political matters. An older sister and brother had already left home and their example influenced his move. In any event, his departure was not without some measure of family approval for his father had arranged an unpaid apprenticeship for the boy with another tanner in St. Peter's Bay. If not a successful adventure, it was an impressionable one. Joe learned that tanning and currying hides was not an occupation he wanted to pursue beyond the term of his apprenticeship. Lighting the tannery's fires in the predawn darkness every day and frequently having to shovel snow out of the shop just to get to the hearths lost its appeal after a few months. Joe was back home in Morell when summer came.

For the next four years, Joe worked the family farm and inn and drove the teams on the Charlottetown-Souris line. As the eldest son at home, he took on greater responsibilities for the family enterprises and their management, especially with his father's growing involvement in colonial economic and political matters. Increasingly, these focused on the possibility of a political union with other provinces of Canada and the potential economic benefits of Canadian

Confederation status for the island. When the British North American Act of 1867 created the new Canadian dominion government, however, Prince Edward Island was not a part of it. The islanders' price for membership, including financial assistance for a railway and the purchase of lands from absentee landowners, was too steep for the other provinces to pay.

P.E.I.'s independent course had dire consequences for the island. It reinforced a sense of political isolation from both the other Maritimes and the new confederation and exposed deep problems with the local economy. The end of the reciprocity agreement with the United States in 1866 had already caused a trade slump, but the failure to gain assistance from the national government for projects deemed necessary for the economic growth of the island shook the confidence and threatened the financial well-being of many who counted on it. Some, like William, had already invested in the construction of an island railway and the project seemed doomed—and their investments lost—unless the dominion government came to the rescue.

An increasing number of islanders, though, had decided that they were not about to wait and see how matters turned out with the dominion government before getting on with their own lives. Beginning in the late 1860s, young men and women in their teens and twenties led an outmigration from Prince Edward Island that would reach epidemic proportions by the end of the century. Rising from thirty-three hundred departures in the 1870s to over eighteen thousand in the 1890s, the latter number representing about 17 percent of the island's population, the P.E.I. emigrants contributed to a mass exodus of nearly half a million people from the Maritime Provinces. Similar conditions throughout the Maritimes prompted the flight – static and outmoded farming and fishing industries unprepared, unorganized, and underfinanced to compete successfully with more modernized market rivals. As the outmigration grew, it undermined the confidence of those who remained and retarded economic development in Atlantic Canada well into the twentieth century.[3]

Now age nineteen and the oldest child still at home, since his sister Mary had left the year before, Joe Hooper decided it was time for him to move on as well. This time he eyed not simply a temporary relocation elsewhere on the island, but a permanent departure from home and Prince Edward itself. On a spring morning in 1870, having sold the only extra shirt he packed with him to a neighbor for three shillings, Joe began his journey with a three-mile walk down

the road to a friend's house. The next day he continued on to Charlottetown, twenty-five miles away.

He found work quickly, an easy task for a young man willing to
bend his back to hard labor. His new job, splitting rails, appealed no
more to Joe than tanning hides. With the help of another family
acquaintance, he accepted an apprenticeship with a butcher. He
stuck with this job for almost a full year before calling it quits. "I left
without saying goodbye," Joe recalled many years later, a succinct
commentary on another career path not chosen. But each job added
a few shillings to his pocket, a few skills to his repertoire. Joe was
slowly acquiring the means, if not the direction, to bid P.E.I. itself
farewell.

In the summer of 1871, Joe set out with Mike Buckley, also late of
the butcher's trade, for Summerside. Located thirty miles west of
Charlottetown on Bedeque Bay, Summerside was the county seat for
Prince County and second only to the provincial capital in size and
importance on the island. Benefiting from its location opposite Shediac on New Brunswick's shore across the Northumberland Strait,
Summerside was the principal port and distribution center for the
western half of the island. For young Hooper, the town's attraction
lay less in its economic characteristics than in its access to the rail-
heads at Shediac through regular steamer service. In short, Summerside was the jumping-off place for the Canadian mainland. After
working for a couple of months caring for livestock, Joe was ready to
jump. With their earnings, Joe and Buckley took the steamer to Shediac and then rode the rails to Moncton, where they switched trains
for Saint John. The pair arrived in the port city on the Bay of Fundy
in September. Joe was only a few months past his twentieth birthday.

With little money left after the trip from P.E.I., Hooper and Buckley immediately looked for work. They found it on a farm at Slocum's
Point, about fifty miles up the Saint John River, where laborers were
needed to bring in the fall harvest. Joe received more than he bar-
gained for in the task—a severe case of dyspepsia. Laid low with
sharp stomach cramps for almost a week, each day costing him
needed wages, Joe concocted his own cure. He took to drinking and
bathing in the waters of the Saint John River. Whether time or the
waters eased his discomfort, Joe was back cutting hay within a few
days. His co-workers marveled at his recovery, teased him about his
daily regimen of a swim in the river, and handed him a nickname—
Salt Water Joe.

But even a healthy Joe Hooper had not left his own farm to work
on someone else's. Soon after his recovery he was ready to move on

again. In November, after the harvest, he and Mike returned to Saint John and landed jobs as stokers for a passenger-carrying steamer line. Through the winter months of 1871–72, the two toiled at yet another physically exhausting job for little pay. This one, though, had an unexpected bonus. It provided transportation and board to new destinations, ever stretching the distance from Prince Edward Island. That distance now transcended national borders when Hooper and Buckley disembarked in Boston, Massachusetts, in early spring.

The city was unlike anything they had seen before. Not only was Boston with its over 250,000 people the most populous place they had ever visited, it manifested a prosperity and expansiveness with which the two Canadians had little familiarity. Boston, like most of the United States outside the war-ravaged South, was prospering in the years after Appomattox. The forces that would enable the United States to become the leading manufacturing nation in the world by the mid-1890s were evident in the commercial, industrial, and agricultural activities of the city and the greater New England area. Factories which had produced the goods to supply the Union armies now equipped a nation whose westward expansion, temporarily slowed during the war years, raced forward. Their output contributed to the fastest growth rate of the country's wealth in its history as the gross national product rose from an average of some $9.1 billion annually in the early 1870s to over $60 billion annually by 1912.[4] Moving from an agricultural nation to an industrial giant, the United States, as reflected in regional centers like Boston, diversified and strengthened its economy while favorable government policies and a generally approving public provided additional supports for economic progress.

Providing labor for the growing economy and a market for its products was a rapidly growing population. From the end of the Civil War to the centennial year of 1876, the nation's population increased nearly one-third, from 35.7 million to 46.1 million.[5] During these years more than 3 million immigrants entered the United States. They were the leading edge of an immigration wave that would bring over 50 million newcomers to American shores during the next half-century. In contrast to the patterns of emigrant settlement before the Civil War, the new arrivals increasingly tended to congregate in the large cities on the eastern seaboard rather than disperse to more rural locations. This was certainly the pattern in Boston, where a large portion of the more than 300,000 Canadians and Newfoundlanders who emigrated in the last quarter of the nineteenth century gravitated to the Hub City itself and to the mill villages and factory towns of New England.[6] By 1890, one-third of Boston's population was foreign born.

Soon after their arrival in Boston, Hooper and Buckley separated. Joe headed south for New Bedford on Buzzards Bay; Mike stopped in North Bridgewater, about halfway between Boston and the south shore of the state. Joe's experience with livestock landed him a job paying fifteen dollars a month to care for the horses of Robert Ashley, a farmer. Ashley had a budding ice business as well, so Joe divided his time between handling horses and hauling ice. He proved adept at both and within a month's time received a salary increase to a dollar a day. For nearly a year, Hooper stuck with the ice business and Ashley's enterprise expanded on the strong back of the young Canadian. Moving ten tons of ice each day, Ashley and Hooper supplied icehouses within a twenty-five-mile radius, which included Brockton to the north, where Joe kept in touch with Buckley. By autumn 1872, Joe's salary was up to two dollars a day, but room and board at five dollars a week left him little to spend and less to save.

Restless for the better livelihood that beckoned him to leave Prince Edward Island, Joe was ready to move on again when spring came. He took a job lasting shoes for Mitchell Campbell, a shoemaker in New Bedford, who paid Joe five and a half cents for each pair he shaped. Molding as many as ninety pairs a day, Hooper doubled his previous salary with Ashley. His efficiency came to the attention of a rival shoemaker in Brockton, who lured Joe away from Campbell's for seven and a half cents per pair. Through the summer of 1873, Joe managed a steady income of about twenty-two dollars a week, hardly a great fortune, but an adequate income for a young man without obligations.

Given his employment pattern since leaving Morell, it is unlikely that Joe would have remained at the last for long. He did not have the chance to decide. After three months in Brockton, the dyspepsia returned, worse than ever. There was no saltwater cure this time. As his savings dwindled with no work and mounting medical bills, Joe paid off his outstanding debts, bought a new suit, swallowed his pride, and purchased a ticket back to P.E.I.

If there had been any doubt in Joe's mind about whether he would remain and work the family lands and businesses after he returned home the first time, there was none now. He intended to stay in Morell with his parents and the three brothers and two sisters who had not yet left home just long enough to recover his health. He was determined to return to the United States when he had the resources to manage it. In the spring he was ready to take on work again. A familiar source of employment offered it—Joe signed on with the railway to build fences for its expanding properties.

Since his brief stint cutting ties three years earlier, the railway's fortunes had improved considerably. It had benefited, in particular, from P.E.I.'s decision finally to join the Canadian Confederation on July 1, 1873. That enabled the dominion government to provide the island with funds for the construction of the railway, a project sorely in need of fresh capital. As chairman of the Board of Railway Appraisers in 1872 and 1873 and a twice-elected member to the House of Assembly for the island, William Hooper played a key role in these developments.

A full year passed before Joe accumulated enough money to leave Morell for the third and last time. Turning responsibilities for management of the family properties over to his twenty-one-year-old brother, Sam, during their father's continuing absences with government matters, Joe sailed to Portland, Maine, just after Christmas 1875. There he visited his sister, Tilly, who had settled in the area with her husband, Phil Hughes, a childhood friend of Joe's. His brother-in-law helped him find work with a logging outfit in New Hampshire and Joe was soon off to the woods.

For the next three months, Joe felled trees in the White Mountains. The grueling work not only taxed his physical strength but tested his mettle in the competitive environment that frequently accompanied manual labor. Loggers generally worked in pairs, and each partner, with the foreman's encouragement, vied to impress the other with his prowess. At 217, Joe's partner outweighed him by about 30 pounds, but backbreaking work was no stranger to Joe and he held his own with the bigger man. Their wages linked to their combined lifts, the Hooper pair made good money during the winter cut. However, more than manly pride motivated Joe's production with the ax. His sights were set on a grander adventure which logger's pay and springtime would bring.

Through Tilly, Joe had kept in touch with his increasingly far-flung family. The two who had wandered the farthest were Mary, the second-oldest sister, now twenty-eight, and brother Bill, two years his senior at twenty-seven. Both had settled in California the year before, from where they wrote Tilly to encourage Joe to join them. Concerned with his wandering ways and unfocused work experiences, Mary suggested that Joe might find employment on her new husband's farm in the Santa Clara Valley south of San Francisco Bay. How much the prospective offer influenced Joe's decision is uncertain, but, no doubt, the firsthand accounts of California's promise he received from Mary and Bill seemed to confirm what he and so many thousands of others had heard about the new El Dorado.

Here was a land "charged with human hope," a place which offered new beginnings, inspired golden dreams, and conjured images of happiness fulfilled.[7] The Santa Clara Valley, the self-proclaimed "Garden of the World," especially seemed to be a place where dreams came true. Described by Bayard Taylor, perhaps the most noted travel writer of the nineteenth century, as one of the three most beautiful valleys in the world and by Chauncey Depew, chairman of the board of the Vanderbilt railway system, as the richest valley in the world, Santa Clara had attracted over twenty-five-thousand settlers by the mid-1870s, making it one of the most populous counties in the state.[8] Promotional literature boasted that the valley offered "Homes for a Million" and that the reality of the American dream fulfilled there was so clearly the case that only the "truth, the whole truth, and nothing but the truth" should be set forth in describing the valley and its attractions.[9] All of this beckoned Salt Water Joe in the spring of 1876, and he eagerly responded.

If California was a place of new beginnings, then 1876 was a time. The nation's centennial year reminded Americans from whence they had come, but more importantly it invited speculation about where they were headed. Evidence of that future abounded, particularly in the formulation of elements that would influence and shape a national culture. In March, Scottish émigré Alexander Graham Bell received the first United States patent for his telephone, magically transforming the way Americans communicated with one another across the miles. Like the telegraph before it and the radio to follow, the telephone put people from all parts of the country in closer contact with one another, reinforcing the same staples of mass culture which pulled them together.

In June a combined force of Sioux and Northern Cheyenne Indians annihilated several troops of the Seventh Cavalry under the command of George Armstrong Custer at the Little Bighorn River in southeastern Montana. It was the last Indian victory in the Great Plains wars and precipitated a swift and vengeful retaliation that subdued the major tribes by the end of the year. Their subjugation removed forever the barrier they posed to settlement and development of the land by non-Indians. The federal government's policies toward the Indians alternately varied between confining them to reservations and forcing their assimilation into the majority white culture. In either case they were the victims of an aggressive expansionism within the country and the instruments—the railroad, new communications technologies, and racial attitudes—which sustained it.

In November the Democrats announced their national political resurgence when the party's presidential nominee, Samuel J. Tilden, outpolled the Republican candidate, Rutherford B. Hayes, by 250,000 popular votes. However, disputed electoral returns from four states cost the Democrats the White House when a special electoral commission awarded all of the contested votes to Hayes. The Democrats made gains in both Houses of Congress, though, and received important concessions from the Republicans in the resolution of the electoral dispute. These ensured their voice in national affairs and reestablished their control of Southern politics. In particular, the electoral compromise officially ended the period of Reconstruction in the South, symbolically signaling the end of the Civil War and announcing a new birth of American nationalism.

Eighteen seventy-six marked the nation's progress in terms of space as well as time. The settlement of the trans-Mississippi West excited and influenced the generation of the centennial era as profoundly as the promise of adventure and opportunity beyond the eastern seaboard and Appalachians had affected Americans a hundred years earlier. In both cases, the attractions of virgin land and new economic and social freedoms pulled men and women to the frontier, helping to define the meaning of the very country they were settling.

The appeal of the West in the American imagination, particularly its depiction as a new Eden, a free and open pastoral paradise, was reinforced through several events in the centennial year. In New York City, Frederick Law Olmsted's crowning achievement of landscape architecture, Central Park, opened. It provided the urban masses with a magnificent green space, an antidote to the concrete canyons and cramped conditions of their daily lives. Mark Twain's *Tom Sawyer*, the major publishing event of 1876, offered a literary escape to the western frontier. His antisentimental portrait of the comic and tragic dimensions of an agrarian society on the verge of transformation appealed to intellectuals and mass audiences alike as he mined the usable past of his own youth to comment on the changes and continuities of the American scene he observed.

The attraction of pastoral images to urban audiences was very much on the mind of a group of businessmen who gathered for a meeting at Manhattan's Grand Central Hotel in February. Called together by William Ambrose Hulbert, a charter stockholder and president of the Chicago White Stockings Club of the National Association of Professional Base Ball Players, the representatives of several eastern and western clubs agreed to establish a new organization for the management of their sport. They called it the National League of Professional Base Ball Clubs.[10] Reflecting the tendencies of big business toward consolidation and control, the group arbitrarily moved to exclude the players on their clubs from any management authority and reconstituted their sport in terms of an owner-labor relationship. Hulbert's coup, in effect the establishment of a closed corporation with the promise of financial gain for the club owners and investors, ushered in a new era for both the game and the business of baseball in its competition for the entertainment dollar and its place in American culture.

Like the other developments, baseball held no immediate interest for Joe Hooper in 1876, but the railroad, which facilitated both the nation's and the game's expansion, did as it continued to play a major role in his life. In April, Joe bought a ticket from a Union Pacific agent in Portland for an emigrant train to the West Coast. Such trains were part of the railroad's efforts to promote settlement on the western lands it had acquired under terms of the Pacific Railway Act of 1862. Awarding federal bonds and large sections of public lands to the railroad companies for each mile of roadbed constructed, the legislation spurred construction of the first transcontinental line. Its completion in May 1869 encouraged other companies to begin alternate routes to the Pacific. By the mid-1870s, four other transcontinental lines were under construction, although only the Union Pacific–Central Pacific line fully linked the Mississippi Valley with the Pacific coast when the Hooper children made their passage. Nevertheless, the competition for riders and settlers had begun. At the height of the railway rivalries a decade later, passenger fares from the Midwest to California dropped from $125 to a $1.[11]

Joe's total fare from coast to coast was seventy-six dollars, of which forty dollars applied to the ticket from Omaha to Sacramento. The price was hard to beat because regular coach fares over the western half of the transcontinental route ran about eighty dollars, while first-class tickets cost one-hundred dollars (four dollars extra per day if the first-class customers wished to dine on board). The traveling conditions for the emigrants, however, were terrible. Unlike those in first-class who crossed the country in resplendent parlor cars with plush upholstery, rich wall hangings, and hand-carved inlaid ceilings, those in the emigrant cars sat cramped together on narrow rows of wooden benches. At one end of their cars sat a wood-burning stove, at the other a "convenience stall," that is, a toilet. Small oil lamps mounted along the walls provided feeble light and a constant threat of fire. While the first-class ticket holders dined on blue-winged teal, antelope steaks, lobster salad, and coconut pudding, the emigrants had no food service on board but grabbed what they could to eat at station stops along the way.

Perhaps the major distinction between the riders in first-class and coach and those in the emigrant cars was that the former got to California much faster. Since the emigrant cars were given lowest priority, they were often coupled to short-run freight cars and constantly shunted aside for the expresses carrying full-fare patrons. For the latter, the trip from Omaha to Sacramento normally took four to four and a half days. The emigrants could count on a trip at least twice that long. On May 10, 1876, fourteen days after he started west, 3,200 miles, more than a hundred station stops, and numerous train changes behind him, Joe Hooper arrived in San Francisco.[12]

The trains which carried Joe and his brother and sister before him to California brought a very different kind of emigrant from those who had arrived during the heady days of the gold rush. Few of the original forty-niners expected to remain in California long. They sought quick riches and an early return to their eastern and midwestern places of origin. The great wave of newcomers to the Pacific coast twenty years after the rush, however, planned on a more permanent stay. Swelling the population of the western states tenfold between 1870 and 1900, they transformed the economic and cultural landscape of the region from a primitive state of speculation and transience to one that was more sophisticated and secure. San Francisco was the hub and mirror of this metamorphosis, changing from a clapboard and tent settlement of hustlers, hopefuls, and whores in 1850 to a confident and cosmopolitan city of diverse tastes and broad opportunities in 1870.

The transformation, of course, was not without struggle. The California which greeted Joe Hooper was in the middle of a turbulent decade that threatened to undo much of the progress of the post–gold rush years.[13] The effects of the panic of 1873, brought on by the failure of Jay Cooke's powerful banking firm and the precipitous national decline in security prices which followed, were felt in the state. The Bank of California was the major West Coast casualty of the country's financial unsteadiness. Its failure in August 1875 deepened a depression which years of drought and crop failure in the early 1870s had already brought to the region. As money became tighter, the Central Pacific Railroad and its subsidiaries, the cattle-

and sheep-ranching barons and the owners of the vast new agricultural industries in the state, increased their competitive hold on state and local governments to protect their interests and profits. While land titles and water rights soared in value, wages fell and widespread unemployment occurred.

Much of the workingmen's anger focused on the Chinese scattered throughout the state. Blaming the Chinese for taking their jobs and driving down wages, loathing their customs and resistance to assimilation, hatemongers encouraged racial violence against the Asians and called for national exclusion laws to halt their immigration. More generally, though, the targets of the discontented were the economic and political powers in the state who seemed indifferent to and removed from their concerns. With over 25 percent of California's farms operated by tenants, the promise of economic freedom and opportunity seemed hollow to many. There was desperation and talk of a popular revolution on the streets when Joe arrived in San Francisco.

The latest Hooper to reach California had other things on his mind, specifically that which he did not have in his pocket—his money pouch. He arrived in San Francisco without it but attributed its loss (and its grand contents of $1.50) not to thieves but to his own carelessness when leaving Portland two weeks earlier. Joe had made new friends on the westbound train, however, and one agreed to lend him the fare he needed to take the train from San Francisco to Gilroy, eighty-one miles to the south in Santa Clara County along the Southern Pacific's main line. There Joe transferred to the Monterey track and rode west for a few miles to Sargent's Station. Mary was waiting to greet him. True to her promise, she also had a job for him.

E. A. Sawyer's farm lay about fifteen miles southeast of Gilroy in San Felipe along Pacheco Creek. In this southernmost corner of the oval-shaped county, the valley between the two low mountain ranges running northwest and southeast on either side narrowed to about seven miles. At this point it was less than half as wide as its broadest stretch a few miles to the north. In contrast to the canyons and slopes of the western chain, with their rich forests of redwood, oak, and madrona, comparatively few trees grew in the valley or on the eastern slopes. Here the land gently rolled and swelled, its many ravines protecting the creeks which sustained the area's agricultural and ranching economy.[14]

Sawyer's spread also employed brother Bill, thus bringing the three transplanted Hoopers together for the first time in nearly five years. The reunion strengthened when Joe overcame whatever uneasiness or reluctance he may have had to accept a job offer from his brother-in-law and moved to the Hageman farm two months later in July. Seven miles east of San Felipe near Bells Station and midway between the south fork of Cedar Creek and Pacheco Creek as the latter turned north, the property reminded Joe of the old family homestead on P.E.I. It produced little in the way of a cash crop, but its variety and freehold were appealing qualities. So, too, was Mary Katherine Keller, the Hagemans' housekeeper. The son was about to take another page from his father's book.

Born in Frankfurt, Germany, in 1852, Mary accompanied her mother, her brother Charles, and a large immigrant party to the United States in 1856. Settling in Lock Haven, Pennsylvania, the Keller family and many of their fellow travelers joined a sizable German community already in the area. The rich farmlands of central Pennsylvania, like those in the midwestern states of Illinois, Michigan, and Wisconsin, had attracted Germans, who since the colonial era had constituted the second-largest non-English European group to settle in the North American colonies.[15] Only the Scotch-Irish had outnumbered the Germans among these white newcomers to America before 1776. From their new homes the German settlers wrote glowing letters to their friends and relatives in the fatherland, further stimulating a steady flow of immigration.

The wave which carried the Kellers to America drew its constituency largely from western and southern Germany. Poor harvests, a potato blight, rising rents and manorial dues, higher farming costs, and the uncertainties and displacements caused by an accelerating changeover to an industrial-based economy raised the level of receptivity to the good news from across the Atlantic. The promise of more political freedom also affected decisions to emigrate, particularly by those intellectuals and middle-class craftsmen whose hopes for a liberal revolution in 1848 had been dashed. During the 1850s more than nine hundred thousand Germans made the crossing, a number not to be surpassed for another generation. For the first time, too, more Germans than Irish entered the United States. This established a pattern that would be reversed only once thereafter—during the period of World War I.[16]

Within four years of the Kellers' arrival in Lock Haven, Mary's mother, Anna Marie, only twenty-nine years old at the time, found a stepfather for her two young children in Jonas Zindel. An established farmer but recent widower when his wife died of complications following the birth of their only child in January 1860, Jonas was also anxious to make his own little family more complete. The wedding of Anna Marie and Jonas a year later brought together the three children of their previous marriages. With the birth of the new couple's first child, Alice, in 1862, followed by six other children in the course of their productive marriage, three sets of half-brothers and sisters grew up together in the Keller-Zindel household.

Within this large and somewhat complicated family, each member was expected to help meet its needs. Mary's main contributions came from her skills as a dressmaker, providing both clothes for the family and some savings for herself. Like Joe Hooper, Mary applied her savings to a train ticket for California. In spring 1878, encouraged by what she, too, had heard about the opportunities for skilled workers in the Bay Area and not exactly thrilled with her prospects in rural Lock Haven, Mary departed for the West Coast on an emigrant train of her own. With assistance from a placement agent in San Francisco, she accepted a job as seamstress and housekeeper for George and Mary Hageman.

Joe's courtship of Mary was short and successful. The two were married in Gilroy on October 17, 1878, less than six months after they had met. Banking on Mary's domestic skills and Joe's abilities from his many previous occupations, including his experience with the family-run inn back in Morell, the newlyweds accepted an offer to run the Tres Piños Hotel. The small hotel in the valley community of the same name twenty-six miles south of Gilroy in San Benito County was not a going concern. It was little more than a station stop for the Southern Pacific. Inelegant but convenient, the hotel offered rudimentary accommodations for passengers waiting overnight for the next day's trains. The Hoopers stuck with the innkeeping business for three years before turning the operation over to Frank Jones. The experience added another job to Joe's long list of former and future professions. The years at Tres Piños had an additive quality in other respects. On August 6, 1879, Mary gave birth to the couple's first children, twin boys, George and Charles.

The three years at Tres Piños represented the longest stretch of employment with the same job that Joe had ever undertaken. True to form, he was restless for a change. Looking to explore other potential livelihoods and locations, he left Mary with the boys in Tres Piños and headed for New Mexico with three companions shortly after turning over the keys of the hotel. Driving two dozen horses the entire way, Joe finally stopped at the Pecos River about a hundred miles east of Albuquerque and over a thousand from the Santa Clara Valley. Like most of his previous work experiences, this sally in search of land to raise cattle and horses did not last long. Joe returned to California by train within five months.

The New Mexico venture seemed to have a settling effect on Joe. Influenced, too, by Mary's new pregnancy, Hooper sought advice from his brother-in-law about the availability of farming properties in the Santa Clara Valley. George suggested that a tract known as Elephant Head, located about a mile east of Bells Station on the Pacheco, might do. Joe agreed. With Hageman's assistance, Joe arranged a tenancy for the land and began construction of a house on it. Shortly after Mary gave birth to their third child, Lulu, in July 1883, the Hoopers took up the Elephant Head homestead. Four years later, their commitment to the farm reinforced with expanding markets for produce from the entire valley, they had their fourth child. Harry Bartholomew was born on August 24, 1887.

2

The Game
of His Youth

What a boyhood! I rode horseback to and from school, six miles each
way. I had a rifle and a shotgun, and there was plenty, as there is
today, of deer, pheasant, ducks, geese and quail. Best of all, I had a
baseball, a bat and a glove.
                                        —Harry Hooper, 1957

Harry Hooper's earliest memory of his childhood was a wagon piled
high with the family's belongings making its way across a sagebrush
plain.[1] The year was 1889 and this was the stuff of high adventure for
a two-year-old boy. Hooper's recollection of the trip revealed just
how impressionable two particular themes in the image were on
him: the transient ways of his father and the rural environment of his
youth. The journey meant that Joe Hooper was restless again for the
success and satisfaction which so many moves before had not realized. Six years on the Elephant Head homestead had turned little
profit. Selling out to his brother-in-law, Joe gathered up his wife and
four children and headed east about twenty miles across the Diablo
Range into Merced County for a tract known as the Garrison Ranch.
Situated on the west bank of the Los Banos Creek, the new property
took Joe out of the rich Santa Clara Valley and, as the sagebrush in
Harry's memory suggested, into country that promised hard challenges for farming and ranching.
     Unlike most of the valley he had left, the land around Volta in the
western reaches of the San Joaquin Valley was parched and flat. The
many streams which drifted down from the Sierra Nevada emptied
into the San Joaquin River and then flowed north to the great delta
where the waters of the San Joaquin merged with those of the Sacramento. On the western side of the San Joaquin, however, close
against the hills which separated the central valley from the Santa

Clara Valley, the streams were fewer and the land less cultivated. These conditions kept the price of land under two dollars an acre, well below property costs in the more fertile regions served directly by the major rivers.[2] This was what Joe could afford to buy for his own. It was no bargain.

The land yielded little in the way of a cash crop yet produced enough vegetables for the family and grains for their livestock to allow a small, diversified operation to survive. Typical of the many family farms throughout the region, it required all members of the family to help in the daily tasks and the annual harvests. As the youngest, Harry had few demands placed on him, but these were testing years nonetheless. He was once assigned the sad task of drowning a batch of unwanted kittens in a nearby creek. After tossing the first one in, he could not bear its pitiful cries and promptly waded in to retrieve it. He had less compunction, however, in tossing fresh eggs against a side of the barn, a habit which he apparently acquired quite early and enjoyed greatly. Although his older brothers reported his behavior to their parents, they paid it little heed. Their indifference encouraged the enjoyment he took in throwing any number of objects and he amused and challenged himself with tosses of increasingly greater distance and accuracy. In the company of his brother George one day, Harry aimed a stone at a moving object in the brush near the chicken yard. The stone found its mark—a small wildcat prowling for a meal—and Harry earned both his brother's admiration and a nickname: Cat.[3]

After three hard years at the Garrison Ranch, the Hoopers had developed the property enough so that its sale and their small savings made possible a move to a more attractive piece of land nearby. The new ranch lay just north of the railroad depot at Volta, closer to the partly shaded western hills of the valley. The alkaline soil and rolling terrain there made for poor pastureland, but the Hoopers still managed to increase their cattle and horse herds and raise a marketable crop of alfalfa. Joe also hired out his prized team of mules to the county for road work, thus adding a few dollars to the family's income.

For the youngest of the Hooper clan, the new ranch meant new places to wander and explore. With sister Lulu and cousin Ray Hooper his steady companions, Harry would ride the back stretches of the ranch or walk the county roads—often with flattened tin cans tied to his feet to protect them from the hot ground—looking for adventure; memories of raiding a neighbor's watermelon patch or playing matador with the family's cows suggest that he had no difficulty finding it. Except for a close call or two when thrown from the saddle or getting cramps while swimming, Harry enjoyed a happy and healthy few years on the Volta ranch. He particularly loved the company of his sister, whose bareback riding at high speed and overall athletic ability impressed him.[4]

These years also marked the beginning of his formal education. With the constant moves and the demands of the home life, his older brothers and sister had very little opportunity for schooling. Their experience might have influenced Harry to resist attending school himself. But with his parents' encouragement, school appealed no less to Harry's curiosity than roaming the high hills or visiting his Uncle Bill's saloon in Volta. At age seven, he started at the Volta elementary school, a two-room schoolhouse accommodating two dozen students, about one in four of the school-age children in the area.

Young Hooper excelled in the classroom and reveled in his new friends, his schoolmates. He suddenly was involved with other children his own age who were neither his siblings nor his cousins. If Harry worked alone to master his studies, he eagerly shared other aspects of his schooling experience with those around him. Included in his socialization were the new games he played, group games. Sled pulls and races, snap-the-whip and tag and red rover. One year, lassoing was the thing to do and Harry joined his schoolmates in roping everything in sight, especially each other.[5]

Of all the games he played, though, none pleased him more than a simple bat and ball game called one-o'-cat. Played with as few as four or five participants, the game required each player to take a turn with the bat while all the others played the field. The batsman's object was to strike the ball beyond the reach of the fielders and then run from his batting spot to a single base and back again without being tagged with the ball by one of the fielders. When a player made "out," he retired to the field and took the last spot in the batting rotation as it continued with a new batter. At this level of competition, the players rarely kept score and the game continued until the school bell or darkness intervened. The game involved both catching and throwing a ball, but it placed a premium on skill with the bat. Although Wee Willie Keeler meant nothing to ten-year-old Harry Hooper in 1897, the simple advice of the National League's best hitter to "hit 'em where they ain't" was the secret to success in one-o'-cat. A player with a keen eye and good speed could stay at bat for quite some time. Harry got plenty of batting practice.

As much as Joe and Mary provided for and indulged their youngest child, they could not ensure that his childhood would be filled only with happy memories of ball games and school days. On March 8, 1897, after fighting a high fever for several days, Lulu died of meningitis. She was four months shy of her fourteenth birthday. Scarcely less so than his mother, Harry was grief striken at the loss of his "great pal."[6]

Despite their limited resources, augmented somewhat by the modest return on a sharecrop lease Joe had taken out in 1896 on a neighbor's parcel of land just north of the Hooper ranch, Harry's parents decided to let him accompany Mary on a trip back to see her mother and relatives in Pennsylvania at the end of the school year. Mary had taken Lulu's death extremely hard, and she and Joe hoped the trip east, as arduous as it would be, would help relieve her sadness. Toward the end of June, Harry and his mother began the long train ride across the country and arrived in Lock Haven just before the Fourth of July.[7]

Things had changed very little there since Mary headed west in 1878. Buoyed by a steady stream of German immigrants, the town and immediate vicinity had grown somewhat and now counted about two thousand inhabitants. But the pace and purpose of the community still focused on the land. The fertile limestone soil, continuously enriched by alluvium from the Susquehanna River flowing to the north, supported a thriving agricultural economy. Neat fields of wheat and corn spread in quilted meticulousness across the landscape. Herds of dairy cows and beef cattle fattened themselves on the unirrigated land, which added texture and color to the great squares of cultivated green and gold. Here lived Harry's grandmother, Anna Marie, and a host of Keller and Zindel aunts, uncles, and cousins. On July 4, they assembled for a grand family picnic to honor Mary and her son. Afterward the men of the families started a game of baseball and Harry got to play. It was a wonderful moment for him.

Once introduced to baseball, there was no containing Harry's excitement about it. He sought to play the game every opportunity he had, and the summer of '97 obliged with both the players and the time to accommodate his enthusiasm. Surrounded by his cousins and their friends, freed from school by summer vacation, and encouraged by his mother, whose own spirits were lifted in the happiness of her son in the game he had discovered, Harry had the time of his life. Like Clarence Darrow, who recalled the "perfect pleasure" that baseball had provided in his youth, Hooper remembered the baseball games of that Pennsylvania summer as the highlight of the "great adventure" which the cross-country trip had been.[8] "That's where I got my love of baseball," Hooper fondly admitted, acknowledging in the same breath the role that his Uncle Mack Zindel had played in fostering both his interest in the game and his skill in playing it.[9]

Uncle Mack, twenty-five at the time, was the youngest half-brother of Harry's mother. He was the last child of the union between Anna Marie Keller and Jonas Zindel, who had died in 1881. Single and still living at home on the family farm, Mack helped his mother host the California kin throughout their stay. He particularly enjoyed young Harry's company and delighted in the boy's enthusiasm for baseball, largely because it reflected his own. An avid fan of the game, Mack perhaps saw Harry as the little brother he did not have and to whom he could impart the wisdom of his experience. At least he could further his nephew's interest in baseball, which he did in games of catch and tales of baseball heroics. More important, however, he also took Harry to his first organized baseball games.

The local team was strictly an amateur contingent that competed against other nines from such neighboring communities in the central part of the state as Williamsport, Flemington, and Bellefonte. Like most teams on the bottom rung of baseball's organizational ladder, the Lock Havens did more to satisfy local interest in the game than to offer skillful play on the field. This was largely because baseball at this level was pursued for the essential enjoyment of the game and the entertainment of the home folks. Unlike competition in either the Eastern League or the Atlantic League, for example, which included representatives from other Pennsylvania towns like Scranton, Wilkes-Barre, Lancaster, and Reading, local amateur ball was oriented neither toward financial profit nor the development of players for higher competitive circles, although the latter in particular was certainly possible. The best example of the local boy making good—and inspiring a few Major League dreams in the process— was John Montgomery Ward. Born and raised in Bellefonte, Ward had played ball for the town team as a teenager before entering Pennsylvania State College and then enjoying a highly successful professional career of seventeen years. The usual circumstances of play offered more modest prospects. Teams—in fact, entire leagues, both amateur and low professional—frequently collapsed before a season ended because of the inattention and ineptitude of owners and league officials, such as there were, and less predictable factors, such as a downturn in the local economy or the decimation of team rosters through the purchase of player contracts by other teams in other leagues. In 1897 alone, seventeen professional baseball leagues started a season, but only ten completed it.[10]

Whatever the uncertain socioeconomic conditions affecting minor league baseball or the amateur brand played in Lock Haven, the game itself unfolded in magnificent splendor before young Harry's eyes. No aspect of the pageantry escaped his notice or failed to excite him. From the simple uniforms and leather gloves of the players to the vendors providing lemonade and peanuts, from the rapid style of play on the field to the reactions it raised among the spectators, the game captivated the boy and filled his summer days with delight. On Saturday afternoons and other game days as Mack's schedule permitted, Harry and his uncle went out to the ball grounds to cheer on the local heroes.

Harry, of course, had no sense of perspective at all for the quality of play on the Lock Haven diamond and the baseball world it represented. The boy's naïveté in these matters no doubt amused Mack as much as his nephew's happiness pleased him. He had another baseball surprise for Harry before the summer ended. In late August, Mack accompanied Harry and his mother to New York City to visit one of the Zindel sisters, Anna Marie, who lived there with her husband, Giuseppe Cavallero. The highlight of the excursion, indeed, the grand event of the entire summer trip, awaited.[11] On Saturday, August 26, Mack and Harry boarded the City Line el for a trip to Brooklyn. Their destination was a large park in the northeastern section of the city where a ball field had been laid out near the intersection of the Eastern Parkway and Liberty Avenue across the tracks of the New York and Manhattan Beach Railroad.[12] This was Eastern Park, the home of the National League—the Major League—Brooklyn Bridegrooms.

Although the Bridegrooms were struggling through the second of three consecutive losing seasons in 1897, there was no better place in all of professional baseball than Brooklyn to appreciate the history and appeal of the national game. Organized ball in the borough traced its roots to the 1850s, when such teams as the Atlantics, the Eckfords, the Putnams, and the Excelsiors formed. By the end of the decade, over seventy baseball clubs existed in Brooklyn and games among them had begun to serve as occasions for neighborhood boosterism and civic pride. Spectator interest in the interclub contests extended to sectional rivalries and prompted the staging of an "all star" series of three games between the representatives of several New York City clubs and members of the Atlantics and Eckfords at the Fashion Race Course on Long Island in the summer of 1858.[13] Although the New Yorkers triumphed in the series two games to one, a Brooklyn contingent won the next all-star matchup, and individual

Brooklyn teams dominated baseball play in the area for the next decade. The fine play of the local teams led the *Brooklyn Eagle* to claim that "nowhere has the National game of Baseball taken a firmer hold than in Brooklyn and nowhere are there better players." Victories over the New Yorkers were especially sweet. "If we are ahead of the big city in nothing else," the *Eagle* observed, "we can beat her in baseball."[14]

Although Brooklyn teams pioneered in both the democratization of the playing field through their mixture of white- and blue-collar workers on their rosters and the professionalization of the game through the payments they provided such skilled players as James Creighton, Joe Start and Dickie Pearce to compete for them, they performed poorly during the brief life of the National Association of Professional Base Ball Players, 1871–75, and failed to elicit an invitation from Hulbert and his partners to join the National League in 1876.[15] Nevertheless, baseball continued to thrive in Brooklyn as a club sport and public entertainment. With a half-dozen first-rate ball fields scattered throughout the increasingly more crowded city of nearly six hundred thousand residents in the early 1880s, there was no lack of interest in the game.

In 1884, Brooklyn returned to the top levels of professional play when the two-year old American Association opened a slot in its eight-team circuit for a club headed by real estate investor and noted gambler Charlie Byrne. The opening of the great bridge between Brooklyn and Manhattan in May 1883 no doubt influenced the association's decision because it linked the nation's most populous cities as never before and rekindled the baseball rivalries between them. The cables of John and Washington Roebling's masterpiece would carry ballplayers and fans—and revenues—both ways.

Within a few years, the club had acquired a nickname—the Bridegrooms—and a championship cast headed by Bob Caruthers, Dave Foutz, Hub Collins, and Tom Lovett. Winning both the American Association's pennant in 1889 and, upon switching to the National League, the senior league's championship the following year, the Brooklyners could not sustain their success into the 1890s. With players returning to their former teams in 1891 after the collapse of the short-lived Players League, both Brooklyn and its American Association opponent in the 1890 "world series," Louisville, failed miserably against sterner competition. The Bridegrooms went from forty-three games over .500 to fifteen under and finished sixth with a 61-76 record. The Cyclones fared even worse, virtually reversing a first place record of 88–44 in 1890 with a 55–84 mark and eighth place finish a year later. When the American Association itself collapsed after the 1891 season, Louisville joined the National League with Baltimore, Saint Louis, and Washington to form a single twelve-team organization. The Cyclones were never contenders in the expanded league. A ninth-place finish in 1892 was the best they would manage during their seven-year membership in the league. For three consecutive years, 1894–96, the Cyclones blew no one away, finishing in the cellar and over fifty games behind the league champion each season. They resided firmly once more in the bottom half of the standings along with Brooklyn when Uncle Mack and Harry took their twenty-five-cent bleacher seats for the afternoon game between the two former champions.

The two teams had more in common than their lowly places in the league standings and distant memories of glory days. Despite the overall lack of talent on their rosters, both clubs had a few men who could have cracked anyone's lineup. Candy LaChance, Mike Griffin, and John Anderson, all of whom had batting averages over .300 and slugging percentages over .425 in 1897, fit this bill for the Bridegrooms. The Cyclones' list was shorter but more impressive. They countered with Fred Clarke, who, at twenty-four, had succeeded Jim Rogers to become the player-manager of the club about a third of the way into the season, and Honus Wagner, a rookie infielder from the coal country of Pennsylvania. Within three years after the Louisville franchise merged with Pittsburgh in the truncated National League of 1900, both Clarke and Wagner would form the nucleus of Pirate teams which captured four pennants and the 1909 World Series before Cap Clarke relinquished the managerial reins in 1915.

More than the players he saw on the field before him, Harry witnessed the professional game as it had evolved by the end of the century. The strategy of the day emphasized bat control, speed on the bases, and aggressiveness.[16] Once the pitching distance was moved from fifty feet to sixty feet, six inches in 1893, batting averages and run production rose dramatically. Whereas team batting averages and runs per game were about .250 and five, respectively, before the longer distance, they jumped to over .280 and seven for the rest of the '90s. Yet the advantages which pitchers enjoyed in the shorter distance—and continued to have with the spit ball, the "dead" ball, and the spacious dimensions of most ball parks behind them—had always been offset somewhat by deficiencies in team defense. Poor playing surfaces, primitive fielding equipment, and little in the way of defensive strategy added uncertainty, if not skill, to the game and made life interesting for even the most overpowering pitchers.[17]

What defenses did not achieve with style, however, they attempted to gain through intimidation. The single umpire usually assigned to games in the nineteenth century could watch and control only so much. His limited view invited exploitation. Fielders employed all kinds of dirty tricks to impede a runner's progress, tripping them as they ran by, grabbing their belts or loose uniform blouses to slow them down, or simply standing in their way on the base paths. Wilbert Robinson, the veteran catcher of the Baltimore Orioles, kept small pebbles in his pocket to drop in the shoes of the batters standing intently in place before him.[18] His tactic had painful consequences for the hitter when he started to run. No less than Robinson, his other teammates on the Orioles of the 1890s seemed to take particular delight in the violence and meanspiritedness that characterized play in the decade. From Dirty Jack Doyle at first to John McGraw at third, the Orioles' infield challenged a runner every step of the way. In less intimate ways the Baltimore outfield contributed to the general mayhem as they often hid balls in the tall grass, far from the umpire's eyes, for retrieval in emergency situations. Crushing a hand reaching for a base with their sharpened spikes, throwing an elbow at a passing runner, or splitting a runner's lip with a viciously applied tag, the Orioles played a brand of ball that was not pretty. It was, though, the order of the day, "as gentlemanly," observed Ty Cobb, "as a kick in the crotch."[19] This brand of ball, perfected by the Orioles but practiced by every team in the league, was the most exciting thing ten-year-old Harry Hooper had ever seen.

Led by Clarke's three hits and Wagner's two, the Cyclones pounded the Brooklyners for nineteen hits and sixteen runs. The Bridegrooms managed eight runs themselves on thirteen hits but saved most of their offense for a six-run ninth inning rally when the game had long since been decided. Although the game lacked suspense after the Cyclones built a 6–0 lead through four innings, it provided quite a hitting exhibition for Harry and the crowd of about twenty-one hundred in attendance. The combined thirty-two hits featured two home runs, two triples, and six doubles. Clarke, who was headed toward a .406 batting average for the season and the runner-up spot for the hitting title behind Keeler's .432, had one of the two-baggers, added a pair of stolen bases, and scored four runs. Only Brooklyn's shortstop, Germany Smith, did not manage at least one safety for the afternoon among the men on both rosters who played. With a couple of wild pitches by Louisville's Bert Cunningham, a hit batsman (Clarke by Harley Payne), and fine defensive play by Wagner at second, the game could not have been more entertaining.

The afternoon at Eastern Park sent Harry back to Lock Haven more eager than ever to play ball with his friends. But the splendid summer was quickly coming to an end. He and his mother had been away from California for over two months and Mary was anxious to return to Joe and the twins. As they bid their farewells, Uncle Mack appeared with one more surprise, a parting gift for his nephew. It was, as Harry recalled many years later, the "best of all" his boyhood joys—a ball, a bat, and a very used, very wonderful fielder's glove.

The return to Volta was not as happy as Mary had hoped. Joe had lost his sharecrop lease and was in danger of losing the ranch itself because he was so far behind on mortgage payments. Much depended on the fall harvest, but Joe had already anticipated the worst. Through the assistance once more of his brother-in-law, George Hageman, he had met Luis Fatyo, a wealthy landholder in the Santa Clara Valley. Luis was the oldest son of Anton Fatyo, a Spanish-born merchant who had arrived in California with the forty-niners after living several years in Chile.[20] The senior Fatyo had established a successful retail store in Santa Clara and expanded his business operations and land holdings over the years. Luis inherited a significant parcel of this land located in the southeastern corner of the valley neighboring on Hageman's property and not far from the original Elephant Head homestead. He offered to build a house for Joe on a sizable tract of his land if Hooper would sharecrop it.

When the Hoopers' alfalfa harvest did not come in as needed, Joe made the move toward which he was probably inclined and certainly prepared. Heading west this time across the Diablo Range in November 1897, he brought his wife, two eighteen-year-old sons, and Harry to land that he would be the first to plow. The five-room house Fatyo had built sat in the middle of two thousand acres of valley land bisected by Pacheco Pass Road and bordered by San Luis Creek on the east and a canyon on the west. The property also included a large barn and corral for Joe's horses and mules, which, until the land was prepared and producing, provided the family's only income as Joe continued to do road work for the county with his teams. The uncleared land and a dry winter prevented the Hoopers from getting a crop in that first planting season, but by the end of 1898 he and the boys had planted about a hundred acres and were praying for a good rain.[21]

Harry, meanwhile, had resumed his studies at the Mendezable

District Grammar School about six miles south of the new Hooper ranch along the county road which crossed San Luis Creek. The school itself was a one-room building and enrolled only a dozen students, eight of them girls. Even so, Harry attempted to get them interested in baseball, but without much success. Harry was back to playing one-o'-cat with the three other boys and sharpening his eye with an occasional shot at a fleeing rattlesnake as he rode back and forth each day on his horse, Melicky. He carried an old .22-caliber rifle with him, a gift from his father, who had enlisted Harry in an effort to kill a passel of squirrels which had taken a particular interest in the barley crop. When Harry proved his ability at handling a gun, Joe gave him a new LaFever shotgun for his thirteenth birthday. It was almost as valuable as his baseball equipment; at least he got to use it more. On outings with his father and brothers, Harry bagged his fair share of ducks and quail. His enthusiasm for the hunt fully matched his marksmanship. Moreover, he had discovered the other great sporting passion of his life.[22]

Like his performance in the Volta school, Harry did well in the classroom, earning high marks in all of his subjects, especially mathematics. His teacher, Mary Sullivan, took a particular interest in him and urged Joe and Mary to allow their youngest child to continue his education beyond a grammar school curriculum.[23] She thought the high school attached to Saint Mary's College in Oakland might be a good place for him to go. Encouraged, too, by their neighbors, county supervisor Jim Hailey and his wife, whose son, George, attended Saint Mary's, the Hoopers agreed that at least one of their children should have the opportunity of an education beyond a few elementary grades. The many moves and the heavy demands of working the family's farms and ranches had limited the prospects for either George or Charlie to have much of a formal education. Impressed with Harry's seriousness about his schooling and his ability, his parents decided to send their youngest to Saint Mary's for a two-year commercial diploma program. "I leapt at the chance," he remembered. Accompanied by George Hailey and another neighbor and Saint Mary's student, George Poultney, Harry left for Oakland in late August 1902. Like his father on his first venture as a young teenager from the family farm on Prince Edward Island, Harry, just a few days past his fifteenth birthday, was eager for what lay ahead. The reason for his excitement was not exactly what his parents had in mind for the $320 annual tuition they would be paying. "I was very well pleased," recounted Harry about the opportunity to attend Saint Mary's, "not because I was particularly interested in getting an education, but because I knew I'd have a chance to play baseball."[24]

3

College Days,
Career Choices

*If they [my parents] hadn't sent me to Saint Mary's College I'd have
turned out to be a dry farmer over in the San Joaquin Valley and
nobody would ever have heard of me.*
—Harry Hooper, August 9, 1971

Young Hooper's interest in baseball matched his scholastic aptitude
and Saint Mary's happily accommodated both. Recognizing his promise in the classroom, especially in mathematics, Harry's teachers
encouraged him to consider undertaking a full baccalaureate degree
program scarcely one semester into the precollegiate curriculum in
which he was initially enrolled. This development took both Harry
and his parents by surprise, and the three consulted about the matter
when Harry returned to the ranch for the Christmas holidays. Although the new educational option would extend Harry's program
from two years to five, placing additional strains on the family's slim
financial resources, Joe and Mary recognized the special opportunity
that their son had; they agreed that Harry should have the chance to
earn a college degree. In the spring term of 1903, Harry continued
with the high school diploma program but added a more advanced
mathematics course in anticipation of starting a degree program in
civil engineering that fall.

As he did in his classroom work, Harry had an early opportunity to
demonstrate his skills on the ball field. When he arrived on campus,
Saint Mary's already fielded three baseball teams on the collegiate
level and was organizing another for students in the secondary-
school curriculum. About twenty of Harry's new classmates joined
him to vie for a spot on the team, which, unfortunately, only had
enough uniforms to dress half of them. The team's coach decided

that a game among the boys would decide who would make the uniformed nine. He named Harry captain and pitcher for one side and gave a fellow newcomer, Harry Davis, similar chores for the other. Hooper's rock-throwing days and Uncle Mack's pointers paid off. His team won the game and earned the uniforms for the school's newest baseball contingent, the Midgets. "We were all," confessed Harry, "quite small."

That Harry Hooper, the youngest son of a poor immigrant farmer, could be playing baseball on a college campus in 1902 was as much a testament to the notable circumstances of his own life as it was a reflection of much larger developments affecting both American higher education and "the national game." For the collegiate scene, the principal development was the dramatic growth in higher-education enrollments in the last quarter of the nineteenth century. For baseball, the keys were the game's surging popularity in the years around the turn of the century and the role it was playing on American campuses. In both cases perceptions of opportunity played a major part in attracting students to college. Most came for the enabling promise of higher education. Some came idly for the fun of it and baseball provided one of their diversions. A few—like the sharecropper's son from the Santa Clara Valley—came for both the degree and the diamond.

Enrollments in American colleges and universities tripled between 1870 and 1890, rising from 52,286 to 154,374, and more than doubled again by 1910.[1] In the last three decades of the nineteenth century, the number of institutions serving this expanding constituency grew almost 80 percent from under six hundred to more than a thousand. Just as significant were the changes affecting the undergraduate curriculum and student life. In 1870 the dominant aim of higher education focused on instilling virtues of discipline, civic responsibility, and morality in students. The primary means to this end was a prescribed classical curriculum offered by strict taskmasters. The course of studies included mathematics, Latin, classical literature, ethics, rhetoric, and, in the church schools, religion. In short, the American university in all aspects of its conduct emphasized a common core of knowledge and the inherent unity of collegiate life.

By 1900 the aspirations of a growing middle class had transformed the college scene. Its members accounted for the increasing enrollments and affected the collegiate culture through the diversity of their social and economic backgrounds and the hopes they pinned on a college education. Social mobility and access to the emerging new professions of the period entered more heavily into the decision to attend college than had previously been the case. Colleges and universities responded with courses of study shaped by utilitarian and vocational values and an elective system designed to deliver them.

Similar changes occurred in student life. Partly a recognition of new attitudes toward such matters, partly an attempt to attract students, colleges and universities began to relax their codes of student discipline (dropping, for example, mandatory chapel attendance) and to support intellectual, social, and recreational programs that added more excitement and variety to the lives of their students. Intercollegiate athletics, in particular, both benefited from and contributed to the new campus milieu.[2]

From the first intercollegiate crew race between Harvard and Yale in 1852 through the heyday of the crew regattas in the early 1870s, the rise of college baseball in the two decades after the Civil War, and the emergence of football by 1900 as the principal sporting spectacle on American campuses, intercollegiate sports competition had evolved from a relatively simple, informal diversion among the sons of the elite in a few northeastern institutions into an instrument of mass entertainment involving entire student bodies, college administrations, faculty, alumni, and thousands of spectators. In the final decades of the nineteenth century, American higher education's first era of spirited competition for students and benefactors, college authorities often equated success on the playing fields with preeminence as an institution of higher learning. With enrollments and prestige hanging in the balance, it did not take many institutions long to define their priorities along both academic and athletic lines.[3]

The crew regattas of the 1870s had demonstrated early the value that could accrue to institutions through the athletic victories of young men wearing the school's colors.[4] The surprising win of Massachusetts Agricultural College over Harvard and Brown in the 1871 regatta not only brought recognition and renown to the tiny land-grant institution of only 150 students, it also encouraged other colleges to bear the considerable financial costs of supporting a crew in the hope of gaining a similar triumph. Regatta victories by Amherst, Columbia, and Cornell between 1872 and 1876 produced jubilation on their campuses and claims of "equality, freedom [and] assured position" vis-à-vis the Ivy giants.[5] By the end of the nineteenth century, football had surpassed crew as the main sporting vehicle to institutional prestige. Similarly, the appeal of intercollegiate athletic victory, which crew first revealed, increased dramatically. At colleges and universities like Chicago, Princeton, Pennsylvania, Kansas, Notre Dame, and numerous land-grant and sectarian institutions throughout the country, campus authorities, alumni, and benefactors linked success on the gridiron with larger student enrollments, more generous donors, and institutional growth.

The early history of Saint Mary's College closely paralleled national developments in higher education in the areas of curriculum development, student life, and expansion.[6] Founded in 1863 by Archbishop Joseph Sadoc Alemany of San Francisco, the college was initially placed under the direction of his diocesan priests. This arrangement proved unsatisfactory almost from the outset, as the priests were neither prepared nor inclined to administer a collegiate institution. With the college's enrollment hovering around thirty a few years later, the archbishop still remained firm in his conviction of the need for the new school. He succeeded in persuading the superior general of the Brothers of the Christian Schools to send a group of nine men to take over the struggling college.[7] They arrived in 1868 and within four years secured from the state of California an official charter for the institution empowering it to grant university degrees. By 1872 the college's enrollment had tripled and its future seemed more secure under the Brothers' direction.

As the collegiate curriculum developed, it reflected both the original interests of the archbishop and the traditional educational mission of the Christian Brothers. The former focused on providing San Francisco immigrants—especially Irish Catholics—with an education that would help them succeed in America and address the many needs of a still frontier society, including preparing men for the priesthood. The Brothers drew upon their order's focus since its founding in France in the late seventeenth century to provide the lower and middle classes with a practical education. The result was a diverse program of studies that expanded upon the original classical curriculum of the college and introduced courses in commercial, scientific, and engineering areas. The distribution of degrees over its first twenty-five years—233 bachelor of arts, 175 bachelor of science in civil and mining engineering, and 459 in business—reflected the different curricular emphases of the college. Conscious of its aim to promote Christian values and responsible citizenship, the college was also clearly attuned to the increasing professionalization and specialization of the American workplace. The young men who attended Saint Mary's, like the first and second generations of new college enrollees throughout the country, did so for the benefits of both liberal and vocational education. Moreover, since the majority of its faculty, students and benefactors were Irish Catholics, the college especially sought to protect the faith as much as to provide a secular education to enable its students to climb society's ladder.

Changes in the circumstances of student life at Saint Mary's in the final quarter of the nineteenth century paralleled those which were occurring within the curriculum. The overall movement was away from strict structure to a more balanced regimen offering students both choice and freedom. In the early years of the college, regulations governed virtually every moment of the student's day, from morning prayers at the rising hour of 6:00 A.M. to lights out at 8:30 P.M. Throughout the day, prescribed times for meals, classes, recreation, and study halls punctuated the lessons of discipline, industry, and spiritual development which formed the center of the Brothers' educational philosophy.[8]

Even within this highly controlled environment, though, there were extracurricular opportunities to give students relief from their studies. These were quite modest initially and focused on occasional picnics and outings and the college's music program. Encouraged by the college's new president, Brother Justin McMahon, students also participated in a variety of athletic activities, including running, rugby, and handball. Although it is not known whether Justin read Thomas Hughes's novels about the education and sporting life of "Tom Brown," the president was apparently familiar with the manner of education practiced in the English public schools of Eton, Harrow, Westminster, and Winchester and likened his role at Saint Mary's to that of headmaster at those places.[9] He particularly saw physical activity as a manly and appropriate element of a Christian education and promoted proficiency in it with the same enthusiasm he accorded academic achievement. In 1872, the same year the state of California authorized Saint Mary's to grant degrees, Justin approved the creation of an organized athletic program at the college. For most of the students this meant intramural sports; for more skillful athletes there was another outlet. Adopting the mythical phoenix as their emblem, these lads turned to the major team sport of the day for the school's first intercollegiate venture and took the field as the Saint Mary's College Base Ball Club.[10]

It was not surprising that the college chose baseball to launch its efforts in sports competition beyond the campus. In the 1870s baseball superseded all collegiate sports in popularity. Whether the Amherst-Williams contest of July 1, 1859, played under "Massachusetts rules" with thirteen men on a side, or the Fordham-Xavier game of November 3, 1859, with nine men on a team, hold the dis-

tinction for the first intercollegiate baseball match, the game had
begun to make headway on many eastern campuses before the outbreak of the Civil War.[11] Although the war generally retarded the
growth of intercollegiate competition, it provided stimulus to baseball and other sports through contests among the men in uniform
and the enthusiasm for the games they played, which the veterans
took home with them after the fighting.[12]

The end of the war signaled a rapid expansion of baseball activity,
and a virtual mania took hold of the sport. The National Association
of Base Ball Players saw its membership leap from thirty clubs in
1864 to ninety-one in 1865 and to more than two hundred in 1866.[13]
The latter number represented seventeen states and the District of
Columbia, whereas the NABBP had originally included clubs from
only New York and New Jersey. *Wilkes' Spirit of the Times* estimated
that there were about two thousand organized baseball clubs in the
nation by the end of the decade.[14]

A similar trend was under way on college campuses. The postwar
matriculation of veterans who had played baseball during the great
conflict gave rise to the game on both sides of the Mason-Dixon Line
and farther west. Within two years of the Confederate surrender at
Appomattox, for example, baseball teams were organized at the University of Virginia, the University of Georgia, Yale, Cornell, the University of Kansas, and Platteville Normal School in Wisconsin.[15] The
latter joined the NABBP's North Western Association, the membership of which stretched from Kenyon College in Ohio to Dubuque,
Iowa.[16]

When the Phoenix made their debut in 1872, they could draw on
an already established baseball tradition in San Francisco. The origins of the game in the Bay Area can be traced to the rowdy days of
the gold rush, when young tradesmen and mechanics headed west
from New York City, Chicago, and other eastern and midwestern
cities to make their fortunes in the capital of the forty-niners. These
men not only contributed to the population boom of the city—from
about one thousand residents in 1848 to nearly thirty-five thousand
just three years later—they brought with them new recreational interests and the critical mass necessary to sustain them.[17] As early as
1852, "full grown persons" could be observed "engaged very indus-
triously in the game known as town ball" on one of the city plazas.[18]
By the decade's end, both cricket and baseball clubs had appeared on
the San Francisco sporting scene, with the latter clearly becoming
the more popular and better organized.[19]

The influence of the New York metropolitan area, the center of the nation's baseball activity, was clearly felt during the early years of baseball on the West Coast.[20] Former New Yorkers, who had gained baseball experience with such clubs as the Knickerbockers and Empires or the Excelsiors and Peconics of Brooklyn, played major roles in developing the game in the Bay Area. San Francisco's first baseball team, the Eagle Base Ball Club, organized in November 1859, drew, for example, on the baseball knowledge of newcomer John Fisher from New York in getting under way.[21] Similarly, the Shephard brothers, William and James, who had played baseball with the Knickerbockers at Hoboken's Elysian Fields, helped organize the Pacific Base Ball Club in 1862. Walter Wallace, who had played with the Peconics, founded, managed, and pitched for the California Theater Baseball Club in 1869.[22] By the late 1860s, there were more than twenty Bay Area teams and they often competed against each other on San Francisco's first enclosed baseball field, the Recreation Grounds at the corner of Twenty-fifth and Folsom streets in the city's heavily Irish Mission District.[23]

The establishment of the Pacific Base Ball Convention in August 1866 gave further impetus to the rise of baseball in San Francisco through the championship matches it promoted and the coveted prizes it awarded, including a "splendid ball bat elaborately mounted in silver."[24] Seeking to advance the game's popularity even more, the convention invited the Cincinnati Red Stockings to play a series of games against Bay Area teams in early fall 1869. The completion of the transcontinental railroad in May of that year made such an invitation possible, and when the Red Stockings accepted, the San Francisco baseball fraternity reacted with joy and optimism about the outcome of the contests. The games themselves, however, were not very competitive, as the eastern visitors dispatched the local nines by a combined score of 289–22 in five games. The lopsided victories extended the undefeated streak of the Red Stockings on their famous nationwide tour that took them nearly twelve thousand miles and attracted more than two hundred thousand fans to their games.[25]

The thrashings at the hands of Harry Wright's boys had an understandably discouraging effect on the baseball enthusiasts in the Bay Area, and attendance fell off at games for a while. By June 1870, though, the press noted "new life" in the game and the Pacific Base Ball Convention encouraged the organization of new clubs.[26] During the next few years, clubs formed in Oakland, Berkeley, Alameda, Occidental, Stockton, Sacramento, and, of course, at Saint Mary's College. By 1876 the men of the Pacific Convention were willing to test their skills on the diamond against national competition again. The occasion this time was the nation's centennial celebration.

Eighteen seventy-six was also the one-hundredth anniversary of the founding of San Francisco. To mark both events, fifteen ballplayers from several clubs in the Bay Area organized an all-star team to compete in a Philadelphia baseball tournament as part of the national festivities. Calling themselves the Centennials, the group headed east by rail in late June.[27] Along the way they competed against local nines whenever station stops allowed. In Atlantic, Iowa, for example, the competition on July 4 was a contingent called the Troublesomes, and nearly one thousand spectators turned out for the contest. They witnessed "one of the finest and most hotly-contested [games] ever played in the State" when the home team unleased a barrage of "heavy and safe hitting" in the bottom of the ninth to push four runs across for a 10–9 victory.[28]

Arriving in Rochester, New York, two weeks later, the weary travelers played poorly in their initial games in the East before gaining a 6–5 victory over the Cricket Club of Binghamton, New York, on July 22 for their first win of the tour.[29] They then headed to Philadelphia for the principal games of the centennial tournament. The Californians responded with their best play. Competing against the finest amateur and semipro teams in the area, the Centennials won six of seven games over an eleven-day period. They avenged their only defeat, 10–5 against Campbell of Philadelphia on August 1, with a 8–6 win just two days before beginning the long journey back to the West Coast.[30]

The Centennials' performance underscored the quality of home-grown baseball talent in the Bay Area and momentarily checked any interest in importing expensive players from other sections of the country to stock the local teams. The example of the 1869 Red Stockings, which fielded only one player who was a native of Cincinnati, however, was not completely lost. The bottom line in the increasingly competitive West Coast baseball world, as elsewhere, was winning, and if that could not be accomplished with a team of local heroes, then the importation of professionals to wear the club colors was recognized as a justifiable and appropriate step to take. It was perhaps fitting that a former member of the Cincinnati team, Cal McVey, should play a key role in this Bay Area development. Moving to Oakland in 1879 after spending the two previous seasons as player-manager for Cincinnati of the National League, McVey organized the Bay City Base Ball Club and immediately established it as one of the best in the area.[31] His players demonstrated their prowess in convincing fashion by beating Cap Anson's Chicago White Stockings, the National League champions of 1880, four games out of six in a postseason series the next year.

But McVey and others like him were both an expensive and often unreliable investment. McVey left baseball a year later to become superintendent of an irrigation company in Hanford, California. His club collapsed without him. James ("Pud") Galvin, who would go on to record 362 wins in a pitching career with Buffalo and Pittsburgh, was offered two thousand dollars by the San Francisco Athletics for the 1880 season. He hung around for only a month before bigger money back east lured him away. Similarly, players like Edward ("The Only") Nolan and William ("Bald Billie") Barnie were barely around long enough for Bay Area fans to appreciate their nicknames before resuming their professional careers with eastern teams.[32] Increasingly, the San Francisco and Oakland clubs returned to the practice of recruiting local talent for their rosters, a decision made easier by the success that such Bay Area products as John Sheridan, Tom Power, Danny Long, Fred Carroll, Bob Blakiston, and Charlie Sweeney enjoyed with the Major League teams of the East in the 1880s.[33] There was no more reliable source of this talent than the Saint Mary's College Phoenix.

The Centennials' tour of 1876 had first brought Saint Mary's to the attention of the eastern baseball world. The Phoenix contributed four players to the all-star squad: catcher Thomas ("Brick") Cullen, center fielder Nicholas Wynn, and pitchers Delos Ashley and William White. Although Wynn and White played only occasionally, White especially after he committed four errors and gave up thirteen hits in the loss to Rochester, Cullen caught most of the games on the tour and even played some center field. Throwing swift "in and out shoots," Ashley earned two victories on the mound for the Bay Area contingent and also played a couple of games in right field.[34]

The honor of being the first man from Saint Mary's to make it to the Majors, though, went not to any of these fellows but to Jeremiah Dennis Eldridge, aka Jerry Denny.[35] A student in the college from 1877 to 1879, Eldridge not only opened the door to the eastern professional leagues for subsequent members of the Phoenix but also contributed to the major controversy in intercollegiate baseball of his time. This centered on the question of whether or not a player could retain his amateur status for his college team and play for pay with professional or semipro clubs during the summer months and off-season.[36] Like others, Eldridge had done this under a thinly disguised pseudonym; he would hold on to his (Jerry Denny) throughout his professional career. The way in which Saint Mary's responded to the play-for-pay issue revealed both the nature of the controversy and one of the key factors that contributed to the Phoenix's great success on the diamond.

The question Eldridge's actions raised focused as much on the distinction between amateur and professional status as it did on notions of what was considered proper behavior or activity for a college gentleman. The latter concern particularly engaged those who looked to English universities for an amateur ideal. In that context, "intercollegiate" sport was the property of an aristocratic sporting elite who generally acknowledged a common body of established customs for their conduct. Foremost in their code was an emphasis on the distinction between work and play. It was simply bad form to commit too much to the pursuit of victory. Accepting pay for play, under any circumstances, violated the English gentleman's concept of fair sporting behavior.

The fluidity and diversity of American society, however, rejected the exclusiveness of the English sporting scene, despite protestations to the contrary, such as that of a Harvard professor who declared in 1889 that "a gentleman has something better to be than a professional athlete."[37] By the time Eldridge had signed a professional contract with Providence in 1881, baseball was well on its way to becoming, in Mark Twain's words, "the very symbol, the outward and visible expression of the drive and push and rush and struggle of the raging, tearing, booming nineteenth century."[38] This meant, particularly with regard to the play-for-pay issue, that neither the sponsors of teams who sought playing talent nor the collegians themselves who appreciated the earning power of their baseball skills looked upon the practice as socially or ethically reprehensible. It seemed consistent with the principles of a free and competitive market environment and the quest to gain an edge in it.

The lack of agreement among colleges and universities on how to deal with the play-for-pay issue and such other eligibility controversies of the late nineteenth century as a minimum residency requirement and the status of transfer, graduate, and professional-school students provided sufficient latitude for institutions and individuals to set their own standards. Saint Mary's was no exception. The college developed an eligibility code for its athletes that focused primarily on their identity as enrolled students of the college, not their status vis-à-vis a strict amateur ideal. Accordingly, the college permitted semiprofessionals to play for the Phoenix and its other athletic teams as long as they fulfilled minimum scholarship requirements and obeyed the college's rules of social conduct.[39] This halfway covenant with standards, lenient by some institutional practices, and firm by others, proved to be not only an effective approach in bringing young men to the college—and hence the Phoenix—but also a beneficial arrangement for them as long as they stayed. It was common practice for Saint Mary's to provide play-for-pay opportunities for its athletes with semipro teams in the local leagues. The best players on the Phoenix could expect to play for these clubs on holidays and Sundays during the regular collegiate playing season, as well as summers and vacations, for anywhere from five to twenty-five dollars per game plus considerations for room, meals, and trip fare. Pitchers and catchers rated the top stipends, but quality players in any position had access to these bonus arrangements.[40]

A generous eligibility policy provided the means for Saint Mary's to field potentially strong teams and such generally supportive conditions for baseball in the Bay Area as an extraordinary amount of sandlot and bush league activity, and a mild year-round climate served to foster playing talent. Yet it was the realization of that potential and the contributory effect of success to further success that largely explained the growing reputation of the Phoenix as a baseball powerhouse. The impressions of Saint Mary's baseball that Jerry (Eldridge) Denny left were positive ones, and his performance in the Majors opened wider the doors to the highest competitive circles for the Phoenix players who followed. In a thirteen-year career with seven different National League teams, Eldridge hit for a lifetime batting average of .260, which included 74 home runs and 512 runs batted in.[41] An ambidextrous third baseman, Eldridge disdained the use of a fielding glove. When he retired after the 1894 season, he was the last player in the professional leagues to go about his defensive chores without the leather.[42]

Following close on Eldridge's success were Saint Mary's alumni Jim Fogarty, Charlie Gagus, and Joe Corbett.[43] Although Fogarty had played second base for the Phoenix in 1883, he found himself in the outfield of the Philadelphia Phils for his Major League debut in 1884. He remained there throughout most of his seven-year career, earning a reputation as one of the most reliable outfielders around. His lifetime batting average of .246 included a career high .293 in 1886. His premature death in 1891, after one year with the Philadelphia entry in the abortive Players League, ended a modest but steady career. Gagus, a student at Saint Mary's from 1875 to 1877, played only one year in the Majors: with Washington of the Union Association in 1884. He compiled a 10–9 pitching record with a team-leading earned run average of 2.54 for a club which finished 46½ games behind league champion Saint Louis in the final standings. His .247 batting average also made him a useful substitute in the outfield.

Corbett, the younger brother of Gentleman Jim, the heavyweight boxing champion, attended the college from 1889 to 1893. He then pitched four years in the National League with Washington, Baltimore, and Saint Louis. His 35–21 career record on the mound included twenty-four wins for second-place Baltimore in 1897.

By 1910, fourteen former Phoenix had made it to the Major Leagues. No college or university west of the Mississippi came close to matching that record, and few elsewhere had comparable or larger numbers.[44] The list of schools that led in sending former students to the Major Leagues included several Catholic institutions, such as Notre Dame, Holy Cross, Georgetown, and Fordham. This phenomenon particularly underscored the conscious attempt of these colleges and universities to use athletics to further their interests. Faced with growing competition for both students and resources from the rapidly expanding land-grant and nonsectarian sectors of the higher-education community and concerned that their visibility was dimming as quickly as their moral authority, these schools increasingly turned to their intercollegiate programs as agents of institutional identity and promotion.[45] Although football and later basketball would be the sports of choice in this effort for Saint Mary's, as well as many other Catholic colleges and universities, baseball put the college on the athletic map first and set the tone for all subsequent forays into the world of intercollegiate athletics.

No one was more important in the effort to develop baseball at Saint Mary's than Brother Agnon McCann. Arriving in 1879, he quickly became the leader of the campus group that supported the growth of athletic programs. In 1883 he helped organize the Saint Mary's College Athletic Association, which raised funds through a five-dollar annual student membership fee to purchase athletic equipment for the school's teams and to keep the playing fields and track in good condition.[46] A staunch advocate of all athletics, Agnon particularly favored baseball and dedicated his energies to promoting and managing the school's program. Arranging games for the Phoenix at Central Park, an enclosed ball field at Eighth and Market streets in San Francisco, Agnon ensured a good audience for his players. Each Saint Mary's boy who made it to the professional leagues underscored for him the appropriateness of a major effort on behalf of baseball at the college.[47] For Agnon, career preparation was not restricted to academic lessons. Although this viewpoint was not shared by all members of the Christian Brothers community— and notwithstanding the summer play-for-pay issue—competitive success in the national game and the resulting favorable publicity for the college kept the pro-athletics group in charge of the situation for many years.[48]

Supported in his efforts by Brother Joseph Fenlon, the college's athletic director from 1905 to 1911, Agnon designed an elaborate infrastructure to develop players for the Phoenix. Harry Hooper's Midgets became the fourth team at Saint Mary's, joining the Phoenix and two junior varsity squads, the Young Phoenix and the Collegians, in Agnon's system. A fifth team would be added during Harry's years at the college. Assisting Agnon with the coaching chores were several Phoenix alumni who had remained in the Bay Area after leaving the college and volunteered their services to the team. Many of these men—like John Brady, Clarence Duggan, Tom Feeney, George Hailey, John McPartland, Joe Nunan, and George Poultney—had enjoyed brief stints with teams in the California, Pacific Coast, and Pacific National leagues. Similarly, the Brothers also attracted the expert help of several present or former Major Leaguers who either lived in the Bay Area during the off-season or had retired near the campus. Included in this group were Parke Wilson and George Van Haltren of the New York Giants, Doc Moskiman of the Boston Red Sox, and Hal Chase of the New York Highlanders.

As the number of talented individuals on the Phoenix suggested, the team enjoyed great success against other collegiate, amateur, semipro, and occasionally Major League competition. The club captured its first title in 1892 (the Pacific Amateur League), added both the California Collegiate and Midwinter Intercollegiate championships in 1893 and 1894, and then ran off twelve consecutive championships in the California-Nevada College Baseball League from 1901 to 1913. When the old California League broke up in 1893, the Phoenix played a large part in keeping baseball alive in the Bay Area by playing teams comprised of former league players. Oftentimes the opposition consisted of players lent from the Phoenix organization to field a full team. This practice allowed Saint Mary's to develop players for its first team. The Saint Mary's boys even proved their prowess against international competition, defeating a touring team from Waseda University of Japan 19–2 in 1902.

This was the scholastic scene and baseball tradition that Harry Hooper found at Saint Mary's. He fit in perfectly. In the classroom, Harry continued to excel, earning straight A's in mathematics and the sciences. Both Brother Bernard Kelly, the head of the college's new program in applied science, and Brother Leo McKinnon, an instructor in the engineering department, took a special interest in Harry and encouraged his work in their areas. This personal attention, which typified the learning environment of the two-hundred-student college, both helped and impressed him. Many years later he showed just how much by sending his own sons to his alma mater.

The well-rounded curriculum of the college gave Harry a chance to shine in other studies as well, and teachers outside his major program were just as eager to support his talents. Required to take music lessons, for example, Harry proved adept with both the violin and the tenor horn and played in the college orchestra and band. His music teacher, Charles Shorts, even thought Harry might have a future as a musician. He had occasionally wandered out to the ball field to watch the boys play and apparently had concluded that young Hooper's energies could be more profitably directed than shagging flies. He cornered Harry one day in the music room and asked, "Why don't you spend more time in here practicing your horn? Some day you might make some money at it." Harry was not persuaded.

Like most college students, career thoughts scarcely distracted Harry's attention from the good times he was having. Most of these centered on athletics. Saint Mary's offered competition in only two sports when Harry attended—baseball and handball. Although his competitive exposure to the former had been limited—in fact, the only time he had played a game with nine players on a side before coming to Saint Mary's was the Fourth of July picnic in Lock Haven—at least he was familiar with the game and the skills it required. Handball was a new sport altogether, yet it demanded the skills Harry had in abundance: quickness, keen hand-eye coordination, and a competitive spirit. During Harry's third year at Saint Mary's, Brother Joseph started an intramural tournament in handball, posting a gold medal on the college's bulletin board and announcing that the winner would claim it. Although he considered himself "more or less the dark horse," Hooper practiced hard with classmates Eddie Burns and Frank Dunn, two of the favorites in the tournament. Again, as with Uncle Mack's tutelage, Harry proved to be an excellent learner. Complementing his natural skills with new lessons in strategy, Harry mixed long and short shots with corner drops on his way to the championship and his first sports trophy, the athletic director's gold medal.

Handball, though, was only a diversion from the game that mattered most.[49] Working his way up through Agnon's system, Hooper became a starting pitcher for the Young Phoenix in his sophomore collegiate year. Weighing barely one hundred pounds and standing slightly over five feet tall, Harry could still whip the ball to the plate with enough speed to make him a formidable hurler for the junior varsity. Cracking the Phoenix lineup, however, was another matter. Although Hooper continued to throw for the Young Phoenix in his junior year, Agnon was becoming increasingly convinced that Harry's physical size and pitching velocity were not sufficient to make it as a pitcher with the first team. He convinced Harry to concentrate his considerable baseball talents on hitting and fielding. Harry's efforts to this end were rewarded with a starting spot in left field for the 1907 Phoenix.

Perhaps the finest Saint Mary's team before World War I and arguably one of the greatest nines in the history of the collegiate game, the Phoenix of Hooper's senior year was loaded with talent. Six future professionals, including Hooper, catcher Eddie Burns, pitcher Harry Krause, outfielders Charlie Enright and Mickey Thompson, and third baseman Joe Hamilton, appeared in the lineup. The College Athletic Association described them as "a neat lot of youngsters, whose laudable desire it is to uphold the laurels of Saint Mary's."[50] They managed to do that nicely. Sweeping through a twenty-seven game schedule without a defeat, the Phoenix took home the championship cups of both the Midwinter Intercollegiate League and the California-Nevada College League. Their victims included Stanford, the University of California, a Pacific Coast League all-star team and, in an exhibition contest before the start of the new Major League season, the Chicago White Sox. Their nineteen-year-old, occasional-horn-blowing left fielder led the College League in hitting with a .371 average. "Their ambition," observed the Athletic Association, was "fully satiated."

The great success of the 1907 Phoenix attracted the attention of scouts from California professional clubs and the Major Leagues. No one on the team received more attention than Hooper. The first to bid for Harry's services was Ray McMenomy, owner of the Alameda club in the California League. He approached Harry just before the end of the 1907 collegiate season and asked him if he would be interested in playing for his club. Hooper, who knew McMenomy from the previous summer, when he had stayed in Oakland to earn some money doing survey work for an engineer, agreed under certain conditions. Since his career sights at the moment were focused on engineering, not baseball, Hooper did not want to commit himself to playing for a club in a geographic area where he thought his long-term job prospects were limited. He told McMenomy that he would play for Alameda just for the stretch between the conclusion of the college season and his graduation from Saint Mary's, a period of only ten days. After that time, Harry wanted his release from the club so that he could pursue employment possibilities in either Sacramento or Stockton, where the operations of the Western Pacific and Southern Pacific railroads held more promise for the kind of job he was seeking. McMenomy agreed, and Hooper signed his first professional contract. It provided a standard guarantee for a percentage of the team's game-day gate receipts. In Harry's case, this meant about ten dollars a game.

Harry was wise in not committing to more than a few games with Alameda for other reasons as well. Foremost among these was the "outlaw" status of the California League.[51] Established in 1885, the CL had never acknowledged the authority of the 1883 National Agreement among the National League, the American Association, and the Northwestern League.[52] That tripartite pact had sought to differentiate between "major" and "minor" leagues and to regulate the competition among the leagues for players and territories. In particular, the agreement formally institutionalized the reserve provision in player contracts, thus binding players to the club for which they initially signed and protecting the clubs from raids on their rosters or defections from them. Enjoying their distance from the baseball wars of the East and convinced that the quality of play on the West Coast was the equal of any league elsewhere, major or minor, the California League defied the National Agreement, even as more and more leagues throughout the country came into its fold.

One of these leagues was the Pacific Coast League. Established in 1903 by baseball men who wished to expand the scope of organized professional play on the West Coast, the PCL initially included clubs from San Francisco, Los Angeles, Oakland, Sacramento, Portland, and Seattle. Like the California League, the PCL did not appreciate being relegated to minor league status by the National Agreement and ignored its authority in the League's first year of operation.[53] Neither, however, did the PCL want to be viewed as an outlaw, especially if that label hurt the career prospects of its players and the credibility of its product. When the three-man National Commission, which governed the National Agreement, declared that any player who broke his contract with an association team to join a club in an outlaw league would be banned from the former for life, the PCL reconsidered its independent status and accepted the National Agreement in 1904. Although the PCL would battle for fan support with the teams of the California League and of other West Coast leagues for several years to come, it had established itself as the dominant western baseball organization by the time Harry Hooper earned his first dollars as a professional ballplayer.

During his brief stint with Alameda, Harry played well at bat and in the field. He had a particularly good day against CL rival Sacramento on May 24, a game played just one week before Harry would graduate from Saint Mary's and complete his contract. Hitting two singles in four trips to the plate, he keyed two Alameda scoring rallies and prevented a Sacramento run when he threw out a runner attempting to go from first to third on a base hit. That evening, Hooper was visited in his room at the Clunie Hotel in Sacramento by Billy Curtin, owner of the Sacramento club. Curtin had been impressed with what he had seen of the young collegian. So, too, had been Sacramento's manager, Charlie Graham. While Curtin asked Hooper if he would be interested in playing for Sacramento, Graham approached McMenomy to see if he would release Harry from his contract. Neither, of course, knew the nature of Harry's short-term agreement with Alameda.

Hooper and McMenomy immediately conferred on the offer. Harry liked the idea of playing for Sacramento, but only if he could land a surveying job in the area. Mac had an angle as well. Since Curtin and Graham were unaware of Harry's expiring contract with Alameda, McMenomy saw an opportunity to profit by their ignorance. He convinced Harry not to say a word about their agreement for his services with Alameda and offered to split with him whatever price he could get in selling Harry to Sacramento. McMenomy then went off to negotiate with Graham.

"So how much do you want for Hooper?" asked Graham.

"How about two hundred dollars?" replied McMenomy.

The Sacramento coach immediately suspected something was amiss. As he told Hooper some time thereafter, "I smelled a rat." McMenomy seemed too eager to unload Hooper and the price was too low for the talent and potential Graham had seen.

"Well, now, Mac," he repled. "I expected to pay four or five hundred dollars for him. How about I give you fifty?"

Caught in his own game, McMenomy agreed.

Meanwhile, the other half of Harry's concerns was being addressed. Curtin had been in touch with Wally Pearson, field engineer for the Western Pacific and avid baseball fan. His father, D. W. Pearson, a supervising engineer for the railroad, was hiring surveyors for some new lines. D.W. agreed to give one of the jobs to Hooper at a starting salary of seventy-five dollars a month. Curtin offered Harry another eighty-five dollars a month to play ball for his team. Pocketing his twenty-five dollar share from the "deal" McMenomy had negotiated, Hooper accepted the offer, although it was clear that his priorities were still not yet set on baseball. "I played with the Sacramento club," Harry explained, "mainly because they promised to get me a surveying job. I guess you might say that was my bonus, a surveying job."[54]

Before donning his new uniform and sighting his level for the Western Pacific, Harry took a trip home to see his parents and brothers. He had to make two stops to catch up with them. He found George and Charles still working the family ranch in the valley. The years had been good to them. They had enjoyed bumper crops in recent years, and not even the great earthquake of 1906 had disrupted their productivity. It had rattled the farm buildings quite a bit, but it caused no real damage. George had also married since Harry started school at Saint Mary's, and the properties on the ranch had been expanded to accommodate his wife and the family they started.

Two good years in 1905 and 1906 had allowed Joe Hooper to fulfill a promise to Mary. He had told her that if they could string a couple of profitable years together, he would leave the ranch in the hands of their sons and retire to Capitola, a small coastal town on Monterey Bay just south of Santa Cruz. As Harry began his senior year at Saint Mary's, Joe and Mary hitched up a team and drove over to Capitola. In June 1907, Harry visited them in their new home and business, a rooming house in the center of the town which catered to vacationers from San Francisco and Oakland who came south for the warm waters of the bay.

Harry heartily approved of their move. Capitola was a charming Victorian community. Situated on the Ocean Shore Rail Line, which ran north all the way to San Francisco, it boasted several fine inns and beaches. They were filled on weekends and holidays throughout the year. Twenty-five years after they had turned over the keys to the Tres Piños Hotel, Joe and Mary were taking in guests again. The setting and circumstances, however, were very different this time around. The pace of their latter-day bed-and-breakfast inn agreed with the retirement couple, as did their steady flow of customers. Joe even managed to acquire additional properties in Capitola with the profits he realized from the boardinghouse. Harry particularly liked the fact that visits to his parents would no longer necessitate his working the harvester in the fields to feel useful around their home.

Harry stayed in Capitola for about two weeks before heading back to Sacramento. Although he was not expected to join the Sacts until the end of June, he needed to find a place to live and to start his job with the Western Pacific. He was fortunate on both accounts. He found a room in the home of William Henderson, whose wife and three sons immediately liked Harry and accepted him as one of the family. His first assignments for the railroad, sighting tracks for new lines heading north out of Sacramento to Pleasant Grove and south to Walnut Grove, were also satisfying. The routine work in the flat country of the central valley gave the novice engineer a chance to gain both confidence and experience.

Traveling in a mule-drawn wagon, Harry supervised a team of three men laying out the grade and slope stakes on the new lines. The work occasionally required that he spend a night or two during the week tenting out at the work site, but never weekends; that's when the Sacts played, every Sunday and every other Saturday, and Hooper quickly demonstrated why he was being paid more to play baseball than to plan trestles.

On July 4, Harry made his debut in center field for Sacramento against arch-rival Stockton. In his first at bat, Hooper singled. In his second, he tripled. In his third, he singled again. By the end of the afternoon, Harry had banged out seven hits in eight trips to the plate, had scored three runs, and had fielded his position flawlessly. It was, observed the *Sacramento Bee,* "an impressive performance."

It was also one that no one could have sustained for long. But a month later and a look at all of the Sacts' opponents, Harry was still hitting at a .471 clip (16 for 34). As is generally the case with an unknown player who starts fast, the next time opposing pitchers faced him, they paid him more heed and gave him less to hit. Harry only managed two hits in his next twenty at bats, then settled into a respectable groove that would carry him the rest of the season. In thirty-three games for the Sacts, Harry compiled a .328 batting average, tallied twenty-one runs, and stole thirteen bases. He was proving himself to be quite a bargain for fifty dollars.

He was also developing into a fine engineer. In 1908, Hooper's responsibilities with the railroad increased as his experience and performance merited more difficult assignments. He was one of the on-site engineers for the construction of the B Street underpass in Sacramento, where he graded and supervised the concrete work. The most elaborate and dangerous project on which he worked was a girder bridge across the American River just east of the city. Building out from both sides of the crossing point, the railroad construction crews placed six eighty-foot spans across the river. Harry was at the site primarily to learn, but he did manage to impress the crew one day with his skills—his baseball skills, that is. Challenged to show the strength of his arm, Harry did his best George Washington imitation and successfully threw a rock across the Sacramento—a toss of over five hundred feet—while the workers cheered. There was no cheering, however, a few months later when the river, swollen from winter rains, threatened to wash out the new bridge. In order to stabilize and weigh down the bridge, Joseph Garibaldi, chief engineer at the site, directed that several gondola cars loaded with rock be moved onto the span's tracks. He was on the section of the bridge with the cars when a key support gave way to the powerful current. It took several weeks to recover the bodies of Garibaldi and the other crewmen who died in the tragedy.

What Harry Hooper had accomplished on the Northern California diamonds during the 1908 season may have saved him from being on the bridge at the time of its collapse. He had a spectacular year. Playing on a team about evenly divided between over-the-hill minor league veterans and young hopefuls like himself, a roster which increasingly looked familiar throughout the Cal State League as it lost playing talent to the Pacific Coast League, the engineer-ball-player hit for a .347 average, scoring thirty-nine runs and stealing thirty-four bases in just sixty-eight games. His performance earned him the accolade "Ty Cobb of the State League," since it reminded many of the Detroit Tigers' star outfielder, who, at age twenty in 1907, became the youngest player in Major League history to win a batting title (.350). Cobb led the American League in batting again in 1908 with a .324 mark on his way to nine consecutive batting titles. The similarities extended to more than just batting averages. Both Cobb and Hooper were natural right-handers who taught themselves to hit left-handed in order to gain an extra step in running to first. Both had excellent speed and an aggressive style on the base paths that translated into stolen bases and extra-base hits. Coupled with powerful throwing arms, their speed underscored their play in the field as well. Both had led their respective leagues in outfield assists in 1908. No one, least of all Harry Hooper, thought his league and Cobb's were comparable, but as he completed his second season of professional ball, Hooper wondered whether his days working on the railroad might be numbered.

Others were raising this question, too. Judge W. W. McCredie, owner of the Portland Beavers in the PCL, had written Hooper to ask whether Harry would be interested in playing for his club. The judge never made a specific offer, though. Meanwhile, Harry's manager had something more concrete in mind. Late in the 1908 season, Charlie Graham approached Hooper and asked, "How would you like to look at the Big Apple?" Harry was not quite sure what he meant. "Well," explained Graham, "I'm a scout for the Boston Red Sox. How would you like to go back and go to the big leagues?" Harry confessed that he had never seriously considered that possibility. Baseball, he felt, "was a sideline to engineering to make enough money for a living."

Graham persisted. He told Harry that he had written Red Sox owner John Taylor on several occasions about his play and potential. Now Taylor was due shortly in the Bay Area to check out some California prospects. Graham encouraged Harry to meet him. Figuring that the worst he would realize from a tryout with Boston was "a nice trip and a chance to see the East," Harry agreed to talk to Taylor. He asked Graham's advice on what kind of money he should expect from him. The man who bought Hooper for fifty dollars was an old hand at such matters. "I think he will offer you about twenty-five hundred dollars a year," Graham thought, "so if I were you I'd ask for about three thousand and see what he says."

A week later, Hooper and Taylor met at one of Harry's favorite haunts in Sacramento, a saloon at Eighth and J streets in which one of his fellow engineers at the Western Pacific, George Newberger, had a part interest. The saloon also served a fine porter which suited Harry's taste. When he had come down with a bad case of dysentery soon after his arrival in the state capital, Harry found that the porter settled his stomach and helped him regain the weight the infection had caused him to lose. For five cents, the establishment served "a great big scuttle" of Harry's medicinal brew, which he was happy to consume with his teammates and co-workers often until the saloon closed at 9:00 P.M. On this occasion, though, Harry was looking for more than a full glass of beer.

As Graham had advised, Hooper responded to Taylor's question of how much it would take for the Red Sox to sign him with a request for three thousand dollars. And as his manager had predicted, Taylor had a counteroffer.

"I had been thinking about twenty-five hundred dollars," replied Taylor. "How about twenty-eight hundred?"

The sum was almost a thousand dollars more than Harry was earning for the year with his engineering and baseball salaries combined. He told Taylor they had a deal.

Harry immediately tendered his resignation to the Western Pacific. Pressed by his mother, who had heard rumors of Boston's interest in her son, Harry went home to Capitola to explain his decision.[55] He was there with the entire family—Joe and Mary, the brothers and George's wife, Molly, Aunt Mary and her husband and children—for Thanksgiving. He was just three months past his twenty-first birthday, a promising career as an engineer declined and an uncertain one as a baseball player awaiting. "I wanted to be an engineer," Hooper would insist later, "but I went to Boston." The game of his youth had become the profession of his future.

A Season
in the Majors

Boston, Mass., February 15th, 1909.

Mr. Harry B. Hooper
c/o Charles Graham
Sacramento, California

Dear Sir:—

You had better arrange to make the trip to Hot Springs so that you
will arrive there not later than February 27th as the team will start
work on March 1st.

The Club will stop at the Majestic Hotel during its stay at Hot
Springs.

Yours sincerely,
Hugh A. McBreen, Treasurer

The instructions to join the Red Sox in Hot Springs, Arkansas, did not
catch Hooper unawares. Through Graham, he had kept in touch with
John Taylor, who had just returned from a trip to China and Japan
and was on the West Coast himself to conclude a contract with another California prospect, Babe Danzig of San Francisco. Taylor had
invited Harry to join him, Danzig, second-year pitcher Frank Arellanes, the New York Highlanders' Hal Chase and his wife, and another Red Sox hopeful, Harry Wolter of Monterey, on their train trip
east, departing Oakland on Sunday, February 28.[1] Although this
would cause Hooper to arrive in Hot Springs a few days later than his
appointed time, he figured that traveling with the club's president
was neither an unwise way to cross the country nor a poor excuse for
missing the opening of training. Harry received a warm send-off
from a few friends who had accompanied him to the Oakland station,
a scene which was repeated when the train made a station stop in
Sacramento two hours later. On March 4, the Boston party—minus

the Chases, who had changed trains in Kansas City—pulled into Hot Springs.

Situated in the piney foothills of the Ozark Mountains fifty-five miles southwest of Little Rock, Hot Springs was a thriving resort community with a resident population of about 12,000. Offering a moderate year-round climate, easy accessibility via three railroad lines, and a beautiful natural setting, the town promised visitors— and 150,000 came annually—"health, pleasure and sightseeing."[2] The centers of attraction were "the wonderful radio-active hot waters" which flowed from forty-six hot springs in the area and soothed the tourists in the pools of nineteen bathhouses. Ten of these were clustered at the base of Hot Springs Mountain and formed Bath House Row. The other nine, including one in the Majestic Hotel, were mainly at either end of Central Avenue, the city's "modern White Way" with its new electric lighting system.

The healing waters and warming temperatures also attracted ballplayers. Albert Spalding, owner of the Chicago White Stockings, sent his manager, Cap Anson, and fourteen of his players there in 1886 to set up what many regard as baseball's first spring training camp.[3] There had been other spring training excursions before Anson sought the baths to "boil out the alcoholic microbes" in his men, but these had been short trips, with little in the way of an established regimen for the players.[4] As early as 1869, for example, Boss Tweed of Tammany Hall had sent his New York Mutuals to New Orleans to prepare for the championship season by playing local teams. The following February, both the Cincinnati Red Stockings and Chicago did the same. But Anson put his charges through a strenuous program of long hikes and twice-daily workouts that proved a lesson to other clubs, especially when his boys won their second consecutive National League title in 1886. By the turn of the century, spring training had become a regular part of the professional baseball scene, with camps operating from West Baden, Indiana, to Mexico City and Savannah, Georgia, to Los Angeles.[5] From the positive effects on the local economies when the clubs were in training to the generation of interest for the approaching season among the fans back home through on-site press reports, the spring camps offered benefits beyond player conditioning that ensured their place in the baseball calendar.

Nineteen nine marked Boston's first spring in the "Valley of the Vapors," although the club was familiar with its attractions since it had trained the two previous years in nearby Little Rock. The Red Sox shared the town's baseball fields with the Pittsburgh Pirates, who started coming to Hot Springs in 1901.[6] The best of the two fields in 1909 adjoined the zoo in spacious Whittington Park. There one could watch the professionals work off the winter beer while a full schedule of balloon ascensions, bicycle races, and grandstand concerts provided additional entertainment. In the south end of the city between an ostrich ranch and an alligator farm lay Majestic Park, the "home" of the Red Sox for thirteen springs between 1909 and 1923.[7] This location afforded spectators more than baseball as well. The sight of an enormous ostrich harnessed to a cart dashing across the grounds was not uncommon. Similarly, H. L. Campbell's nearby alligator farm boasted several hundred of the reptiles and an elaborate chute system on which they performed. The whole scene suggested the day when theme parks and amusement centers in California and Florida would add to the attraction of following one's favorite team to spring training. The sights of Hot Springs would have to wait for Hooper to enjoy, however, as he dutifully reported to the practice field shortly after his noon arrival at the Majestic.

With the four Californians now in camp, the Red Sox had twenty-seven men vying for the twenty-three spots on the team. Boston was a team in transition in 1909 and the faces at Hot Springs clearly revealed that. Gone were the great veterans Cy Young, Jimmy Collins, and Bill Dinneen, who had led the club to consecutive league championships in 1903 and 1904. With the productive years of these stars passing and the club failing to find adequate talent to support them, Boston slipped badly in the standings over the next few years. From 1905 to 1908, the Red Sox finished no higher than fourth in the league. In only one of these seasons, 1905, had the club managed a winning season (78–74). In 1906, they suffered through the humiliation of a 49–105 record leaving them 45½ games behind league champion Chicago in the standings. It was little consolation that Boston's other Major League team, the National League Braves, finished further back in their pennant race. Fred Tenney's boys barely glimpsed the champion Cubs from 66½ games behind at the season's end, although their overall record, 49–102, was a few percentage points better than that of the Red Sox.

Much of the criticism for the team's disappointing performance during these years focused on new owner John I. Taylor. John, the son of *Boston Globe* publisher Charles Taylor, had acquired the club in 1904 as a gift from his father, as many observed, to give him something useful to do. The team's record in the early years of young Taylor's ownership convinced his detractors that his usefulness, such as it was, could be better demonstrated in other ways. So far, it seemed that all Taylor had done was to change the club's name from the Pilgrims to the Red Sox and preside over a reversal of the team's fortunes on the field. Although the team had shown signs of renewed life in 1908 with a fifth-place finish and a 75–79 record, Hooper's rookie season was a critical test for the owner as well.

What was on the line for the Red Sox in the new season was the owner's strategy to build a pennant contender around an entirely new nucleus of young arms, power at the plate, and speed on the base paths. The keys to the starting rotation were right-handers Eddie Cicotte, Joe Wood, and Frank Arellanes and a lefty, Fred Burchell. Cicotte had joined the Red Sox for the 1908 season after only one previous season in the Majors with Detroit in 1905. Working beside Cy Young during the veteran's last year with Boston, Cicotte had developed an effective knuckleball and spitball on his way to an 11–12 season with a 2.43 ERA. His 207 innings pitched were second only to Young's 299. Wood had made his Boston debut in 1908 as well, but appeared in only six games, earning a win and a loss in his two decisions. But the blazing fastball and overall athletic ability he demonstrated in his few outings convinced Taylor and manager Freddie Lake that he was a player with a future. They looked to Wood as a starter in 1909. San Jose's Arellanes had appeared in eleven games for Boston in 1908, eight as a starter, and earned four wins against three defeats. Although he did not possess a great pitch or two like Cicotte and Wood, Arellanes had impressed Lake with his stamina and the manager expected to use him both as a starter and for late-inning relief. Burchell had posted respectable numbers in 1908, his second season with Boston. His 10–8 record, though with a relatively high ERA of 2.96, merited serious consideration for a spot in the regular rotation, especially with a staff short on left-handers. Other contenders for the Boston rotation would likely be drawn from newcomers Charlie Chech and Jack Ryan, both of whom had come to the Red Sox in the trade which sent Young to Cleveland; Charlie Hall, another big right-handed thrower from California who had spent two mediocre seasons with the Indians in 1906–7; and Hooper's traveling companion, Harry Wolter, who offered versatility as a first baseman, outfielder, and left-handed pitcher.

Like the pitching staff, the Boston roster registered newcomers at virtually every field position. Only Heinie Wagner at shortstop and Bill Carrigan behind the plate had at least two complete seasons of experience with the Red Sox to their credit. Tris Speaker, for example, although he had joined the club in 1907, had appeared in only thirty-eight games prior to the 1909 season. Returning for only their second full season in a Red Sox uniform were, with the exception of Wagner, the entire Boston infield: Jake Stahl at first, Amby McConnell at second, and Harry Lord at third. Both Harry Niles and Larry Gardner had been with the Red Sox in 1908 but had seen little playing time at second and third base, respectively. Matters were no different in the outfield. Jack Thoney and Doc Gessler were the two veterans, but both had had modest journeyman careers, playing for four Major League teams apiece before joining Boston in 1908. The other contender for a spot in the starting outfield was Wolter, but the Sox's dearth of left-handed pitching had him slated for work on the mound unless one of the regular outfielders faltered.

This was the situation that greeted Hooper when he and the other late arrivals from California reached Hot Springs. Since he had played ball into November in Sacramento and spent the winter months strengthening his legs running on the Capitola beaches, Harry was already in good baseball shape. His readiness for work and eagerness to make a favorable impression, however, drew mixed reactions from those who were watching him. Harry Casey, one of the *Boston Globe*'s reporters in the Red Sox camp, characterized Hooper as "particularly ambitious" and noted how manager Lake had reprimanded him for throwing too hard in the early going.[8] The *Globe*'s man cited the opinions of "old-timers" who had seen Hooper play on the West Coast that the twenty-one-year-old was "ready to become a regular in any fast company."[9] Conceding that Hooper was "a clever young student" who reminded some observers of Ty Cobb, the correspondent balked at other comparisons with another San Francisco area product, Bill Lange, whose short but brilliant career with Chicago in the 1890s had set the standard by which all West Coast players were measured.[10] With a lifetime batting average of .330 and such heroic exploits to his credit as a game-saving catch allegedly made after crashing through a wooden fence, Little Eva Lange ranked among the finest all-around talents in the game.[11]

The suggestion that Hooper was a "second Bill Lange" only underscored for Casey that a high recommendation "means very little in baseball." Players "touted as wonders" like Hooper, he wrote, "are usually the ones to become a bit nervous and fail to make good from the jump." Calling Lange "one of the rarest stones ever picked up on the diamond fields," the reporter felt that "young Hooper will be lucky if he comes within 20 points of the record left by Sir William Lange." Apparently, Hooper's drive, intensity and style of play, notably his sliding catch, came across as cockiness, even showboating, to the reporter, for he turned to another new player as the object of his plaudits. "The prize package" among the Californians, he observed, was not Hooper but Harry Wolter, "a man who wins your admiration by every move." Extolling Wolter's knowledge of the game and virtuosity as a pitcher, fielder, and "natural batsman," he advised the *Globe*'s readership to look for good things from this "young fellow from the golden shores of the Pacific."[12]

Hooper saw things differently and sought to demonstrate to Boston's manager and players, if not the press, that he belonged with the club. After only a few days in Hot Springs, Harry had assessed his competition and concluded that "the only outfielder there that looked any good" was Tris Speaker. The others, he observed, either "weren't fast enough, or couldn't field, or couldn't throw." He dismissed Thoney, for example, as someone who "couldn't throw a ball thirty feet," an estimate not far from the truth owing to an arm injury Thoney had suffered sliding into second a couple of seasons earlier. Another unidentified contender for a spot in the outfield, Harry felt, apparently had little idea of how to field a fly ball, as his backpedaling to retrieve them frequently ended with him flat on his rump on the ground. The fact that the Boston papers did not see things quite this way only made Hooper "boiling hot."[13]

His treatment at the hands of the veterans in camp did not cool his fire much. The returning players for Boston, particularly those who may have been threatened by the talents of Hooper and the other newcomers, were not about to make things easy for the rookies, much less concede a place in the lineup to any of them. The veterans monopolized the batting cage, for example, forcing Hooper and his rookie teammates to take bats and balls to other areas of the practice field to conduct their own batting practice. Hooper was angered by this practice, finding it detrimental to both team spirit and player development. Moreover, it seemed an unnecessary humiliation of the younger players. It was an experience he would not forget when he joined the ranks of the veterans. For the moment, though, Harry grabbed what batting practice he could and augmented the team's workout sessions with runs in the nearby hills, especially when bad weather kept him off the diamond.

His first opportunity to display his talents in competition came on March 9 when the Red Sox squared off for their first intrasquad game of spring training. Hooper found himself positioned in left field and batting seventh in the order for the Regulars, captained by Doc Gessler. Their opponents, under Harry Niles's direction, were designated the Yannigans, a popular term of the day connoting rookie or second-string status. Hooper was the only one of the California contingent on the Regulars' roster.

He played, as he had figured, like he belonged. In three trips to the plate in the seven-inning game, Harry hammered out two singles and a double.[14] The two-base hit in the second off Jack Ryan drove in Jake Stahl with the Regulars' first run of the game, although Harry was thrown out at third trying to stretch the hit into a triple. Both of his singles contributed to innings of four runs each in the fourth and fifth frames. He came around to score after both hits, one tally aided by a stolen base. In the field, Hooper hauled in one fly ball but let a hard liner off the bat of Elmer Steele get through him for an extra-base error which allowed two runs to score. Nevertheless, the Regulars rallied from a 7–2 deficit after two innings to pound out a 10–7 win.[15]

The Red Sox got in another game the next day—Harry was hitless in three at bats but fielded four chances flawlessly in left—before the skies opened and a heavy spring rain interrupted practice for several days. The absence of activity on the ball field gave Hooper and his teammates ample opportunity to explore the wonders of Hot Springs. His diary entries for these days provide a charming picture of a young man on holiday.[16] With his steady companion, Harry Wolter, Hooper seemed very much the tourist, picking up a souvenir shaving mug, getting measured for a new suit, joining the other Boston rookies for a traditional picture in an ox-drawn cart, hiking to the top of the 165-foot-tall steel tower atop West Mountain for a panoramic view of Hot Springs Valley and the surrounding countryside. Forsaking the dark pleasures of the Black Orchid, the town's notorious dance hall with its black "hostesses," Harry opted instead for the theater and tenpins. A production at the opera house, entitled "Dolly Dimples," merited a one-word review in his diary: "poor." The bowling proved more enjoyable as Hooper joined his teammates to defeat a foursome of Chicago Cubs who were in town for several days to prepare for the new season.

When the weather permitted intrasquad games to resume on March 15, Hooper continued his fine play. He had a run-scoring single in three at bats for the Regulars in a 5–2 win over the Yannigans. His play featured a bullet throw to the plate to hold a runner on third after Harry had hauled in a long drive down the left field line. The next day he slugged his first home run as a Red Sox in two plate appearances as the Regulars defeated the second-stringers again, 5–3.

The press finally began to take notice of his play and potential.

Hooper "seemed to get plenty of ginger in him when it came to being placed under fire," observed Boston reporter Tim Murnane. Another noted how Hooper "awakened" in game situations, dispelling those critics who had previously labeled the young man from California as "a bit lazy and unambitious." "He is working diligently," said the *Globe*'s Casey, "correcting some of the poor impressions he made his first few days out."[17]

What these accounts had captured, barely two weeks into Hooper's first year as a Major League professional, were qualities that would characterize his play throughout his entire career—a graceful, efficient playing manner and performance under pressure. His effortless running style and quick reflexes belied his actual speed afoot. Later, as he carefully studied opposing pitchers and batters, he added a calculated anticipation to his repertoire as a fielder and base runner. His successful start in spring training recalled his debut for Sacramento and presaged performances in other pressure situations during regular season and World Series play. As the Red Sox prepared to leave Hot Springs for a long train tour which would eventually bring them to Philadelphia for the opening of the 1909 season, Hooper's persistent critic with the *Globe* conceded that Harry "will become a fine ball player in time, and the Red Sox will have use for him."[18]

For the next three weeks the Red Sox were on the road. The rains in Hot Springs had turned the nearly grassless ball park into a sea of mud, so Lake decided to cut short their stay by a week and begin a series of scheduled games against local professional teams in several station-stop cities that much earlier. Their itinerary included a week in Memphis, several days each in Nashville and Cincinnati, then a circuitous swing east through Indianapolis, Dayton, Wilkes-Barre, and Buffalo. The wet weather followed them north, turned colder, and caused as many games to be canceled as were played. On the weekend before the opening game in the City of Brotherly Love, Harry and his teammates conducted practice in a light snowfall.

Hooper's place on the Boston roster, if not his role in the starting lineup, seemed assured through his steady play during spring training. Since the Regulars' Speaker and Gessler were slated to open the season in center and right, respectively, Lake occasionally moved Hooper to the Yannigans to test him in an outfield position other than left. Although this gave Hooper an opportunity to display his versatility and fielding range, the move particularly benefited Harry Niles. For with his infield set, Lake looked to utilize Niles in other ways and experimented throughout the spring with him in the outfield. Niles, who had broken into the Major Leagues as a right fielder with the Saint Louis Browns in 1906, and in fact led the league at his position that rookie year with thirty-four assists, had played a few games in the outfield for Boston as well in 1908. His play in left for the Regulars when Hooper moved to the Yannigans convinced Lake that Niles would do a better job there than Jack Thoney, who had reported to Hot Springs overweight and had progressed very slowly in getting into playing shape.

Hooper did not take these developments particularly well. He confided to his diary that he was "quite frankly, disappointed" that Niles and, occasionally, Wolter, replaced him in left with the first-stringers.[19] A cryptic notation, "Played the bench," suggested his frustration.[20] On one occasion after the Red Sox had dropped a 2–0 decision to Memphis of the Southern Association on a hit that dropped between Niles and Speaker, Harry critically noted that the runs came "on a ball that no one goes after."[21] It was clear to Hooper that he belonged in the starting lineup on opening day. He continued to hit and field well in those games in which he played—a single in four trips against Nashville, two for five against Cincinnati in the finale of the three-game set there—but Niles seemed to have the edge. His "sweet fielding" and surprising power at the plate, including a home run for "one of the longest hits made on the trip," improved the chances of the twenty-nine-year-old veteran of three seasons for the left-field assignment in Philadelphia.[22]

Lake erased any doubts about the starting lineup for opening day when he informed the team in Buffalo on April 10 that Arellanes would be on the mound and Niles in left. Elsewhere, the Red Sox showed Stahl, McConnell, and Lord on the bases, Wagner at short, Carrigan behind the plate, Speaker in center, and, a mild surprise, Thoney in the other outfield spot. With the news, Lake, the starters, and most of the pitching staff headed on to Philadelphia, while the subs stayed over in Wilkes-Barre for a final practice game, a 1–0 win against the local entry in the New York State League. The next day, Monday the twelfth, Hooper and his teammates took the 7:40 A.M. train out of Wilkes-Barre for Philadelphia. They pulled into the Thirtieth Street Station before noon and a quick carriage ride later arrived at Shibe Park for the first game of the 1909 season.[23]

It was a grand day. The cold snap broke and pleasant temperatures in the low sixties warmed the crowd of more than thirty thousand who packed the new park for its debut as well. Shortly before three in the afternoon, both teams marched out to center field where the Stars and Stripes were raised and the ballplayers joined the crowd in a rendition of "America." Mayor John Reyburn tossed out the first ball a few minutes later and Eddie Plank took the hill for Connie Mack's Athletics. Gettysburg Eddie kept the home fans happy. Scattering six hits and striking out five, Plank gave up only one run to the visitors as Philadelphia opened with a solid 8–1 win. Danny Murphy's four hits, including two doubles, and Simon Nicholls's three singles paced the A's as they chased Arellanes in the seventh inning.[24]

The Red Sox notched their first win of the 1909 campaign the next day as Charlie Chech went the distance against Jack Coombs in a 4–2 decision. Hooper watched this game, as he had the opener, from the bench. Two games into the championship season, Harry was learning some new and particularly harsh lessons about a rookie's lot on a Major League team. Not only did he sit out the entire Philadelphia series (games 3 and 4 were rained out), he never even had a chance to take the field; he sat in the dugout in his home uniform, his road uniform having been lent to Charlie French, who had been recalled to the roster to play second when a family emergency took Wagner out of the lineup and illness felled his backup.[25] Despite his impressive and promising work in the preseason, Hooper was blocked in his quest for playing time just as his participation in batting practice had been restricted during spring training. This time his foil was the entrenched preference of baseball management to stick with a veteran lineup in the early going and while the games still mattered. Thoney's place in the starting outfield underscored this decision. Hooper's uncertainty about his status was also fueled through disturbing rumors in the press that he shortly would be sent to Saint Paul of the American Association for more seasoning.[26]

Nevertheless, when the team arrived in Washington for the second series of the young season, Hooper was still with it, although he was not optimistic that things would be any different against the capital city club. Lake's announcement at breakfast on the morning of the series opener that he would play the same lineup as the Philadelphia games seemed to confirm Harry's assessment of the situation. He vented his frustration through a climb to the top of the Washington Monument before heading to the ballpark. To his surprise, Lake was waiting for him when he arrived with the appropriate uniform and an assignment: starting left field, batting seventh. With Thoney ill and Wagner still absent, the manager had moved Niles to short and inserted Hooper in the lineup.[27]

Hooper barely had time to appreciate this turn of events before he was thrust into a critical game situation. In the top of the second,

Harry came to the plate with two out and a runner on second. On the mound for Washington was Bill Burns, a burly six-foot two-inch left-hander. The chance to break through early against the big man cheered the Red Sox and they asked excitedly, "Who's up? Who's up?" as Hooper made his way to the batter's box. The rookie recalled that his teammates were not exactly brimming with confidence about his chances. "'Hooper's up' someone said, and I could see everyone thinking, 'Oh, well, that's too bad.'"[28]

Harry chased their gloom with one swing. He lined a Burns fast-ball for a single, driving in his first Major League run. He collected a second single before the afternoon was over and almost nailed a third when Burns instinctively threw his glove in front of a line drive that shot off Harry's bat to rob him of another base hit. In the field, the young Californian snagged three fly balls and recorded his first assist when he threw out a man at the plate. "Got off lucky," Harry noted in his diary, although he added that "with more luck would have had four hits."[29]

The Red Sox lost the game, 3–2, but no one was happier in the Boston dressing room afterward than John Taylor. "That's the boy I signed in California," he declared to anyone who would listen as he shook every hand in sight.[30] Lake agreed that "there is awful good material in that boy" and added that "he will make his mark in the big league just as Speaker is doing now."[31] Hooper acknowledged the "combination of circumstances" that had opened a spot for him in the lineup but knew that he still had to prove that he belonged there. Lake rewarded Harry's performance with starts in the other two games of the Washington series and the rookie played well. Although hitless in Boston's 6–1 win the next day, Hooper stole a base after a walk and handled three chances in the outfield without a problem. In the finale of the series, attended by President William Howard Taft, Hooper contributed a hit in three plate appearances to an 8–4 Red Sox victory, scored two runs, and recorded six putouts in left.[32] Heading to Boston for the home opener, the Red Sox sported a 3–2 record. Hooper showed a respectable .273 average for his first week in the Majors at bat and a perfect mark in the field.

Harry got his first look at Boston's home field, the Huntington Avenue Baseball Grounds, on the afternoon before the series opener against the Athletics. Without the ring of spectators who often lined up ten deep or more on raised ground that swept from one foul line to the other across the far reaches of the outfield, the playing area seemed to stretch forever. By most ballpark dimensions, it did. The former site of circuses and carnivals, Huntington Grounds did not lack for space. From home plate to the left-field fence, behind which ran Huntington Avenue, the line traveled 440 feet. As distant as this fence was, it was almost 200 feet *shorter* than straightaway center. From there, home was a mere speck in the infield diamond, 635 feet distant, nearly one-eighth of a mile away. By comparison, the 280-foot right-field line scarcely seemed more than a step or two behind first base.[33]

Since the seating capacity in the old wooden grandstand was only 9,000, several thousand more fans frequently stood in the outfield, especially for big games. The first and third games of the 1903 World Series, for example, drew 16,242 and 18,801, respectively, to the grounds.[34] The early arrivals claimed space on the low, semicircular hill across the outfield. The wall they created reduced the dimensions of the park by over one-hundred feet in left and two-hundred feet in center. Other patrons gathered on a second hill that stretched from left center to dead center. From this vantage point they could view the field over the heads of the spectators on the inner hill, which was about fifty feet in front of them.

Despite morning temperatures barely above freezing, the fans packed the twin rises of the Huntington Grounds outfield early on April 21 for the Red Sox home opener. Hooper had a closer view than any of them, but a view was all he had. Lake put Thoney back in the lineup for the game, a courtesy to the veteran and an indication that the manager was not about to assign left field to a rookie with only three games of experience. Hooper simply reported his status as "benched," from where he watched Charlie Chech notch his second win of the young season.[35] A triple steal involving Lord, Gessler, and Speaker highlighted Boston's 6–2 victory. The fleet Speaker added two more stolen bases of his own as some of the speed which Taylor had acquired with him, Wagner, Gardner, Stahl, and Hooper began to manifest itself.

Harry found himself back in the starting lineup for the second and third games of the Athletics series but could not manage a hit in either game against Philadelphia's outstanding pitching. In addition to Plank, the formidable A's rotation included Chief Bender, Jack Coombs, and fellow Saint Mary's College alumnus Hal Krause. They would produce the American League's best team ERA in 1909, 1.92. Krause, like the other starters one of Connie Mack's college boys, was embarked on his best season in the Majors. His 1.39 earned run average and strikeout rate of 5.87 per nine innings led his league in both categories. In this first series of the 1909 campaign between the Red Sox and the A's, Krause contributed to his former teammate's poor showing at the plate and Hooper went to the bench again as a result. It was becoming clear to Harry that Lake intended to alternate him and Thoney, going with whoever had the hot bat.

Harry's turn came again quickly. It began rather innocently when Lake sent him in to pinch-run for Tubby Spencer in the ninth inning of the series opener against New York on May 6. Harry eventually came around to score Boston's winning run in the game. Although Hooper failed as a pinch hitter for Spencer in the ninth inning of the next game, the manager increasingly liked what he saw in the Californian and decided to give him some regular playing time. Hooper responded to the challenge in typical fashion—he launched the first batting streak of his Major League career. From May 8 to May 17, against New York, Cleveland, and Detroit, Hooper batted .500 (12 for 24). His work at the plate during this stretch included two four-hit games, one coming against Cy Young and the other off Tiger pitching in his first appearance on a playing field with Ty Cobb.

As the Red Sox began their second cycle through the American League, the opposing pitchers also got their second look at Hooper. By this time they had begun to form a book on him, appreciating his strengths, noting his weaknesses. At bat, Hooper seemed to offer no surprises as he appeared to fit the mold of most Major League hitters of his day. Since offensive strategy focused on manufacturing one run at a time, the ability to get on base, to build a score through smart base running, and to advance runners ahead of you mattered highly. Hooper tailored his batting style accordingly. A natural right-handed thrower and batter, Harry had experimented as a switch hitter at Saint Mary's and with Alameda. He decided to make the conversion completely to left-handed hitting in order to gain the extra step in leaving the batter's box from the first-base side. His batting stance eschewed power for dependable contact. Standing in a slight crouch, bent at the waist, hands slightly separated on the bat, Hooper would swing his arms back and forth in front of him like a pendulum while he eyed the pitcher. As the pitcher began his windup, Hooper would settle his hands at chest level, his bat extended backward at an angle slightly higher than the parallel of his shoulders. His slightly open stance afforded a full view of the pitcher and the ball once it left his hand. Relaxed at the plate, loose and graceful in his manner, Harry showed his teammates other reasons why he wore the nickname "Cat." By midseason the rookie had acquired a not entirely uncomplimentary variation of his moniker: Pussy Foot.

His inexperience and conventional appearance at the plate affected the way pitchers threw to him initially. Fastballs on the inside of the plate tested his nerve and bat speed. Balls thrown to the outside explored his batting eye, patience, and inclination either to go with a pitch or attempt to pull it. The early line on Hooper, not uncommon for many rookies, suggested vulnerability to sharp breaking pitches. As a result, Harry saw more curves and spitters as the season developed. This strategy seemed an effective one, because no sooner had the Red Sox started their second swing through the league then Harry's hitting streak came to an end. He was back on the bench for almost a month from late May to late June.

In dealing with the first slump of his Major League career, Hooper revealed more to opposing managers and pitchers about his baseball ability and attitude than the mechanics of his batting stance and swing. Hooper had learned his lessons well from Brother Agnon. Speed, timing, and a good eye, as solidly as one possessed these physical assets, would not guarantee success at the plate. They had to be tempered with patience, especially an appreciation of the breaks of the game, and honed with hard work. Although Hooper would become a better hitter as he became familiar with the pitchers he faced and the strengths of his teammates in the lineup with him, he brought an intensity and intelligence to the Major Leagues that his experience there confirmed.

Hooper's approach to the many aspects of the game consistently revealed these qualities. On his problems at bat in his rookie season, Hooper recognized that slumps are a part of the game which affect everyone.[36] Although "hard to figure," they usually start, he explained, "by having some bad luck, when the hard hit balls are at somebody." They are compounded by a loss of confidence. Acknowledging that any advice on getting out of a slump is "much easier to give than to do," Harry stressed the mental part of the game as the key to dealing with a bad string at the plate. "Put everything you have in each game," he advised, but "when it is over, regardless what happened, dismiss it from your mind." Since an off day will inevitably come, "there is no use in getting in a bad mood and brooding over it. Remember in the course of the season, luck will pretty near even up and you will get bloopers to make up for the line drives that are caught. Your big days will make up for your bad days."

Although this conventional perspective on baseball fortune was not as fully developed in the young Californian during his first year in the Majors as it would become, Hooper understood very clearly, even at this early stage of his career, that its complement was hard work. His diary recorded his work habits in the extra batting practice he frequently took to shake off a slump or groove his swing. As a spray hitter, Hooper concentrated on his timing to meet the ball and drive it to any field. The percentages, he felt, were with a left-handed batter who could hit to left field rather than attempt to pull every pitch to the right side.[37] If the first baseman was holding a runner on first, then the odds improved for the left-handed hitter to try to shoot a pitch through the hole between first and second. Similarly, if a fast runner came to the plate with the third baseman playing behind the bag, then Hooper liked to see the batter lay down a bunt. But timing, he thought, developed primarily from hitting the ball to the opposite field.[38] Whatever the infield alignment, bat control was an extension of Hooper's relaxed manner at the plate and sound fundamentals. These were particularly essential in resisting every batsman's urge to try to power a pitch. "You will hit your hardest balls," Harry observed, "when you are not trying to."[39]

Whatever Jack Thoney's intentions at the plate, his dismal batting average of .125 convinced Lake to reinsert Hooper in the starting lineup. Harry celebrated his return with three hits in five trips to the plate against New York's Joe Doyle on June 23. As noteworthy as his work with the bat, Hooper took over Speaker's chores in center for the game when Lake decided to give the Texan the day off. In Washington a few days later, Hooper collected three more hits in the first game of the Senators series and delivered a clutch single off Walter Johnson to drive in the winning Red Sox run in the finale. The victory, Boston's sixteenth against only nine defeats for the month of June, raised the team's season record to 35–25 and into second place in the league standings, 5½ games behind front-runner Detroit and a game ahead of Connie Mack's A's. Not since 1904 had the Red Sox appeared so high in the standings two months into a season.

Boston's fine showing seemed to confirm Taylor's plan to make a quick transition from a veteran ball club to a youthful one. Not only were the new-look Red Sox winning once again, they were playing an exciting brand of ball. Their nickname—the Speed Boys—suggested its basis. On offense, team speed translated into extra-base hits and stolen bases. Speaker led the way in the first category with twenty-six doubles and thirteen triples, the latter the fourth-best total in the league for the season. Spoke also pilfered thirty-five bases in 1909, one fewer than club leader Harry Lord. The team's 215 stolen bases for the year were second best in the circuit behind Detroit. Led by their swift twosome, Cobb (76) and Donie Bush (53), the Tigers swiped 280. Speaker also paced the Red Sox defensively. His 319 putouts, thirty-five assists, and twelve double plays led the league in each category for outfielders. The four Red Sox who saw the most time in the outfield in 1909 (Speaker, Niles, Gessler, and Hooper) threw out eighty-seven runners and started nineteen double plays. These were the league's best defensive numbers for any outfield combination.

Boston was not the only American League team enjoying success with new faces in 1909. Despite winning consecutive league championships in 1907 and 1908, Detroit revamped virtually its entire infield during the season, replacing veterans Claude Rossman, Germany Schaefer, and Bill Coughlin with Tom Jones, Jim Delahanty, and George Moriarty at first, second, and third, respectively. Only shortstop Bush, with just twenty Major League games' experience to his credit before the 1909 campaign, maintained his spot in the lineup throughout the season. The principal difference between the youth movements in Boston and Detroit, however, was that the Tigers sought a better balance of veterans and newcomers, especially in their pitching. The mainstays of the Tiger staff—George Mullin, Ed Willett, Ed Summers, Ed Killian, and Bill Donovan—had twenty-eight years' experience pitching in the Major Leagues among them prior to the 1909 season. Twenty-two of these years were with Detroit. In contrast, Boston's rotation of Arellanes, Cicotte, Wood, Chech, and Hall counted nine years' Major League experience among them, only three of which were with the Red Sox.

As the season wore on, the relative inexperience of the Boston staff began to take its toll. Throughout the summer, the Red Sox strengthened their place in the first division of the league, but unsteadiness on the mound effected inconsistency in the overall play of the club and prevented any serious contention for a pennant. Taylor attempted to shore up his young pitching staff—a move further necessitated when Wood suffered a knee injury that hampered his work in the second half of the season—through the acquisition of veterans wherever he could find them. He signed the Highlanders' Jack Chesbro and Ed Karger of Cincinnati after both had been released from their clubs. In September, Taylor added Washington's Charlie Smith to the Boston roster. This last move not only helped the team the most as Smith won all three of his outings for Boston in the last month of the season, it also signaled Taylor's decision about the Sox outfield of the future, for he obtained Smith for Doc Gessler. Since Thoney had already dropped out of the outfield picture with his poor batting average and a career-threatening ankle injury in late June, Gessler's departure announced Hooper's arrival as a regular in the Boston outfield.

Harry's play throughout his rookie year certainly made personnel decisions on the club easier to make. Thoney's injury elevated

Hooper to Boston's fourth outfielder for the second half of the season. Although Speaker, Niles, and Gessler were the designated starters, especially during most of July and August, when Boston compiled a league-best record of 38–22, Harry played sparingly but well. Anticipating a strategy that became routine many years later, Lake occasionally inserted Hooper as a defensive replacement for Niles or Gessler in the late innings. These playing opportunities generally did not lead to plate appearances, but Hooper kept his batting eye sharp with extra hitting practice and careful study of opposing pitchers. He continued to work on his fielding as well, especially practicing in right field, the "sun" field, until he "was good at it."[40] His ability to play any position in the outfield increased his value, and his work habits underscored his potential. The decision to trade Gessler reflected both Boston's need for pitching down the stretch and the club's appreciation of Harry's improved skills and versatility.

Detroit's overall balance, depth, and experience and Philadelphia's powerful pitching gradually put distance between them and the Red Sox as the season entered its final weeks. Boston's strong showing in early August briefly closed the gap among the top three teams in the league, but the Speed Boys could not keep pace with either the Tigers or the Athletics in September. After dropping three of four to the A's in Philadelphia to start their final swing through the East, Detroit swept Washington, New York, and Boston. The Tigers' momentum carried them to nineteen wins in their last twenty-six games and their third straight American League title. Connie Mack's boys, perhaps exhausted from their successful series against Detroit in early September, faded against lesser competition and finished 3½ games behind Hughie Jennings's talented club. Still, the A's compiled an impressive 95–58 record, their winningest season since the American League began play in 1901. With such young stars as Eddie Collins, Frank Baker, and Jack Barry to provide runs and defense for their great pitching, Philadelphia promised to be a pennant contender for many years to come.

Boston's fine year suggested no less. Though 9½ games behind Detroit at the end, the Red Sox finished twenty-five games over .500. This performance marked a significant improvement over their 75–79 record of the previous year for their best showing since the championship season of 1904. No one deserved more credit than Tris Speaker. With a .309 batting average (sixth best in the league), .443 slugging percentage (fifth), seven home runs (second), seventy-seven runs batted in (fourth), 241 total bases (fifth), and thirty-five stolen bases (sixth), the young Texan had established himself as one of the premier players in the Major Leagues. Harry Lord's .311 batting average and thirty-six stolen bases, Jake Stahl's .294 plate average, six home runs, and twelve triples, and Bill Carrigan's .296 batting average represented a solid supporting cast. Gone was Gessler's .298 bat, but the Sox clearly felt that Hooper would be posting enough impressive numbers of his own that the Doc's presence would not be missed.

Harry's first year in the Majors gave the club good reason for optimism. Batting .282 in eighty-one games, the rookie brought speed and occasional power to the plate. His seven extra-base hits for the season included three doubles and four triples. His fifteen stolen bases underscored his offensive value, contributing to his twenty-nine runs scored. Seven times during the season he collected three or more hits in a game, although his diary often recorded the times he came up empty handed as balls hit "on a rope" found a fielder's glove. The hits fell often enough, however, to avoid any prolonged slumps as his batting average ranged between .275 and .295 most of the year. More important, the former "Ty Cobb of the California League" was learning patience and acquiring perspective at the plate. Both curbed his temper and calmed the frustrations of a bad day with the bat or a long day on the bench. In short, Harry was maturing as a hitter, gaining a better sense of his own capabilities and how they could contribute to his team's offensive production.

Hooper displayed a similar steadiness in the field. The defensive requirements of the vast outfield expanses of Huntington Grounds put a premium on speed and a powerful, accurate arm. Harry had both. His fielding range frequently carried him into Speaker's territory in center, but Hooper generally deferred to Spoke in his rookie season. The two early developed a mutual respect for each other's play in the field that generally avoided any territorial tensions. Speaker—and opposing players—quickly came to appreciate Hooper's arm as he gunned down fourteen runners on the base paths in only seventy-four games in the outfield his first year. Harry's assists ratio per games played (.189) was second only among Boston outfielders to Speaker (.246).

As Hooper prepared to leave Boston for the off-season in California, he could look back with a good deal of satisfaction on his first year in the Majors. Not only had he emerged as the best of the lot from the Pacific Coast, but his abilities and potential had effected roster changes in order to make room for him. The confidence he brought to spring training, tested during the course of the season, proved neither false nor unrealistic. He showed he could play with the big boys. The years to come would determine how well.

$$5$$

Trial and Triumph

Boy, if there was any one characteristic of Harry Hooper's, it was that
he was a clutch player. When the chips were down that guy played
like wildfire.

—Smoky Joe Wood, 1966

As the Red Sox assembled in Hot Springs for spring training in 1910,
there was good reason to be optimistic about the approaching pennant race. Virtually the entire lineup that had completed the previous season, including the mainstays of the pitching staff, had returned. Jake Stahl, Heinie Wagner, and Harry Lord at first, short, and
third, respectively, were certain starters at their positions. A preseason duel between Amby McConnell and Larry Gardner would
determine who completed the infield. With Tubby Spencer released
from the club and Pat Donahue soon to follow in the early going, Bill
Carrigan had the catching chores to himself. He would be handling
the pitches of a mounds corps headed by Frank Arellanes, Eddie
Cicotte, Ray Collins, Charlie Hall, Charlie Smith, and Smoky Joe
Wood. In 1909 they had accounted for over 60 percent of the team's
wins with a combined record of 53–31 and an ERA of 2.31.

With Doc Gessler gone to Washington, Harry Wolter not slated for
much action in the field or on the mound, and the oft-injured Jack
Thoney scheduled for a quick departure once the season started, the
status of the Boston outfield was clearer, and far less crowded, than
it was the previous year. Since Speaker was set in center and Hooper
in left or right, only one spot remained to be determined as the Red
Sox reported to camp. The contenders were Harry Niles, who had
kept Hooper on the bench at the start of the 1909 season, and another highly touted prospect from California, a twenty-two-year-old
San Franciscan who had spent the last two years with the Oakland
Oaks of the Pacific Coast League, George ("Duffy") Lewis. Hooper
knew Lewis very well. They had played together for Alameda in 1907

during Harry's brief stint with Ray McMenomy's club, and Harry had followed Duffy's performance throughout the 1908 season, although they competed in different leagues. But Hooper's familiarity with Lewis went back even further, for Duffy had preceded Hooper at Saint Mary's and had played for the Phoenix in 1903–4, his only year in attendance at the college.

Although a rookie in the Red Sox camp, Lewis had three years of professional ball behind him already and did not appreciate the snubs and insults from the veterans which first-year players traditionally endured. Unlike Hooper, who had channeled his anger at this treatment to greater intensity in his training regimen and game play, Duffy was more pugnacious and not reluctant to express his displeasure in confrontational terms with the veterans and management. He refused, for example, to relinquish his time in the batting cage to the regulars or to suffer lightly the various indignities of rookie status. His attitude particularly put Lewis on a collision course with Speaker and initiated ill feeling between them that lasted throughout their careers. Duffy's disregard of other training traditions irritated the new Boston manager, Patsy Donovan, a strict disciplinarian who attempted to condition Lewis with fines and a seat on the bench.[1] That was where Duffy found himself when the season began. He did not stay there long.

Opening at home against New York, the Red Sox started a lineup that featured five left-handed hitters. The Highlanders countered with left-handed pitching throughout the series. The matchup produced only one Boston victory in three games as the Red Sox managed just three runs a game. Lewis's right-handed bat soon found its way into the lineup. He pinch-hit in two of Boston's next four games, registering his first Major League hit in two plate appearances. On April 25, however, with the Red Sox record at 4–4, Duffy got his first start as Boston faced Eddie Plank and the Athletics. Ironically, he replaced Hooper in left in the lineup, one of only three games which Harry would miss playing all season. Harry had started slowly, too, hitting only .240 at the time and Donovan thought that Lewis's insertion into the lineup might provide a spur to Hooper. On April 27, as the Red Sox prepared to take on Washington in the first game of the teams' opening series in the capital city, Hooper was back in the starting lineup, this time in right field in order to accommodate Duffy in left. It was the first time that Hooper, Speaker, and Lewis appeared in the Boston outfield together.

They enjoyed an auspicious debut. Harry and Duffy each knocked out three hits in five trips to the plate, Spoke added four of his own, including a home run and a triple, and the trio scored five runs among them in leading the Red Sox to an 11–1 rout of the Senators. Three wins followed in Boston's next four games to solidify the new outfield lineup. Through the course of the 1910 season and over the next five years, Hooper, Speaker, and Lewis would play together in over 90 percent of Boston's games.

Except for a few games late in the campaign, Lewis remained in left the entire year as he enjoyed a rookie season that was even more impressive than Hooper's had been. Playing in 149 games, Duffy added balance and power to the Boston batting order. His .283 average was second best on the club behind Speaker's .340 and included forty-four extra base hits, eight for the circuit. Both totals trailed only Jake Stahl's forty-five and ten, respectively, the latter the Majors' highest home run output as well. Duffy's work in the outfield was just as solid. Although he did not have the speed of Hooper or Speaker, he possessed sound fielding instincts and an arm to reinforce them. In 1910 he threw out twenty-eight runners who unsuccessfully tested him. Only Hooper, with thirty assists, gunned down more on the base paths. In their first season playing together, Hoop, Spoke, and Duffy participated in twenty-three double plays, a phenomenal figure for a team which turned only eighty, just one more than Detroit's worst mark in the Majors in this category.

The play of the Boston fly catchers, however, both in the field and at the plate, where they hit for a combined .296 average, was not enough to carry the Red Sox to a pennant. Recovering from an opening-day loss to Washington on Walter Johnson's one-hit shutout, a game marked by President Taft's initiating a tradition in tossing out the first ball, the Philadelphia Athletics won the next three games in the series and scarcely interrupted their momentum thereafter on their way to an American League record of 102 wins in the championship season. With Eddie Collins, Danny Murphy, and Rube Oldring all hitting .300 or better and Jack Coombs, Chief Bender, Cy Morgan, and Plank combining for eighty-eight wins and a 1.61 ERA, Connie Mack's boys took command of the pennant race in late June, gradually widened their lead throughout the summer, and clinched the flag on September 20 with almost three weeks still remaining in the regular season.

The quality of the Athletics' play held the Red Sox in check, just as it did everyone else in the league. But Boston's failure to improve on its 1909 record was not entirely attributable to the strength of the opposition. The team was still relatively young. When the season started, Hooper, Speaker, and Lewis were all only twenty-two years old; Gardner was twenty-three, and Wood, already in his third season with the Red Sox, was just twenty. Their youth would not necessarily have been a liability, even in the tightest pennant race, if conditions around them were more stable. But such was not the case, particularly in the managerial department.

Patsy Donovan, who had starred as an outfielder for Pittsburgh and Saint Louis of the National League before assuming the managerial reins of those clubs and, most recently, Brooklyn for three undistinguished seasons, was the *seventh* Red Sox manager since 1906. Only Freddie Lake, who had headed across town to the Boston Braves after the 1909 season when he and Taylor could not settle on the manager's salary for 1910, had completed a full year at the helm for the Red Sox since Jimmy Collins in 1905. Chick Stahl had replaced Collins at the end of 1906, but when he took his own life shortly before the beginning of the 1907 season, Boston's manager situation collapsed in complete disarray. Cy Young, George Huff, and Bob Unglaub, all briefly and ineptly, tried to run the club before Deacon McGuire took the job. The old veteran of the American Association lasted until August 1908, when Lake took over.

With a more experienced and mature team, the changing face of the manager might not have had an ill effect on the club's fortunes. The professional game was not that far removed from a time when the manager's principal tasks were to handle the details of club administration, not the conduct of game play. But as Johnny Evers observed, times had changed and so had the duties of a manager. The evolution of the "scientific game" in the 1890s placed more interest and importance on a manager's strategic leadership. But, Evers noted, this was "the lightest part of his work."[2] With twenty-three men, "the majority of them grown children, under his charge, [the manager] is forced to soothe their injured feelings, condole with them in their troubles, cheer them in their blues, and check them in their exuberance." Such responsibilities required not only special skills in handling the diverse needs and personalities of nearly two dozen players but also the time to get to know them. The revolving door which characterized Boston's managerial situation effectively prevented the latter from occurring.

Another key factor frustrating Boston's pennant hopes in 1910 was the team's defensive play, or, more accurately, the lack of it apart from the outfield. Only the last-place Saint Louis Browns in the American League had a poorer fielding average among all the Major League teams than the Red Sox. A good defensive club often hinges on solid play in the middle of the diamond and the corners, namely, catcher, center field, first, and third. The Red Sox were strong in only one of these positions, but no one played it better than Tris Speaker. Positioning himself only thirty or forty feet, and often closer, behind second base, Speaker played the shallowest center field of any of his dead-ball contemporaries and certainly anyone who came after him. His shallow set actually allowed him to become an additional in-fielder at times. Sneaking in behind runners to take pickoff throws from the catcher or pitcher, throwing batters out at first on hard-hit balls up the middle, or turning the pivot on double plays, Speaker was an intrusive presence who transformed the very concept of play for his position.[3] The four unassisted double plays he made through-out his career, including one in the 1912 World Series, were as sure a testimony to his fielding and sense of the strategic role of the center fielder as the innumerable balls he outraced in the deepest parts of the ballpark. "Spoke was something extra special," his future team-mate, Babe Ruth, would recall. "In my Red Sox pitching days I would hear the crack of the bat and say, 'There goes the ball game.' But Tris would turn his back to the plate, race far out to the fences and at the last moment make a diving catch. Not once . . . but a thousand times."[4]

In front of Speaker, however, were decidedly lesser defensive lights at the other important middle position and the corners. The best of the lot with a glove was Stahl at first, but he was playing his last full season in the Majors in 1910 and an increase in his errors and decreases in his assists and double-play participation marked the fading of his once reliable fielding skills. Carrigan, who had been platooned at catcher his first three years with the Red Sox, had earned the everyday assignment on the strength of his solid year at bat and behind the plate in 1909. But 1910 was a year like his nickname—rough. His batting average slipped forty-seven points and his errors increased almost twofold, although he appeared in only twenty more games than he played the previous season. Things were no better at third. Lord's deficiencies as a fielder focused less on what he did when he had the ball than on whether he got it. Al-though he ran well on the base paths, he seemed to lose his mobility with a glove on his hand. In 1908 and 1909, he ranked near the bottom among the regular third basemen in the Majors for chances accepted and assists. A few years later, in fact, he would establish the single-season American League mark for inactivity by a third base-man playing in 150 or more games with 364 chances accepted and 281 assists. This achievement, such as it was, would not be in the uniform of the Red Sox. After losing nine of twelve games in a poor stretch in early August that dropped them 8½ games behind Phila-delphia, Boston traded Lord and the seldom-used McConnell to the White Sox in a move to strengthen the left side of their infield.

The trade also acknowledged some dissension on the club that centered on Lord. The third baseman had broken a finger in June and been replaced with Clyde Engle, a versatile performer in both the outfield and infield who had recently been acquired from New York in exchange for Wolter. With Engle installed at third, the Red Sox had played their best ball of the season and Donovan was reluc-tant to take him out of the starting lineup even when Lord was ready to play again. The manager's decision angered Lord, who not only wanted his job back at third but now wondered aloud whether he should have Donovan's as well. Lord's increasing unhappiness with his lack of playing time and Donovan's direction of the club made the decision to unload him an easy one to make. In return, the Red Sox got third baseman Billy Purtell and a right-handed pitcher named Nig Smith. Purtell plugged the hole at third but created one in the batting order. He hit only .208 for Boston in forty-nine games, while a healthier and happier Lord, feeling more appreciated with his new club, finished the season batting .297 for Chicago. Smith appeared in only four games for Boston the rest of the way, winning one and losing two.

Hooper's second season in the Majors confirmed the solid play of his rookie year. Although his batting average slipped from .282 to .267, placing him only above Carrigan's .249 among the Red Sox regulars, he demonstrated his worth to the club in many other cate-gories. Appearing in 155 of Boston's 158 games in the season (four ended in ties or rainouts and had to be rescheduled), Harry led the league in games played. His 584 at bats were third in the league behind Napoleon Lajoie of Cleveland (591) and Detroit's Sam Craw-ford (588). His speed on the bases translated into ten triples and forty stolen bases, the latter leading the club. Moreover, Harry showed a mature patience at the plate that resulted in better pitch selection and frequent bases on balls. His sixty-two walks led the Red Sox in this department and was the fifth-highest total in the free-swinging American League.

As the season had progressed, so, too, had Harry's place in the batting order. Opening the season batting seventh, Hooper had moved to sixth and then to fourth by May. But the cleanup spot neither suited Harry's temperament nor complemented his offensive strengths. His own analysis of his baseball skills—a keen eye, a good judge of the strike zone, speed afoot, and a studious approach to the

game—suggested a more appropriate place at the top of the lineup.[5]
Donovan thought so too. On May 9 against New York, the manager
penciled in Hooper in the leadoff position. Although Harry would
alternate between first and second with Lord in the batting order
over the next few weeks, once Lord suffered his broken finger and
dropped from the lineup, Harry moved to the leadoff spot permanently.

Despite a relatively modest batting average, Hooper tallied eighty-
one runs in the 1910 season, second only on the club to Speaker's
ninety-two. Perhaps more than any other statistic, his runs scored
revealed how well Harry understood the role of the leadoff hitter and
how successfully he brought his skills to bear on that position. "The
leadoff man's job," Harry said simply, "is to reach base, then with the
cooperation of following batters to work his way around and score."[6]
This basic formula underscored Hooper's sense of both individual
responsibility and team play that the game demanded. The former
placed the burden of getting something started offensively squarely
on the shoulders of the leadoff hitter. Eschewing power and often a
higher batting average in passing up good pitches while working the
count to a possible walk or looking to lay down a bunt, the leadoff
batter, Harry explained, ought to make the opposing pitcher work
hard against the first batter he faces. Once on base, the leadoff man
should be a threat to steal, thereby further upsetting the pitcher's
rhythm and his attempt to control the flow of the game.

The cooperative nature of producing runs focused primarily on
the hitter's ability to advance runners on base ahead of him, but
owing to his spot in the lineup, the chances for a leadoff hitter's
doing this were less frequent than a batter in the heart of the order.
If the leadoff man found any runners on base when he came to the
plate, these were the lower hitters in the lineup, often the pitcher or
a weak-hitting, slow-running position player. In such circumstances,
the leadoff hitter must be an accomplished sacrifice bunter, for slow
and inexperienced base runners ahead of him generally limited his
options for moving them along, especially employing the hit-and-run
play. Moreover, the baserunning deficiencies of these players particularly required another quality of the leadoff hitter—a balanced perspective on the breaks of the game. Slow runners were bound to cost
the batter a few hits over the course of a season. The leadoff spot was
not suited for someone whose contribution to the team was measured solely in terms of a batting average or whose concern focused
largely on his personal statistics.

While the regular season schedule presented an almost daily opportunity for Harry to demonstrate his skills, one event during the 1910 campaign provided a particularly interesting showcase for them. This was Doc Powers Day at Shibe Park, Philadelphia, on May 30. Michael ("Doc") Powers, the popular Philadelphia catcher for eight seasons, had died on April 26, 1909, of complications stemming from violent stomach pains he had suffered during the Athletics' opening game a couple of weeks earlier.[7] This, of course, had been Harry's first Major League game as well and the sight of the stricken Powers being carried off the field after his collapse in the seventh inning amid all the ceremony of Shibe Park's inaugural added to the lasting impressions of that day. To honor Powers and to benefit his widow and three children through the proceeds of the occasion, the American League set aside an off-day in its eastern schedule for an exhibition game between the Athletics and "a picked team composed of the star players of the New York, Boston and Washington clubs." In addition, as Connie Mack described in his announcement of the day, a series of "special events" testing the running, throwing, and hitting skills of the players would be conducted. The winners of these events would receive "handsome Loving Cups."[8]

A crowd of more than twelve thousand showed up for the exhibition, raising nearly seven thousand dollars for Powers's family. No one impressed the crowd more than Hooper. Competing in two events, the long-distance throw and the 100-yard dash, Harry placed first and second, respectively. In the throwing contest, Harry led a Red Sox sweep of the event as Speaker and Lewis finished in that order behind him. In the dash, Harry finished second to Jimmy Austin, the swift, slick-fielding third baseman of the New York Highlanders, who, like Hooper, averaged about thirty stolen bases a season during his first five years in the Majors, 1909–13. A year later, incidentally, at a similar field day at Chicago's new Comiskey Park with representatives of all the American League clubs on hand, Harry outraced Austin, although he placed second again in the dash to the White Sox's Bobby Messenger. Harry's arm was just as strong in 1911, though, as he won an accuracy event, which required the players to throw a ball from the outfield through a barrel suspended at second base.[9]

As Harry headed home to California at the end of the 1910 season, he took with him more than just the Powers Day trophies. Both right field and the leadoff spot in the Red Sox lineup were his. Hooper's "continuous development" in both posts was a key factor in lending "renewed hope" for Boston in the next season.[10] Harry shared this optimism. Lord's departure arrested the dissension on the club, although it came too late for the Red Sox to overtake the Athletics. The Boston outfield was the strongest defensively in the American League and its only rival at bat was the Detroit trio of Cobb, Crawford, and Davy Jones. Both Gardner at second and Engle at third had strengthened their holds on their positions with solid play, particularly in the latter half of the season. Finally, a respectable if not formidable pitching rotation of Cicotte, Collins, Hall, Karger and Wood suggested that a pennant-contending year lay ahead.

Nineteen eleven was not that year. Stumbling at the gate from the outset, the Red Sox never mounted a serious challenge to either the Athletics or the Tigers, who had distanced themselves from the rest of the pack by the end of May and battled evenly through midsummer until the Athletics' overall strength carried them to their second consecutive league championship. Philadelphia's comfortable margin of victory at the end—13½ games—belied how tough the race had been. On June 1, for example, the Athletics trailed the Tigers, who had been breezing along winning three out of every four games, by 9½ games. But Detroit's pace was as unsustainable as the A's surge was irresistible. With Coombs, Plank, and Bender again leading the way on the mound and Collins, Murphy, and Frank Baker pacing A's hitters to an impressive .296 team batting average, the highest in either league and the strongest since Philadelphia's .301 mark in 1899, Connie Mack's boys passed Detroit on August 4 and reached the century mark in wins again (101) on their way to a successful date with John McGraw's Giants in the World Series.

Perhaps the most fitting commentary on Boston's year was that the Red Sox had to mount their longest winning streak of the season—six games—in their final week to finish above .500 and avoid sixth place. Their final mark of 78–75 earned them a virtual tie for fourth place in the standings with the White Sox, twenty-four games behind Philadelphia. Since Boston faded from pennant contention so early in 1911, clues to the club's disappointing performance can be found in events at the top of the season. One game in particular, played even before the season got under way, provided a hint of the struggles to follow. Two others, one in the early going and another in midseason, were tantalizing indicators of the talent that Taylor's money had assembled. Taken together, the three games especially demonstrated the keenly felt frustration in the continued deferral of the promise of the Red Sox that had first been glimpsed in 1909.

The rains which Hooper had described as interrupting the Red Sox spring training schedule in Hot Springs in his rookie year plagued the club again in 1910. Taylor attributed part of his club's slow start in each of these years to the wet weather and its effect on the conditioning of his players. He decided to move the club to a new training site in 1911, Redondo Beach near Los Angeles in Southern California. The move, though, had as much to do with escaping the inclemency of an Arkansas spring as it did in satisfying Taylor's personal schedule. Married to a former San Francisco socialite, Dorothy Van Ness, Taylor made frequent trips to the West Coast during their courtship and wished to accompany his wife when she visited her family.[11] Not incidentally, Taylor's familiarity with the California baseball scene, which had already yielded Hooper, Lewis, Arellanes, and Wolter for his club, also influenced the decision to train on the coast since it might strengthen Boston's access to the talent of the PCL and other California leagues.

If the Red Sox had restricted their stay to sunny Southern California, the West Coast spring might have served the club well. But, as in previous years, Boston scheduled a series of exhibition games at various station stops along their long route back to the East. Two games were slated to be played against the PCL's Oakland and Sacramento teams in San Francisco's Bay Area in early April as Boston headed for the season opener in Chicago a week later. Unfortunately, the seasonal rains of Northern California had made the Oaks' and Sacts' diamonds, as well as most others in the area, unplayable. There was one notable exception—Brother Agnon's carefully maintained and well-drained field at Saint Mary's College. Although the Phoenix did not have a home game on April 8, they were scheduled to play the University of California at Berkeley at four o'clock that afternoon. Agnon saw an opportunity to display his current players and provide a homecoming for Hooper and Lewis. He convinced Donovan that his California intercollegiate champions could provide a good contest for the Red Sox. Anxious to get his team some playing time after ten straight days of rain, the Boston manager accepted the challenge. At 1:30 P.M., with a grand crowd on hand, having been drawn to the field by students on horseback racing throughout Oakland and Berkeley announcing the game, Elmer ("Tiny") Leonard threw the first pitch of the Phoenix's oddly constructed doubleheader.[12]

It was the start of a great day for Saint Mary's, a disastrous one for Boston. Leonard pitched masterfully, keeping the Red Sox bats almost completely in check, spinning a 1–0 shutout. The game's last out came when the Phoenix's Ed Lynch gunned down Speaker at the plate as he attempted to score on a long fly-out in foul territory in left field. Embarrassed by his out, Spoke tried to deflect attention from himself in suggesting that Hooper, perhaps wishing to help his old team get on the scoreboard, had misplayed the ball that led to the only Saint Mary's run. But Harry would have none of this, nor let Speaker off the hook so easily for his baserunning gaffe. "No, I did not let it go by," he pointedly explained to an Oakland reporter. "You know me and you know that I could not have done that." Indicating that he would seek out Speaker to clarify his comments, Harry added, "We have no excuse for losing that game. We were warned by Danny Long of the San Francisco team to take no chances or we would be beaten. We could not hit Tiny and we had two of our best pitchers in the game—Wood and Bedient."[13]

Less than an hour after Speaker's out, the Phoenix took the field again against California. The exhilaration of the Boston victory carried over. Mike Cann tossed a no-hitter and Saint Mary's shut out the Bears 6–0 in a seven-inning game. Before the end of the 1911 professional season, both Leonard and Cann, the hurling heroes of the Phoenix sweep, were with Major League clubs. Tiny, following up on Connie Mack's standing offer to sign the best Saint Mary's pitcher each year, joined the Athletics and Mike agreed to terms with the Highlanders.[14]

Notwithstanding the slight tension between Hooper and Speaker regarding their play in the game, the real harbinger of the approaching season was a broken leg suffered in a freak accident by Hugh Bradley, the designated successor to Stahl at first. Slipping on the wet slope which led from the Saint Mary's College gymnasium to the ball field, Bradley was lost for all but a few meaningless games at the end of the season. More so than the key injuries that had hampered the club's play in the two previous years, Bradley's loss on the heels of Stahl's retirement to accept an executive position at one of his father-in-law's banks in Chicago was decisive. Unfortunately, he was not the only player to go down during 1911. At one time or another, every regular in the Red Sox lineup missed playing time because of illness or injury.

Despite the "deplorable" decimation of Boston's ranks for three consecutive seasons, its roster, when healthy and intact, was as formidable as any in either league.[15] Two games during the 1911 season underscored their strength at bat and on the mound. On April 21, with Massachusetts Governor Foss occupying the dignitaries' box and Boston Mayor John F. Fitzgerald throwing out the first ball, the Red Sox opened their home schedule at Huntington Grounds by crushing Mack's defending world champions 13-4. The Red Sox pounded A's pitching for seventeen hits, including two Larry Gardner doubles and additional two-baggers from Hooper, Speaker, Engle, and rookie shortstop Steve Yerkes. Engle, batting fifth and playing at third this day, also cleared the left-field fence for one of his only two home runs on the season. Philadelphia's ace, Jack Coombs, who had led the league with thirty-one wins in 1910 and a sparkling 1.30 ERA and was headed toward another league-leading season with twenty-eight wins in 1911, lasted only two innings before the Boston onslaught.

The other game of the 1911 season that dramatically provided a lens on the future was a quick little hour-and-a-half gem spun by Joe Wood against the hapless Saint Louis Browns on July 29. Heading for 107 losses and a last-place finish in the American League in 1911, the Browns had rarely provided stiff competition for anyone in recent years. Their main problem was a serious lack of pitching, as the team's 3.83 ERA was the worst in the Majors besides the Boston Nationals' truly miserable 5.08. But the Browns could brighten on occasion and for this game they had Joe Lake, their most effective pitcher, on the mound and a lineup that included three good contact men in Burt Shotten, Jimmy Austin, and Frank LaPorte. They knocked out over 140 hits apiece in 1911. They and their teammates got none this day. Relying almost exclusively on his blazing fastball, Smoky Joe struck out twelve Browns, walked just two, and allowed only three balls to be hit beyond the infield as he recorded the fifth no-hitter in Boston's American League history. Speaker's solo home run and Gardner's run-scoring triple highlighted Boston's five-run, seven-hit attack.

The game announced Wood's arrival on the top plateau of the Majors' pitching ranks after three years of steady improvement. Wood first attracted the attention of Boston scouts when he won eighteen games for Hutchinson, Kansas, of the Western Association in 1907. He was then only sixteen years old but had already earned his first dollars as a baseball player when he played out the last three weeks of the 1906 season with the Bloomer Girls, a thinly disguised "all-female" barnstorming team in Kansas. As fair as Joe's complexion was, he no more fooled anyone about his sex than his play as an infielder suggested that this was the best way to employ his powerful arm. Wood joined the Red Sox at the very end of the 1908 season and appeared in six games, splitting two decisions with a respectable 2.38 ERA.

In spring training with Hooper in 1909, Wood was observed throwing batting practice by Paul Shannon of the *Boston Post*. "That fellow really throws smoke," the sportswriter commented and the former Bloomer had a nickname.[16] Working as hard as anyone in the Boston camp, a quality that greatly impressed Hooper and cemented the close friendship between the two in succeeding years, Joe developed a wicked curve to complement his swift pitch. As he learned to control it, his pitching became more effective and his fastball more overpowering. In 1909, despite a knee injury which kept him out of the rotation for over a month, he went 11–7 with an ERA of 2.21. In 1910 he recorded twelve wins against thirteen defeats but dropped his ERA to 1.68. Moreover, his dedication to mastering his pitching mechanics and studying the habits of the batters he faced resulted in improving his strikeout rate per nine innings to 6.6. Only Walter Johnson in the second of ten consecutive seasons over which he would average more than twenty-six wins a year was better with 7.6. In the year of his no-hitter, Smoky Joe improved his strikeout ratio to a league-leading 7.5 and his victories to twenty-three, the most a Red Sox hurler had recorded since Cy Young notched twenty-six in the championship year of 1904. No slouch with a bat, either, Wood added a decent .261 batting average to the lineup on the days he pitched. All this ability in a twenty-one-year-old body led his teammate, Charlie Hall, to conclude that Smoky Joe "was the most natural and talented" ballplayer he had ever seen.[17]

Wood's no-hitter was the single most eye-catching event of the Red Sox season. He was not alone, however, in having a successful year individually. The Boston outfield continued to impress at bat and through their play in the field. They hit for a combined .315, built on Spoke's .327, Harry's .311, and Lewis's .307 averages. Speaker and Lewis with eight and seven round trippers, respectively, trailed only the Athletics' Home Run Baker with eleven of his trademark blasts. Harry even socked four himself, accounting for a few of the team-leading ninety-three runs he scored. Hooper paced Boston in other categories as well. For the second straight year, he led the team in at bats (524), stolen bases (38), and walks (73), the latter the league's third-highest total. His on-base percentage, perhaps the best measurement of his work as a leadoff hitter, was .399, second on the club to Speaker's .411 and the strongest among all leadoff men in the league.

Elsewhere in the Boston lineup, a few nagging questions from previous seasons were being addressed. When the peripatetic Engle was not positioned at third, Larry Gardner was. Like his teammate and close friend, pitcher Ray Collins, Gardner had come to the attention of the Boston organization through his collegiate play at the University of Vermont. He played only sparingly with the Red Sox in

1908 and 1909, spending most of his time with Lynn of the New England League, where he batted .305. With Lord at third, at least until his departure, Gardner played second for Boston in 1910. His strong arm and quickness, if not his mild manner, suggested that Larry may have been better suited for third. If there were any doubts about his courage for the hot corner, they were erased in the way he stood up to the fiercest base runners wherever he encountered them. An incident with Cobb while Gardner was still becoming accustomed to play at second early in the 1910 season said much about both men. Taking a throw in the baseline as Cobb bore down on him, Gardner was an inviting target as he stood his ground. But instead of taking out the youngster, Cobb attempted to sidestep him and was tagged out. As he walked off the field, Cobb told Heinie Wagner at short, "Tell the kid I won't give him a break like that again. I could have cut him in two."[18]

Gardner learned quickly and perhaps too well as far as Cobb was concerned. Moved to third permanently midway through the 1911 season, Gardner enjoyed the most success of any third baseman in the league in frustrating Cobb's attempts to bunt his way on base. For not only had Gardner failed to be intimidated by the Georgia Peach, but he had learned a secret about Cobb's bunting manner-isms that he kept to himself until long after both had retired. Cobb, it seemed, had a habit of licking his lips and then tightening them before laying down a bunt. Gardner noticed these telltale signs early in his career at third. Before Cobb squared to bunt, Gardner was moving down the line, depriving Ty of the element of surprise. "I don't think Ty ever bunted for a hit against me," Gardner proudly claimed.[19]

The Vermonter's partner on the left side of the infield was Heinie Wagner, a thirty-year-old veteran of six seasons with the Red Sox. He shared seniority honors on the club with catcher Bill Carrigan. Both were remarkably alike. Tough, steady competitors, they were yeo-man performers whose contributions to the team focused less on their statistics than on the experience of their years in the Majors and the instructive influence they had on the younger players around them. Both, in fact, would eventually manage the club. In 1911 they also shared the list of Red Sox wounded as Heinie suffered a series of slow-healing sprains and Bill a broken hand. Their misfortune side-lined both of them for more than half the season. They put their bench time to good use, though, in helping the two rookies who largely replaced them—Yerkes and Les Nunamaker, respectively—develop nicely.

If Boston and the rest of the baseball world wondered what would happen if the Red Sox were ever unencumbered with casts on their limbs and third-string replacements in their lineup, they did not have to wait long to find out. Nineteen twelve was a year like none other in Red Sox history. The fresh winds of spring that carry pennant hopes, no matter how faint, to even the most desperate ranks of the league brought more than just renewed expectations to Boston. They swept in newness everywhere—new owners, a new manager, and a new ballpark. Perhaps more than anything, though, they carried an air of surprise, and for once it was pleasant.

With Connie Mack claiming that his 1912 team was the "best of that era" and few pundits in the sporting press rising to dispute him, the American League flag seemed all but conceded to the Athletics for a third consecutive championship before the first pitch was thrown. A curious thing happened on the way to the World Series, though. Philadelphia won enough games (90) to have captured the pennant in both 1910 and 1911, but so did Washington, rising from the depths behind the Big Train, Walter Johnson, on the hill and with Clark Griffith directing action in the dugout to pass the A's with one more victory, one fewer defeat. The Nats' resurrection might have been the story of the year in the American League. It was, after all, the only time in the league's brief history so far that they had finished above .500 and better than sixth place in the final standings. As impressive as Washington's performance had been, however, it achieved only runner-up honors in the league for the Senators, for fourteen games ahead of them, sporting the most wins (105) and the highest winning percentage (.691) of any previous AL champion, were the Red Sox.

The new elements in the Boston organization at the top of the season were connected with a local and league-wide quest for more respectability, both as a competitive product on the field and as a worthy attraction for the public's increasing entertainment dollar. The guiding hand for both developments in the American League belonged to its president, Ban Johnson. A former sports editor at the *Cincinnati Commercial-Gazette,* Johnson had taken a leave of absence from the paper to help revive the Midwest's folded Western League in 1894 with his friend Charlie Comiskey. They turned it into one of baseball's best-directed circuits, and Johnson never looked back on his brief career as a sportswriter. In 1900, he changed the name of his organization to the American League and initiated a series of bold maneuvers—in particular the establishment of competing franchises in eastern cities where the National League already had teams—that led to a costly bidding war for the services of top players. Part of the price Johnson extracted to halt the raiding was recognition of equal status for his league by the older circuit in 1903.

Financially backed by Charles Somers, a wealthy Cleveland industrialist whose fortune derived from his father's coal and lumber interests, Johnson tabbed Connie Mack, the field and business manager of the Western League's Milwaukee club, to take the lead in organizing new teams for the AL in both Boston and Philadelphia. Mack had immediate success in Philadelphia, where he found in sporting-goods manufacturer Benjamin Shibe a kindred spirit in appreciating the business aspects—and profit objectives—of the game of baseball.[20] Johnson and Mack, however, were less successful in Boston in finding local backers who were willing to risk investment in a rival club to the city's popular National League entry. With the 1901 season rapidly approaching and Mack needed in Philadelphia as the manager of the new Athletics, Johnson turned the Boston franchise completely over to Somers.[21] Two owners later (Milwaukee attorney Henry J. Killilea and Charles Henry Taylor), Johnson had the opportunity to exert the kind of control over the Boston franchise that he had planned initially.

Two factors prompted his move. First, the Mack-Shibe arrangement in Philadelphia had proved particularly successful and suggested a formula that could be replicated elsewhere. Shibe, a businessman who enjoyed baseball, provided the capital for the franchise. His interests focused as much on the financial return of his investment as, like other nouveau riche, the social status that accompanied his visible association with an attractive popular enterprise. Mack, a baseball man who enjoyed the living he could earn from the game he played and managed, brought an insider's expertise to the operations of the club. Their roles and perspectives complemented each other well.

Second, the staid and humorless Johnson had never been comfortable with General Taylor's son in control of the Boston franchise. John's playboy reputation, built on his country-club habits and expensive tastes, did not appeal to Johnson, the son of a minister, nor, in his view, did they serve the best interests of his league and the image of the game he was trying to foster.[22] So in late 1911, when the general indicated he was thinking about putting 50 percent of the club up for sale, Johnson was quick to act. He persuaded Taylor to sell the shares to a group headed by Jimmy McAleer and Robert McRoy, a combination in the Mack-Shibe mold. McAleer, the baseball man, had played ball for thirteen seasons, most notably as a light-hitting but stylish outfielder for the Cleveland Spiders of the National League in the 1890s. He followed his playing career with managerial stints at Cleveland, Saint Louis, and Washington of the American League for another eleven years. McRoy, the organization man, was a loyal associate of Johnson, having served as the secretary of the American League for many years. In January 1912 the Red Sox announced their new executive team: McAleer as president, McRoy as treasurer, and, with the other half of the club's stock, John I. as vice-president and his father as a member of the board of directors. The shake-up was not confined to the front office. It was also announced that Patsy Donovan had been released as manager. The new man was an old hand. Wooed away from his banker's desk in Chicago for a piece of the club and the opportunity to play first again was Jake Stahl.

The changes in the Red Sox executive administration provided the kind of leadership for the organization that reflected Johnson's notions of a properly run baseball franchise. This was particularly important as the club prepared to move into its new home, Fenway Park.[23] This elegant, 27,000-seat facility, similar to the new steel and reinforced concrete ballparks in Philadelphia (Shibe Park), Pittsburgh (Forbes Field), and New York (Polo Grounds), was as much a monument to the man who built it—General Taylor—as it was a testimonial to the enormous popularity of Major League baseball. With the turnstiles recording a twofold rise in attendance at regular season games between 1901 and 1910, Johnson and league officials were most concerned that the operations of the parks and the conduct of the game project a sense of worthiness and propriety that would keep the crowds coming. Attempts "to drive ruffianism out of the game" by suppressing "obscene, indecent and vulgar language on the ball field" or upgrading the status of umpires coincided with an interest in playing the game in attractive, inviting, and well-maintained environs.[24] After Boston had led the Majors in attendance in 1910 with just over 740,000 admissions, Taylor decided to build his new park on an oddly configured piece of land that his real estate company owned in a marshy section of the city known as the Fens. The general fully reflected Johnson's views when he described the facility as "a proper viewing grounds for championship play."[25]

It took awhile for the Red Sox finally to get to play on their new field, but once they did, they put on quite a show for the home folks. Returning to Boston after sweeping New York in three games and splitting a pair with the Athletics in Philadelphia to open the 1912 season with a 4-1 mark, the Red Sox then had to wait several days for the skies to clear before the new ball field in the Fens could be inaugurated. After three rain-outs, Honey Fitz at last got to toss out the first ball on April 20 as Boston hosted the Highlanders. When the Red Sox came to bat in their half of the first, Harry Hooper had the honor of taking the first swing for the home team in the new park. The New Yorkers fared no better than their own home opener as successive singles by Yerkes and Speaker in the bottom of the eleventh off Jim Vaughn gave Charlie ("Sea Lion") Hall the victory in relief of Bucky O'Brien.

The Red Sox rarely disappointed the fans at Fenway the rest of the season. Winning fifty-seven of seventy-seven decisions in their new surroundings, they matched the American League record for home victories shared by Detroit and Philadelphia in their championship years of 1909 and 1910, respectively. Combined with a .640 winning percentage on the road, the Red Sox seized the league lead from Chicago in early June, built a seven-game cushion by July 4, and pushed it to sixteen before clinching the pennant on September 18. Their pennant-winning celebration occurred earlier than any previous AL champion.

There was no shortage of heroes on the Boston roster to account for the spectacular season. Returning to Hot Springs to train, Stahl set his veteran lineup early, which, enjoying "the inspiring effect upon a team of comparative immunity from injury," stayed virtually intact the entire season.[26] Every position regular except Jake, who alternated at first with Engle and Bradley, and Carrigan, who shared the backup chores with Forrest Cady, a burly six-foot two-inch rookie acquired from Newark of the International League, played in at least 131 games, all at their assigned posts. Gardner continued to master his play at third and contributed a .315 batting average to give the Red Sox—with Stahl (.301) in the lineup—.300 hitters at both corners. Wagner and Yerkes provided solid play up the middle, and Heinie enjoyed his best year in the Majors at the plate, batting .274 with career-high RBIs (68) and runs scored (75).

Flanking Speaker in center, Hooper and Lewis solidified the reputation of the trio as the best defensive outfield in the Majors. Neither Harry nor Duffy, though, had as strong a year at the plate as 1911. Hooper's average fell to .242, a mark he failed to exceed only once in his career. Yet, for the third consecutive season, he led the club in plate appearances (590) and placed high in other categories as well. His runs scored (98), bases on balls (66), and stolen bases (29) were second on the team behind Speaker and his twelve triples tied Tris behind Gardner's eighteen. This kind of output underscored both his ability to get on base and to make things happen once he was there. Curiously, Harry's only poorer year in terms of batting average was 1915, another pennant-winning season for the Red Sox. But then, as in the World Series about to commence, Harry saved his best for October. Unlike Harry, Duffy's .284 average reflected his hitting ability more accurately than the .307 level he had achieved the previous season. Though falling off in average, Lewis timed his hits well as his 109 RBIs, second best in the league to the 130 of the Athletics' Baker, led the Red Sox in one of the few offensive categories that Spoke did not.

It was Speaker, though, "the king of the outfield," as Duffy dubbed him, whom opposing pitchers feared most in the Boston lineup.[27] The intense Texan, driven by a desire for athletic perfection, elevated his game to a new level of performance in 1912. Battling Cobb and Joe Jackson of the Indians for the hitting title all season, Tris ended with a .383 mark but finished third behind Ty's .410, the second of two consecutive .400-plus seasons for the Tiger star, and Shoeless Joe's .395, an average bettered only once in his career, .408 in 1911. Banging out 222 hits, including fifty-three doubles, tops in the Majors, and ten home runs, the most with Baker again in the AL, Spoke led both leagues in on-base percentage (.464) and finished just behind Cobb and Jackson in slugging percentage. The latter two's edge in triples, twenty-three and twenty-six, respectively, to Speaker's twelve, accounted for their advantage in the slugging category. Spoke's 136 runs scored, second best in the Majors to the one more tallied by Eddie Collins of the A's, and team-leading fifty-two stolen bases rounded out his contributions to the Boston offense. In the field, Tris led his talented teammates and all other outfielders in both leagues with thirty-five assists and nine double plays. His year earned him the most valuable player award of his day, a four-cylinder, nickel-trimmed Chalmers 30 automobile valued at $1,900, presented by the Chalmers Motor Company to the player in each league who "should prove himself as the most important and useful player to his club and to the league at large in point of deportment and value of services rendered."[28]

Despite his spectacular season, it was not a foregone conclusion that Speaker would drive off with the Chalmers. The surprising performance of the Senators, owed largely to the pitching of Johnson and the fine all-around play of fleet center fielder Clyde Milan, moved the baseball writers who selected the award recipients to cast several votes their way. Similarly, the popular Ed Walsh, workhorse of the White Sox staff, who led the Majors in innings pitched for the fourth time in six years with 393, drew support for another "iron man" performance and his second straight season of twenty-seven wins. For many writers, however, consideration of a player to challenge Speaker for the award was a simpler and more familiar matter. They thought about his teammate and roommate, Joe Wood.

"Can I throw harder than Joe Wood?" Walter Johnson repeated the interviewer's question. "Listen, my friend," he replied, "there's no man alive who can throw harder than Smoky Joe Wood."[29] Not only in velocity, but by any measurement of pitching prowess, there was no pitcher in the game better than Wood in 1912. Few ever have put together a season to rival his, which, said Damon Runyon, placed him on "the pinnacle of pitching greatness."[30]

Coming off a year when he had led the Red Sox in wins and ERA (23 and 2.02), though still the youngest hurler on the club at twenty-two, Wood was expected to lead a staff whose ability was somewhat of a mystery. Despite posting the best team ERA in the league in 1911, 2.73, the pitching corps had faltered in stretches throughout the season, raising doubts about its depth and durability. Jake Stahl hoped to address both issues through a stronger preseason conditioning program for his pitchers and, like the rest of his lineup, the creation of a set rotation. Joining Wood in it were the returning veterans O'Brien, Hall, and Collins and a rookie just two days older than Joe, Hugh Bedient, who had been obtained from Jersey City of the International League. Only Collins with a knee injury lost any meaningful time out of the rotation in the new season as the five accounted for 102 of the club's 105 victories. Bedient was the most pleasant surprise with a 20-9 log which garnered him very favorable reviews. But the headlines belonged to Smoky Joe.

Beginning with his win over New York in the opening game of the season, Wood paced the Boston staff all the way. More than simply leading them in the victory column, Joe inspired them with the brilliance of his craft. On May 20, for example, with six victories in the young season already to his credit, he tossed the first shutout at Fenway Park, blanking the first-place White Sox, 2–0. Nine more of his thirty-four victories in 1912 would be shutouts. The closest after him in both categories was Walter Johnson with seven no-run games among his thirty-three wins.

Like his no-hitter of the previous season, Wood determined the game that would be the benchmark of the 1912 season for the Red Sox. It came against Johnson, Smoky Joe's own choice for "the greatest pitcher who ever lived."[31] Through the middle months of the season, Johnson had been even more formidable than usual. Humming his pitches with relentless efficiency, the Big Train began a string of sixteen consecutive wins on July 3 before suffering a loss in relief against Saint Louis on August 26. During much of the same period, Wood had mounted a winning streak of his own. On September 3 it reached thirteen. With the Senators scheduled for a weekend series in Boston a few days later, the interest in a Johnson-Wood duel was irresistible. Clark Griffith persuaded Stahl to move Joe's spot in the rotation up a day so that the matchup could occur.

As Wood recalled, the press built the game up like a championship prizefight, listing the two players' physical statistics along with the details of their winning streaks and careers.[32] Filling every seat in the new park and spilling out onto the field, where they were contained behind ropes along the foul lines and in front of the right-field bleachers, the record crowd, estimated at thirty-two thousand, watched the two best pitchers in the league live up to their billing. Johnson, the "champion," threw only ninety-seven pitches, seventy for strikes, as he fanned five, walked none, and allowed just five Boston hits. But successive two-out doubles by Speaker and Lewis in the sixth inning gave Smoky Joe, the "challenger," the only run he needed—the only one that Johnson allowed. Duffy's hit, a lazy fly ball down the right-field line, barely dropped in fair territory beyond the desperate reach of the onrushing Dan Moeller. Wood's six-hit, nine-strikeout 1–0 victory, the sixth shutout of his streak, kept it going at fourteen. Ironically, it was halted at Johnson's mark—sixteen—two weeks later when Joe Lake of the Tigers, in relief of Tex Covington, held off Boston for a 6–4 Detroit victory on September 20. The victory streak, since tied by Lefty Grove in 1931 and Schoolboy Rowe in 1934, still stands as the American League record.

The heroics of Wood, Speaker, and their teammates carried the Red Sox to one of the most eagerly anticipated World Series in years. Their opponents would be McGraw's New York Giants, the same team that had refused to meet the Boston Pilgrims in postseason play in 1904 to determine baseball's world champion. Loathing AL President Johnson for his league's encroachment on his baseball territory in New York, John T. Brush, the Giants' owner, had dismissed the American League pennant winners then as "a bunch of bush leaguers" whom he would not lower his own champions to meet.[33]

McGraw had his own reasons for not wanting to play Boston in 1904, not the least of which was a similar contempt for Johnson that stemmed from several confrontations between the two during McGraw's brief tenure as a manager in Johnson's American League in 1901–2.[34] McGraw also bitterly recalled the successive losses his champion Baltimore Orioles had suffered in the contrived postseason series for the Temple Cup in 1894 and 1895 between the first- and second-place finishers in the National League. Winning his league's pennant by thirteen games in 1904, McGraw was in no mood to risk diminution of his team's achievement in another unnecessary postseason tournament. The fact that the American League Pilgrims had surprised Pittsburgh, the NL representative in the first World Series of 1903, winning five out of eight games in a scheduled nine-game set, did not lessen McGraw's wariness of the value of such a competition.

By 1912, however, the matter of a postseason meeting of the two Major League winners had become an established—and required— climax to the baseball season. As the Giants and Red Sox prepared to face each other, each league had won four of the previous championships. But the American League had won two in succession, including Philadelphia's triumph in six games over McGraw's team in 1911. Looking for revenge this October, McGraw also recalled how Boston had defeated his club four games to one in a postseason exhibition series between the two third place finishers in the 1909 regular campaign. He particularly remembered how the young Texan in the Boston outfield had ripped his pitching for twelve hits, including two doubles and two home runs, in twenty trips to the plate. "I never believed a player could be that good," said John Taylor of Speaker's exhibition then.[35] McGraw concurred. The New York manager, who had passed on an opportunity to sign Speaker when he showed up at the Giants' camp in 1908, considered Spoke the one man his boys had to stop to win the Series. Otherwise, he figured, the Red Sox would not be as tough as the Athletics had been a year ago.

McGraw's assessment of Speaker was correct; his view of the rest of the club was not. If not cleanly played—the two teams made a combined thirty errors, contributing to nineteen unearned runs—the Series pitted two evenly matched opponents against each other in a struggle that would not be decided until there were two out in the bottom of the tenth inning of the final game. The pitchers at that time were Joe Wood and Christy Mathewson, a fitting pairing since so much of the Series had revolved around that which they had controlled and that which they had suffered at the often fumbling hands of others throughout the championship. The drama of their final confrontation had largely been made possible by the man whom McGraw feared the most—Speaker—and the Boston player whom he learned to respect the most—Harry Hooper.

"It would not surprise me a little bit to see Joe Wood win three games in the first four days of the contests," predicted Clark Griffith about the only man he considered the equal of Walter Johnson.[36] Instead, Joe settled for two. In game 1, played in New York, Wood faced the Giants' rookie sensation, Jeff Tesreau, McGraw's surprising starter over his aces Mathewson and Rube Marquard. With the first game in the Polo Grounds, McGraw gambled that his young right-hander would more likely handle the pressure of the Series better before the home crowd than in the hostile confines of Fenway Park. Mac could then come back with the veteran Mathewson in Boston, whose task at worst would be to even the Series for the Giants.

Considering the season that Tesreau had just had, seventeen wins and an ERA of 1.96, the lowest on the staff, it was not a bad decision. It just did not work out. Although he carried a 2–1 lead into the seventh inning, Tesreau could not hold it. With two out and runners on first and third, Hooper tied the game on a hard shot down the first-base line to the wall. Yerkes followed Harry's double with a single, scoring two runs and putting Boston ahead 4–2. With the score unchanged in the bottom of the ninth, Wood got the first out before successive singles off the bats of Fred Merkle and Buck Herzog and Chief Meyers's double pushed one run across and put the potential tying and winning runs on second and third. The Chief's hit should have scored another run had not Hooper turned in the defensive play of the day. Racing to the right-field line to scoop up Meyers's hit with his bare hand, Harry then fired the ball on a line to Cady at the plate. Seeing the perfect throw headed for home, McGraw held Herzog at third. "That throw," said Hughie Jennings, "saved the Series."[37] Harry's play was all the inspiration Wood needed to finish. Throwing "so hard I thought my arm would fly right off my body," Joe blazed third strikes past both Art Fletcher and Doc Crandall to end the game.[38] The Red Sox had their victory and Wood his "biggest thrill" in baseball.[39]

After the second game had been called because of darkness with the score knotted at 6–6 through eleven innings and after Marquard had scattered seven Red Sox hits to best O'Brien 2–1 and even the Series at a win apiece the next day, Smoky Joe was back on the hill for game 4. Despite only two days' rest, Wood threw another complete-game victory. His familiar allies in the effort were Hooper, Speaker, and his fastball. Harry and Spoke each collected their fifth hit of the Series to frustrate Tesreau again, and Hoop's quick retrieval of a ball hit for a single through the right side of the infield in the Giants seventh enabled Yerkes to gun down Fletcher at the plate and end a brief New York rally. Wood fanned eight more Giants to raise his strikeout total to nineteen in eighteen innings pitched.

Smoky Joe's second win in New York sent the Red Sox back to Boston to face Matty again in game 5. Like the scenario after game 1, the Giants needed a victory from their great star to even the Series. Mathewson pitched well enough to earn it, but as in game 2, when shoddy defense allowed four unearned runs to score, his fielders failed him again. After back-to-back triples by Hooper and Yerkes in the third, Larry Doyle, the Chalmers Award winner in the National League, let Speaker's ground ball get through him to allow Yerkes to score Boston's second run of the inning. The Red Sox could push no more across as Matty set down every batter he faced the rest of the afternoon. But Bedient was just as effective, allowing the Giants only three hits. An unearned run in the seventh was all the Giants could muster. With four games now decided, Boston held a 3-1 edge. Mathewson, meanwhile, had allowed but four earned runs in nineteen innings and had only a loss and a no-decision to show for it. Hooper, fielding his position flawlessly through five games, led the Red Sox hitters with seven hits for a .368 average. Moreover, he had reached base in every game so far, four times leading off the Boston first with either a hit or a walk.

With their backs to the wall, McGraw's men suddenly found the offense that had produced the highest team batting average in the Majors in 1912, .286. They were helped when Wood unexpectedly did not take the mound for the Red Sox in game 6. Stahl apparently had been persuaded by McAleer to give O'Brien another chance and to rest Joe an extra day just in case. Like McGraw's gamble with Tesreau in game 1, Stahl's decision to start O'Brien did not pay off. With two out and two on in the New York half of the first inning, O'Brien balked in the Giants' first run. His false move on the mound completely unhinged him and the Giants capitalized quickly. Two doubles, two singles, and a double steal followed to push four more runs across before Bucky picked off Fletcher at first to end the frame. Collins relieved O'Brien in the second inning and held the Giants in check the rest of the game. But Boston only managed two unearned runs of its own against Marquard, who went the distance for his second complete-game win of the Series. Rube had allowed only one earned run in the eighteen innings he had worked.

With Boston still needing one win for the title, the Series shifted back to Fenway, where the Red Sox and their supporters confidently expected Wood to end matters in the sixth decisive game. But this was not, in fact, the sixth game to be played. The tie in game 2 had added an extra game to the schedule so that this third Wood-Tesreau matchup was actually game 7. The folks who seemed most confused by the expanded schedule were in Fenway's ticket office. Series tickets had been sold in strips of three. If a seventh game was necessary to break a 3–3 deadlock, the site for that game to be decided on a coin flip, then admissions to that contest would be a separate matter through game-day sales. The Boston administration had counted the tie game as one of the three allotted to the Series strip holders; hence they viewed the game of October 15—the seventh actually to be played—as open to spectators on a first-come, first-served basis.

This view was not shared by the Red Sox's most raucous supporters, a group known as the Royal Rooters. Headed by Mayor Fitzgerald, accompanied by brass bands, singing their favorite song, "Tessie," at the top of their lungs, and well fortified for the occasion after a lengthy pregame meeting at Nuf Ced McGreevey's Whittier Street saloon, the gang of about three hundred paraded onto the field about fifteen minutes before game time, heading for their accustomed seats in the left-field stands. The Rooters were not happy to find that their usual location was now occupied by patrons who had purchased tickets for the game that day. Demanding that their seats be cleared, Honey Fitz caucused with the group around the pitcher's mound. When it became apparent that no one in the sold-out park was going to give up a seat to the mayor and his company, the indignant Royal Rooters refused to leave the playing field. In desperation, McAleer directed several mounted policemen to persuade the group otherwise. Finally, after the mob had been herded behind the low left-field bleacher fence and the parts of it that had been knocked down in the process had been repaired, the game was ready to begin about thirty minutes after its scheduled start.

Unfortunately, Smoky Joe was not. Never one to make excuses for a poor performance, Wood denied that the fracas on the field and the long wait it had caused affected his pitching. Whether his arm had stiffened or not after he was warm and ready to go, Joe was not the pitcher he had been in the earlier games. Before he retired his first batter, New York had tallied twice on three straight hits, aided by another successful double steal. Before Wood returned to the bench, the Giants had batted around, scoring six runs on seven hits. Like the previous game, the Red Sox never recovered from the first-inning disaster. The Giants pounded Hall in relief of Wood for nine more hits, five more runs, and coasted to an easy 11–4 win to even the Series at three games apiece.

And so this "most agitatious, most soul-searching series ever played since the big leagues began" came down to one more game for the championship.[40] Although New York lost the coin flip to decide where the game would be held, they had every reason to be optimistic about its outcome. Their two decisive victories in games 6 and 7 signaled that life was back in their bats. Their fielding had been anything but championship caliber, but, no worse than Boston's glove work, it had not cost them the Series—yet. At times the Giants' defense had actually sparkled, such as when Fred Snodgrass, running full speed with his back to the plate, hauled in Wagner's long drive to right center with a man on in the fourth inning of Marquard's 5–2 win. Hugh Fullerton of the *New York Times* called it a "miracle catch."[41] But the reason for the most confidence among the Giants and their followers was that Matty would be on the mound. In two previous World Series, Mathewson had not failed to win at least one game. Surely he was pitching well enough not to be denied this October.

Things were less sanguine in the Boston camp. The last two games, especially the rout of Wood, had demoralized the team and angered its fans. Still smarting from their treatment in game 7, the Royal Rooters announced that none of their ranks would be attending the final game and urged other fans to stay away as well. The *Boston Globe* sympathized with the Rooters and censured the Red Sox management for employing police who allegedly used tactics more appropriate to Russian cossacks controlling the peasants in Moscow than handling the citizens of the commonwealth.[42] Whether because of the Rooters' boycott or doubts that Bedient could keep the Giants at bay again, only 17,034 people, less than half the turnout for previous games in Boston, showed up for the finale. They would have a lot to tell their absent friends for years to come.

Every time someone in the sparse crowd looked up that afternoon, there were men on base for one team or the other. But as the game headed into the bottom of the seventh, New York clung to a 1–0 lead. Both Mathewson and Bedient had been saved by timely fielding or particularly effective work of their own when it was needed most. Matty pitched out of scoring threats in four of the first six innings, retiring the Red Sox in order in the other two. Twice the Giants had gunned down Boston base runners who had tried to stretch base hits into something more; three times Matty had ended an inning with a strikeout. Bedient had allowed a run in the third when Red Murray doubled home Josh Devore, who had reached base on a two-out walk. But, though the Giants put men aboard in every inning, twice getting them to third base, they had not been able to push across another run.

Thwarting the Giants on one occasion was Boston's own miracle catch, one which immediately overshadowed Snodgrass's grab and every other defensive gem in the Series for its timing and execution. The miracle worker was Harry Hooper. In the top of the fifth, Doyle blasted a pitch directly over Harry's head toward the temporary fence in deep right field. The thirty-inch-high fence had been erected about ten feet in front of the permanent wall in order to pack a few hundred more spectators into rows of chairs behind it. Harry raced for the fence, his back to the ball. At the last instant, as he planted his right foot to leap for the ball, he looked back over his left shoulder to find it. Instinctively, as his momentum carried him over the low railing, he reached up with his right hand—his bare hand— and felt the ball smack into his palm. He held on to it as he disappeared into the crowd. McGraw and the Giants immediately claimed that Hooper had made the catch while off the playing field, thus disallowing it and awarding a home run to Doyle. But the National League's Bill Klem, the crew chief of the Series umpires, ruled that Harry's catch was a fair one.

How spectacular was Hooper's grab? *Base Ball Magazine*'s editor, William Phelon, called it "unequaled, unexampled."[43] Speaker said it was the greatest catch he had ever seen.[44] Richter of the *Reach Guide* bestowed "the honor of saving the final game" on Harry for making "the most wonderful catch ever seen in a World's Series."[45] Wood thought his catch "was almost impossible to believe even when you saw it."[46] Hooper placed the catch at the very top of the long list of those Major League accomplishments of which he was most proud.[47] Harry also acknowledged that he may have had some help in making it. As he took his position in the outfield in the top of the first inning, Hooper noticed a piece of paper on the grass. He picked it up to discover that it was a Catholic prayer card, a small picture depicting the Sacred Heart of Jesus with a few words of intercession printed on it. Thinking the card had been left by a fan who intended for him to find it, Harry recited the prayer to himself and stuck the card in his pants pocket. As the magnitude of his catch grew with the years, so, too, did Harry's wonderment at a connection between his discovery and the good fortune that followed.[48]

Indeed, perhaps no mere mortal could have scripted what was to follow. In the home seventh, the Red Sox finally broke through against Mathewson. With two out and runners on first and second, Stahl sent Olaf Henriksen up to pinch-hit for Bedient. Though nicknamed "Swede," the Danish-born reserve was a solid ballplayer who had to suffer the consequences of being the fourth-best outfielder on the Boston roster. He never got more than ninety-nine at bats in any of the seven seasons he played with the Red Sox, but he generally made the most of the chances he did have. In 1912 he had batted .321 in thirty-seven game appearances, driving in eight runs on his eighteen hits. He delivered this day as well, tying the game on a screaming shot down the left-field line. Stahl then called on Wood to finish the game for Boston. As he took the mound in the top of the eighth, the pitching matchup which so many had anticipated at the outset of the Series—Wood vs. Mathewson—had finally materialized. "I don't know if I had any butterflies," Smoky Joe recalled of the moment, "but let's say I was definitely impressed by the situation."[49]

For two innings, the eighth and ninth, both pitchers were superb, setting down their opposition with little difficulty. The game now moved to an extra frame. In the top of the tenth with one out, Murray, who had two hits off Wood already in the Series, doubled into the gap between Lewis and Speaker in left. Merkle then followed with a single to center which Tris juggled briefly in his haste to hold Murray on third. His miscue, however, gave Murray the opening he needed to score. Wood struck out Herzog and induced Meyers to bounce one back to the mound to prevent any further damage and end the inning. But Boston now trailed by a run, heading to the bottom of the tenth, facing Mathewson in a game situation the master relished.

What followed then was one of the most storied sequences in the annals of World Series play. Engle, pinch-hitting for Wood, who had injured his pitching hand fielding Meyers's grounder, lofted an easy fly ball to Snodgrass, who simply dropped it; Engle wound up at second on the error. Hooper then smashed a drive to deep right center—"a sure triple," recollected Harry[50]—which Snodgrass outran and caught in a diving lunge at the last moment; Engle moved to third after the catch. Yerkes walked to set up a possible game-ending double play. Speaker then popped a high foul between home and first base. Matty, Merkle, and Meyers converged on the ball, with Mathewson calling for the Chief to take it. But he could not reach it and the ball fell harmlessly in foul ground. "Matty," said Speaker as the two passed each other to resume their battle, "that play will cost you the game and the Series."[51] Spoke then delivered on his word, stroking a game-tying single to right to score Engle and cancel the run that his error in the top of the inning had allowed. McGraw directed Matty to walk Lewis intentionally to load the bases and set up a force play at any bag. But Larry Gardner, struggling at bat and in the field the entire Series, now had his own redemptive opportunity. He made the most of it as his long sacrifice fly to Devore in right field brought in Yerkes with the winning run of the Series.

For Wood, Gardner's RBI meant his third win of the Series. For Mathewson, it meant his second loss, despite relinquishing only five earned runs in 28⅔ innings pitched, an ERA of 1.57. For Snodgrass, it meant baseball immortality for his "$30,000 muff," the share of the players' receipts his error supposedly had cost his teammates. For the Giants, the loss was their second consecutive failure in World Series play; their third awaited them a year later. For Boston, the improbable ending capped a magnificent season. Although outhit by New York .270 to .220 and posting a higher ERA than the Giants, 2.80 to 1.71, the Red Sox had rallied against the odds, the despair of their fans, and the momentum of McGraw's club. They were rewarded with a huge parade and rally the next day at Fanueil Hall, where Honey Fitz presented the players with keys to the city and proclaimed them to be "the greatest club ever."[52]

As only the center stage of the World Series can command, the performances on the field received the most intense scrutiny of the press. Replaying the game and casting about for heroes and goats, the typewriter corps had little difficulty agreeing on who should wear those mantles. The muff that ever after would be mentioned in the same breath as his name earned Fred Snodgrass the most blame for the Giants' defeat. The catch, that "paralyzing catch on the final afternoon" which saved his team from "the deep tureen," brought Harry the greatest share of credit for the Red Sox victory.[53] Perhaps more meaningful than any of the bouquets which the press threw his way, though, Hooper's play against a John McGraw–coached team so impressed the old man that he praised Harry as "one of the most dangerous hitters in a pinch that the game has ever known."[54] Tying Speaker for most hits on the club in the Series with nine, including three for extra bases; reaching base six times in his first at bat in the eight games; and alone among the Boston regulars in not making an error in the field, Harry indeed had "played like wildfire" when the chips were down. He had also earned a winner's share of $4,025, the richest payoff in Series history for the players. It would come in handy as he headed west to Capitola for the winter. For not only were his family and friends waiting there to celebrate his triumph but so, too, was Esther Henchy, and Harry had a date with her at the altar in November.

Harry's father, Joe, his twin brothers, George and Charlie, his sister, Lulu, and his mother, Mary Katherine, in 1889. Harry is seated in front. (Courtesy of John Hooper)

The Young Phoenix Base Ball Club of Saint Mary's College, 1903. Harry, seated in the front row (on the left), was one of the team's mascots. (Courtesy of Saint Mary's College Archives, Moraga, Calif.)

Harry as a young engineer-surveyor for the Western Pacific Railroad, 1908. (Courtesy of John Hooper)

Spring training, Hot Springs, Arkansas, 1909. Harry, on the front of the ox, poses with three other rookies and two Boston reporters. (Courtesy of John Hooper)

Harry, in the Boston Red Sox outfield, 1909. (National Baseball Library, Cooperstown, N.Y.)

Harry, with Larry Gardner and Jake Stahl, the Red Sox manager, at spring training, 1912. (National Baseball Library, Cooperstown, N.Y.)

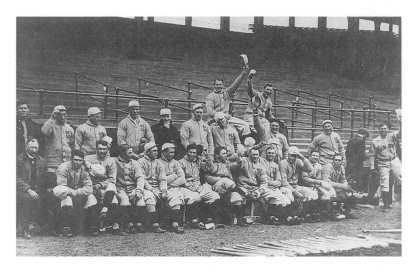

The Red Sox pose in their new ballpark, Fenway Park, in April 1912. Harry is seated in the front row (sixth player from the left). (National Baseball Library, Cooperstown, N.Y.)

Harry takes batting practice as Larry Gardner waits his turn, ca. 1912. (National Baseball Library, Cooperstown, N.Y.)

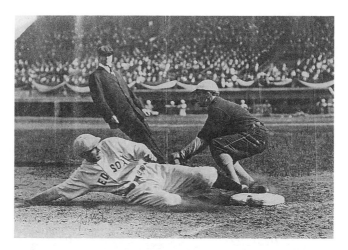

Harry slides into third against Harry Lord of the Chicago
White Sox during the official opening of Fenway Park, May
17, 1912. Silk O'Loughlin makes the call. The first game at
Fenway had taken place on April 20, but the park was still
under construction. (National Baseball Library, Cooperstown, N.Y.)

The 1912 Boston outfield: Olaf Henrikson, Harry, Tris
Speaker, and Duffy Lewis. Henrikson batted .321 in 1912
and .375 in 1913 but couldn't crack the starting line-up.
(National Baseball Library, Cooperstown, N.Y.)

"Speed Boys in a Speedy Car" proclaimed the ad copy for this photo of Larry Gardner and Harry sitting in a Stutz roadster after the 1912 World Series. (Courtesy of John Hooper).

6

Dearest Esther

Today has been a long, dreary day. Most of the fellows went out to see the races, but I didn't. Instead I loafed around and read. I am going to bed as soon as I finish this. This makes my second letter to you today. But I have been lonesome for you all day.
—Harry Hooper, July 17, 1913

The three Henchy sisters—Kathleen, Molly and Esther—turned the boys' heads when they visited the Capitola beaches and ball fields. The daughters of an Irishman, who had arrived in the United States from County Limerick as a sixteen-year-old stowaway, and his New England–born wife, who had met and married him while visiting her brother in the Santa Clara Valley, the girls were inseparable, venturing forth together and creating a stir with their liveliness and beauty. The youngest was Esther, four years junior to Kathleen and a year behind Molly. If her order in the family required some deference to her sisters, Esther ignored such conventions when it came to the suitors who frequented the Henchy home. One of them was the ballplaying son of Joe and Mary Hooper.

Harry had courted Kathleen initially, but Esther's sunny personality and shocking red hair quickly shifted his attention. Sharing long walks on the beach and Sunday concerts at the band pavilion in town, the two found their fondness for each other growing during the winter months of 1911–12. Before Harry headed east for the championship season that would carry the Red Sox to the World Series, he and Esther agreed to set a wedding date around Thanksgiving. On November 26, with Larry Gardner serving as best man and Molly as maid of honor, the two were married in a Catholic ceremony before embarking by motorcar on a honeymoon tour of the California missions that took them all the way to San Diego. Esther was just nineteen, Harry twenty-five. Returning to Capitola three weeks later, they made their first home in a small cottage near the inn Harry's parents owned.

Harry's new marital status had no immediate effect on his routine as he reported on March 1 for the now familiar ritual of spring training in Hot Springs. Although he was not eager to leave Esther in California, Harry looked forward to the new season and the rumors of its approach which the twice-daily workouts at Whittington Park confirmed. Unlike many players who despised the tedium and generally poor playing conditions of the spring sites, Hooper enjoyed the camaraderie and relaxed atmosphere of these weeks. Unlike Cobb, specifically, who had no one on the Tigers he particularly wanted to see after the winter's separation, Hooper had several close friends among the Red Sox players and the sporting press.[1] His favorites were Gardner and Wood, whose quiet manner and devotion to hard work closely mirrored Harry's own personality and habits.

Although not reluctant to join his more boisterous teammates like Lewis, Wagner, or Carrigan for a day at the Essex Park or Oaklawn race tracks or a night on the town sampling the wares of the Opera House Bar or the Happy Hollow Saloon, Harry preferred to spend time catching up on the winter's news, reminiscing about the previous season, or simply talking baseball over a game of bridge or checkers. These latter activities, in fact, though considerably less colorful and crude than the midnight revelries and stunts that grabbed headlines and fed the popular view of professional ballplayers as largely unsavory characters, were more reflective of the way the idle hours would be filled in the long months of the regular season. Like his approach to matters on the field, Harry saw no reason to rehearse the time away from the ballpark any differently in the spring from the way it would be spent once the championship campaign had begun.

Hooper also appreciated the value of the spring weeks in setting a tone for the kind of "extra effort that spells the difference between a winner or a loser."[2] In his few years in the Majors already, Hooper had seen the dramatic difference that good conditioning, or the lack thereof, could make in the way a club began a season and stayed competitive in it. The quick starts of the Tigers in 1911 and the White Sox in 1912, for example, were partly attributable to successful preseasons from which they emerged with their players in shape and their games in good form. Although neither Detroit nor Chicago won pennants in those years, they managed to throw quite a scare at the clubs which did in the big leads they built early in the pennant race. Conditioning, Harry knew, was not simply a matter of concern that began when the players arrived in camp. Well aware of the disruptive effects uncertain spring weather could have on the best preseason plans of any club, Hooper stressed the individual player's responsibility to achieve a competitive edge physically "whether you are in the game or on the bench."[3] He maintained a rigorous year-round regimen himself, running on the sands of Capitola and in the hills above Santa Cruz and sharpening his hand-eye coordination in the hunting and golfing he enjoyed in the off-season. No less than his rookie year, Hooper worked extremely hard once he was in camp. This spring he especially spent more time working on his hitting fundamentals, hoping to avoid the slow start which had affected his batting average all season in 1912.

To a far greater extent than he had done since his rookie season, Harry also spent more time writing about his experiences. Unlike 1909, though, his thoughts were not given to solitary entries in a diary but to a shared and steady correspondence with his young wife. The letters between them, sweet and confiding, reveal as much about their longing for each other as about Harry's life away from the ballpark. The latter point is particularly important to note, for Harry, like so many husbands in other professions who decided it was best to leave their work at the office when they came home, rarely referred to the games he played and his performance in them when he "came home" to Esther in his letters. In this respect, his letters were very different from his diary notations, which essentially chronicled his own performance and observations about his teammates and the progress of the season. His correspondence was less critical of his daily work on the field but more confessional of his feelings. He missed Esther terribly and lovingly told her so.

"Reading your daily messages is the bright shining feature of my otherwise dull existence here," Harry wrote Esther from Hot Springs. Between practice and an occasional golf game, "if the weather permits," Harry reported, "there isn't any news." Esther's letters, he assured her, put him to "the pleasant task" of responding, although he spent much of his time counting the days "till I see you." Esther was scheduled to join Harry in Boston before the season began, at which time, Harry promised her, "I shall try to repay you in love's desire" for being "the best little wife anybody ever had." Thanking her for her prayers and the Sunday communion she regularly offered for his well-being, a gesture which he dutifully returned, Harry warned that "I am afraid you are in danger of being loved to death when I see you."[4]

Such affection and the religious dimensions of its expression characterized their entire correspondence. Although neither Harry nor Esther practiced their Catholicism in other than an ordinary manner, they carefully respected the performance obligations of the church calendar and minded their faith in an unassuming fashion. Performing their Easter duty of confession and communion during the Lenten season, attending Sunday Mass regularly, and remembering each other in their prayers, the two affirmed the value of their faith and its place in their lives. Easter seemed a particularly important time for them, perhaps because it was the major holy day of the year when they were unlikely to be with each other. Falling either at the end of spring training or at the very beginning of the baseball season, Easter coincided with a hectic time in Harry's schedule when he was often on the road and gearing himself up for the start of the new campaign. Yet as the Easter season and Harry's professional one both signaled a spirit of renewal in the spring, their Easter cards carried similar expressions of reassurance and replenishment.

"A happy joyful Easter is hard to spend, my dear," Harry wrote, "without my lovely Esther, my lonely heart to cheer." Harry's poems were never more sophisticated, but their simplicity effectively conveyed his loneliness and love for his wife. "I hope this finds you happy, and I'll be happy too," he penned another year, "in the hope that in the future on Easter I'll be with you." Perhaps the Arkansas rains inspired a similar wish: "But may God who regulates the Happiness Bureau of Weather make the only cloud upon your sky the fact we're not together."[5] Signed "Your Worshipful Husband," "Your loving Harry," or "Yours in love, Harry," the messages often bore a single fingerprint. As verse, Harry's words form the simplest kind of rhyming couplet, an innocence of meter appropriate to the lightness of the sentiments. But it is the very gentleness and ingenuousness of his expressions that provide another window on his character. They also explain why finding the prayer card in the outfield in the final game of the 1912 World Series so impressed Harry and provoked his sense of wonderment at the good fortune that followed.

There were, of course, ways to remedy the longing Harry had for Esther, namely, to move her to Boston or to have her travel with the team on the road occasionally. The former, however, was not a realistic step for the young couple to take. Setting up a residence in or near Boston was neither a practical matter economically nor a wise one emotionally. With both sets of parents and Esther's sisters and friends in the Capitola–Santa Cruz area, Harry convinced his wife that she was better off where she was, living near their parents' homes, than keeping house in a strange city while her husband was away two weeks out of every four for the six months of the regular season.

As for traveling with the team, this was a matter that had economic implications as well but, more fundamentally, raised questions regarding the role of a baseball wife. The Red Sox, like most clubs in the Majors, prohibited wives from joining their husbands in spring training but had no expressed policy against their attending games at home or on the road once the regular season had commenced. Generally, however, wives did not travel in the company of their player-husbands or stay with them in their hotels. If they ventured out on the road, wives usually did so in the company of the wives of their husbands' friends on the team or caught up with the team in cities where they had other friends or relatives with whom they could stay. In the first season after their marriage, for example, Esther joined Harry for occasional two-week stretches at a time, usually in Boston for home stands.

The awkward conditions affecting spousal relationships during the season reflected the uncertain judgment regarding the value of a baseball wife. Although John McGraw was "convinced that nothing helps a young man so much in baseball or in any other profession as a good wife," he did not approve a wife's accompanying her husband on road trips because "she seems to distract his attention."[6] Distraction, of course, in McGraw's opinion, was a threat to a player's performance no matter where or when it occurred and he warned against the "foolish wives or sweethearts who sit in the stand and yell out endearing encouragement to their husbands. They not only embarrass the player but often make it very uncomfortable for those about them in the stands." If experienced husband-wife relationships were potentially distractive, the Giants manager had a special set of concerns for players contemplating marriage. "When a young fellow gets into his head to get married, there's no stopping him," McGraw explained. "He thinks of nothing else." In particular, he complained, they "think their marriage is the most important thing in the world . . . they forget all about baseball." McGraw's advice in these matters was simple. A baseball player should not get married until after the World Series. By the time the next season comes around, then, he and his bride should "be able to understand things," presumably the line between a wife's foolish and helpful behavior. McGraw's views were generally held by baseball people. Wives were acknowledged for the stabilizing effect they could have on their husbands but essentially marginalized for the "problems" they were perceived as causing.[7]

If Harry's decision to marry at the end of the 1912 season had any adverse effect on his play, his heroics during the World Series as his

November wedding day approached dispelled McGraw's notion of conjugal distraction. As the 1913 campaign progressed, it was obvious that Harry's newlywed status did not inhibit his play on the field. Proving that his performance at the plate in the Series was more indicative of his work than that he had shown during the regular season, Hooper raised his batting average over forty points to .288. Playing in 148 games, exceeded previously only by his 155 game appearances in 1910, he led the team in at bats (586) for the fourth consecutive year. His 169 hits, the most he would collect in a season in a Red Sox uniform, contributed to a team-leading one hundred runs scored. His stolen bases (26), doubles (29), and triples (12) placed him second or third on the club in each of these categories. He also matched his 1911 home run output, leading the team with four round-trippers. Remarkably, he collected two of these on the same day as he led off the Red Sox's first inning in each game of a Memorial Day doubleheader against Washington with a homer. He has been the only player in Major League history to accomplish such a feat.

Although he did not mention these clouts to Esther, Harry was excited enough by another of his homers—a three-run blast that won the game against Saint Louis on May 16—that he uncharacteristically wrote her about it. He reported that he "only got one hit" in the game, "but it was a good one."[8] Nevertheless, Harry told his wife, overall "there is no news. All I have done since I wrote you last is to sleep, eat, and play a ball game." His agenda that evening called for a game of checkers with Hugh Bedient.

For her part, Esther even more rarely brought up the subject of baseball in her correspondence with Harry. In this respect she seemed to defer to his example, choosing not to press for news about his work unless she felt he wanted to talk about it. She underscored her sense of place in his world in generally staying away from the ballpark when Harry was playing, a decision which McGraw and others would heartily approve. Her absence, however, reflected less a concern that her nervousness might make her conspicuous than a desire not to intrude in the professional side of his life. As much as Harry missed Esther, he never expressed his longing in terms of wishing to see her at the ballpark. Typically he declared: "I am very lonesome for you, and wish I were there or you were here."[9] But those places where he wished to join her were far from the public arenas of his career.

Since the newlyweds were unlikely to find the privacy they desired at Putnam's, the residential hotel which catered to ballplayers and where Harry lived his first few years with the Red Sox, he rented a cottage for the two of them in Winthrop, a seaside community on a peninsula jutting into Massachusetts Bay a few miles northeast of Boston. In 1913 they spent only a couple of weeks during a summer home stand in the cottage, but in subsequent years they would rent a place in the area for the entire summer season. In 1914 and 1915, for example, they stayed in a cottage alongside one occupied by Larry and Margaret Gardner and hosted Joe and May Wood, Tris Speaker, and others quite regularly. Otherwise, Esther occasionally stayed with an aunt in Lawrence on her trips east.

Hooper's off-field associations with Wood and Gardner, in particular, reflected the closeness of their friendships and revealed the way in which cliques among teammates could be formed. Alike in age, temperament, and interests away from the ballpark, especially golf and hunting, they spent most of their time during the season in each other's company and found numerous occasions in the off-season to get together as well. Hooper and Gardner, Duffy Lewis said, "were inseparable," and Speaker was pulled into their circle with Smoky Joe because he and Tris roomed together.[10]

They were particularly eager to visit Harry in California and he usually hosted one or more of them for a week or two of vacation once the season had ended. After the 1914 campaign, for example, Harry organized a hunting trip for Joe, Spoke, and a few of his California friends. It was such a successful venture that the three Red Sox teammates decided to establish the Hooper Outing Club to commemorate the occasion and plan for future events. The three celebrated the organization of the club with a grand concert and dance in Boston's convention hall at the start of the 1915 season.[11] With Hooper installed as honorary president and chairman of the ball, assisted by floor marshals Wood and Speaker, the gala attracted more than four hundred guests from the Red Sox, the Boston Braves, and the Royal Rooters; city dignitaries; and the sporting press. Dancing until two o'clock in the morning to the music of Poole's Orchestra, the guests applauded Harry and Esther, who led the order of dances with a "one-step" before joining them for a full program of waltzes, fox trots, galops, and schottisches. At intermission the revelers were treated to the inaugural performance of the official song of the Hooper Outing and Athletic Club, a little ditty to the tune of "There's a Girl in the Heart of Maryland":

> Our club has a name of the Hooper O.C.
> and we surely cannot be beat.

> We are named after Harry Hooper of the Red Sox
> To watch him run the bases is a treat.
> So Hooper up, for Hooper boys
> And our hips for him might and may
> For we'll all be with him, all summer long
> Till his team wins the pennant again.

Although Hooper's friendships with other members of the Red Sox were not as close as they were with his colleagues in the Outing Club, he enjoyed a remarkable camaraderie with all of them. Considering the intense dislike which characterized some of the personal relationships on the team, this was no mean feat. Speaker and Lewis, for example, had little use for each other beyond the playing field. The origins of their mutual animosity probably stemmed from Duffy's swaggering manner and its less than endearing effect on Spoke. It first manifested itself in spring training in 1910 when Duffy did not defer to the veterans in a way that Tris expected. However, their problems with each other erupted in the summer of 1913 when Speaker persisted in embarrassing Lewis by sneaking up behind him to knock off his cap and expose his balding scalp. Spoke's behavior added insult to injury because Lewis had shaved his own head in Saint Louis to gain some relief from a sweltering heat wave which had accompanied the club on a western swing in July. His teammates had done the same thing, but Duffy's hair never fully grew back. When Speaker snatched Duffy's hat before the home folks in Boston, Lewis had had enough. "Do that again and I'll kill you," Duffy warned. Spoke did it again. Duffy promptly threw his bat at Speaker, striking him in the shins so hard that he had to be helped from the field.[12] The two rarely talked to each other off the field after that, but Lewis asserted that "once a game started we forgot personal feelings. We helped each other as willingly as we helped anybody else in the lineup."[13]

The ill feeling between Lewis and Speaker flowed over to the cliques to which they each belonged. But there were more fundamental differences that separated Duffy's camp from Spoke's. Duffy's companions included a bar-hopping and card-playing crowd, most notably Carrigan and Wagner. In 1914 they added a newcomer to their ranks, a rough-mannered nineteen-year-old rookie who already knew his way around saloons from his bartending days at his father's place: Babe Ruth. Speaker's friends reflected his serious demeanor and conservative tastes. They were more inclined to keep to themselves, less interested in the lights and action that Duffy sought.

Some of them were also Masons, members of a fraternal order whose secrecy and rites were not viewed with favor by the Catholics on the team. The Irish Lewis and his gang, of course, were solidly Catholic.

Hooper, though Catholic, preferred the company of a quieter lot, no matter what their politics or religion. For example, he enjoyed a lifelong friendship with Lewis, although its form away from the ball field usually focused on correspondence between them, not trips or vacations together. Harry, like Duffy and his buddies, enjoyed his card playing and shows as well, but his choices were bridge and musical theater, not poker and burlesque.

Harry did agree with Duffy's assessment of how he and his outfield partners worked together in the field. Although Carrigan recalled that Speaker would occasionally invade Lewis's territory in left, the trio played as a unit, respecting each other's abilities, particularly as they applied to the unique demands of play in Fenway.[14] In his sector, Duffy had to contend with a ten-foot-high embankment in front of the left-field wall that extended from the foul line to the flagpole in center field. The slope served to warn fielders of the proximity of the wall and was a common feature of ballparks before warning tracks were built. There were no inclines anywhere else as steep as Fenway's, though, and Lewis's mastery of it earned the area its nickname: Duffy's Cliff.

Over in right, because of the strange configuration of the park, Harry had the most territory to cover, even more than Spoke in center. Although the right-field corner was only 313½ feet from home plate, the low fence that swept out from the foul pole merged with a higher wall and then headed toward a corner in right center some 550 feet from the batter's box. Odd angles formed by the bullpen and the joining of the two fences complicated the spacious dimensions. Moreover, the tricky shadows and glare of what was generally acknowledged to be the toughest sun field in the Majors added adventure to the right fielder's afternoon. But no one handled these conditions better than Hooper.

Borrowing an innovation he had learned from Fred Clarke of the Pirates, Hooper was the first American Leaguer to use flip-down sunglasses in the field. He punched two holes in his cap for the string which secured them under the bill, ready to use instantly. They provided the advantage he needed to handle high flies when the sun played havoc with a fielder's vision. Harry claimed he never lost a ball in the sun at Fenway and no one remembered otherwise. Another characteristic of his play was an invention of his own doing—

the sliding catch. Hooper discovered that he could more effectively handle low line drives without loss of momentum or balance by sliding into the ball rather than doing the more conventional nose-dive toward it. Folding his left leg under him as he approached the ball, his outstretched and trailing right leg providing guidance for the slide, Harry retained complete freedom for his throwing arm and avoided any jarring contact with the ground that could knock a ball loose or cause injury. The move could be employed for a better body block of grounders as well. Moreover, the slide always kept the play in front of him and permitted a quick recovery to a throwing position.

But the most lethal weapon in his defensive arsenal was his arm. As Harry's saving throw in the first game of the World Series had demonstrated, the power and accuracy of his arm were as impressive and steady under pressure as they were when he was winning throwing contests in field exhibitions. Those who watched him play on a regular basis particularly understood this. Asked to identify the best thrower among the Hooper-Speaker-Lewis outfield, their teammate and manager, Bill Carrigan, replied, "Hooper, for day-in and day-out pegging."[15] Carrigan explained that Harry "had the toughest throwing job" of the three because of the depth of right field at Fenway and the very nature of right-field play, which required him to make more long throws over the course of the season, especially to third base, than the other outfielders. "Harry," added Carrigan, "threw to all spots with amazing accuracy." Speaker agreed. "He had the best arm of the three of us," said Spoke. "He actually threw strikes from the outfield."[16] Tom Connolly, who umpired in the American League throughout Harry's career, judged his arm to be "the finest" of all the great fielders he had watched perform.[17] And Ruth, who would learn a few things about outfield play from Harry during their years together on the Red Sox, tabbed him "the greatest defensive rightfielder" who had ever played the game.[18]

More than praise, though, Hooper's play earned him the respect of teammate and opponent alike. But more than his performance on the field, how he conducted himself as a Major League ballplayer both deepened and widened that respect, allowing him to cross the cliquish lines on his own club and challenge the hackneyed perceptions that often disregarded the new breed of professional athlete he represented. Harry's letters to Esther provide a warm and candid commentary on a professional and his world that portrayed both in distinctive yet reassuringly ordinary terms. If his letters suggested dullness in his habits, they also revealed the tedium of his schedule.

If they lacked exuberance in relating the practice of his profession, they added emphasis to the recognition that what often provided a firmly etched memory of heroic performance for the casual fan was merely a matter of routine for the men who took the field every day. If his correspondence chronicled a nomadic existence, its regularity and tone conveyed an appreciation of stable values, a mark of the "home boy" quality in him which Lewis observed.[19] If it signaled a devotion to duty, it did so within a moral framework that stressed industry and integrity. In short, both on and off the field, revealed in his play and recorded in his words, Hooper presented an image of the professional ballplayer that fostered the rising respectability of the game itself.

There were, of course, many elements that shaped and defined respectability. Some, like efforts to rid the game of ruffianism, to improve the players' salaries, or to provide more attractive playing and viewing facilities, were matters that had been addressed with noteworthy success before Hooper signed his first contract with the Red Sox. Others, such as the increased representation of former collegians on the Major League rosters or the emergence of a new professional work ethic among the players, one which emphasized year-round attention to their physical conditioning, concern about their off-field image, and an analytical approach to their play, were reflected more directly in Hooper's own experience. Whether in the vanguard of change or swept along in its currents, Hooper was both witness and agent to the respectability of his sport and profession.

Notwithstanding his love of baseball, it is unlikely that Harry would have considered it as a career path unless the professional scene had not already taken significant steps to escape a relatively recent past in which "the moral and intellectual atmosphere was murky, to say the least."[20] Led by Albert Spalding and Henry Chadwick, baseball owners, publicists, and entrepreneurs in other aspects of the business of sport extolled the alleged virtues of the "American game" and tried to market its appeal around a set of traditional middle-class ideas and values.[21] This was no small challenge for a world which Chadwick himself described as contaminated by the twin evils of "the saloon and the brothel."[22] Yet, despite their efforts, the paradox affecting professional ballplayers—practitioners of a game that was hailed for its embodiment of cherished national virtues and values yet possessors of very little social standing themselves—persisted into the twentieth century. Sam Crawford, whose nineteen-year career in the Majors started in 1899, typically recalled how "baseball players weren't too much accepted . . .

were considered pretty crude . . . couldn't get into the best hotels and all that."[23] The list of fathers who denounced the intentions of their daughters to marry a baseball player included Robert Todd Lincoln.[24]

The arrival of the American League on a par with the National in 1901 had two immediate effects on the status of the professional game. On one hand, the new circuit of eight teams doubled the number of spots on Major League rosters. On the other, the competition for player talent posed by the AL forced the older league to abolish its official salary cap of $2,400, which had been in place since 1894, as a means to hold down club payrolls and reinforce the owners' domination of the game. Harry's rookie salary of $2,850 in 1909, though double what most first-year players could expect, placed him close to the mean of what his fellow Major Leaguers were earning. His salary was less than half the amount established stars received, but it was considerably more than that which the average American worker earned in a year. The estimated annual earnings of a skilled urban mechanic, for example, were approximately $900, the same salary Harry got with the Western Pacific Railroad, while unskilled workers rarely earned more than $12 to $14 a week.[25]

Beyond the intrinsic appeal of the game as a sporting activity, a test of skill, and a matter, quite basically, of fun, the relatively high pay of a Major League ballplayer and the opportunity to earn it particularly enlarged the pool of young men interested in pursuing a professional career. Like Hooper, many in these ranks were former collegiate players who increasingly looked upon baseball as a legitimate means to earn a livelihood. Harry was surrounded by such men on his Boston teams. At a time when only 7 percent of the traditional college-age population was enrolled in the nation's institutions of higher education, the Red Sox teams of the 1910s could count ten to twelve former collegians on their rosters every year.[26] Moreover, nearly half of them had graduated from the colleges where they had played baseball.

By mid-decade the rosters of the American and National League teams included 163 players who had previously played college ball. Their numbers had risen steadily from the 1870s when Cap Anson (Notre Dame and Iowa), Steve Bellan (Fordham), Denny Mack (Villanova), and Spalding (Rockford, Illinois, Commercial College) had appeared in the lineups of teams in the National Association. By 1880 the National League counted twenty players with some collegiate experience among the 489 who had joined its ranks over the previous decade. These twenty represented only 4.1 percent of the total number of men who had played for the teams of the National Association and the National League throughout the 1870s. But even then the percentage of professional ballplayers with college experience surpassed the proportion of eighteen- to twenty-one-year-old Americans in college. With the exception of the decade of the 1880s, a clear and consistent pattern of overrepresentation of college men among Major League ballplayers had been established before Harry took his first swings for Boston.[27]

Hooper represented exactly what the professional clubs hoped they would get in mining the collegiate leagues. He offered a proven talent developed in one of the most successful collegiate baseball programs in the country. Although he did not possess the star quality and impact potential of Bucknell's Mathewson, the most celebrated model of the new baseball professional at the turn of the century, Harry exhibited a similar intensity and intelligence. Both qualities promised to elevate the image of the game.

Just as respectability had several meanings, in fact different meanings for different players—attractive wages, social standing, community influence, off-season and postcareer business opportunities, public acclaim—it appealed to club owners and managers on many levels as well. Foremost among these was the gate attraction of a competitive team which contended for pennants on the field and whose members conducted themselves with propriety off of it. Yet, as the degenerate reputation of ballplayers was probably overemphasized in the attention which a few well-publicized escapades received, so, too, the moderating effect of the former collegians on the social behavior of Major Leaguers was undoubtedly exaggerated. President Charles Eliot of Harvard, for example, could question the appropriateness of college men playing games against professional teams, but it was not necessarily clear whose virtue he was trying to protect. One newspaperman suggested that a ban on such contests would save the professionals from sinking to the "lowest level of depravity" at the hands of the "rat-killing, cock-fighting" collegians.[28] Nevertheless, players with a collegiate background, no matter how brief or accomplished, provided a cachet which club authorities appreciated.

Connie Mack was the most avid recruiter of college players in the early twentieth century, and his success with such men as Chief Bender (Carlisle), Eddie Plank (Gettysburg), Jack Coombs (Colby), Harry Davis (Girard), Al Orth (DePauw), Eddie Collins (Columbia), Jack Barry (Holy Cross), and Andy Coakley (Holy Cross) influenced others to look to the playing fields of academe for baseball talent.[29]

From 1902 to 1914, Mack's Athletics won six pennants while the number of new players on Major League rosters with previous college playing experience increased from twenty-one to fifty-seven.[30] To help locate and assess talent in the collegiate ranks and to gain an edge in the recruitment battles, Major League clubs expanded their scouting systems and established ties with the coaches of the leading college nines. Mack's arrangement with Brother Agnon at Saint Mary's, for example, brought Hal Krause to Philadelphia in 1908 and Tiny Leonard in 1911.

Both 1913 and 1914 were years when Mack's collegiate connections paid off with big dividends. Leading the league for all but the first two weeks of the immediate season after Boston's championship, Philadelphia shook off one contender after another on a steady drive to the club's third World Series appearance in four years. Leading the Majors in runs scored, runs batted in, home runs, and team batting average, the Athletics offered power and consistency at the plate to match their balance and talent on the mound. They coasted to a 6½ game margin of victory over Washington, which finished second again on the wonderful arm of Walter Johnson, whose thirty-six victories and 1.14 ERA earned him the Chalmers Award for the AL.

Further back in the pack, just managing to avoid a second-division finish, were the Red Sox, 15½ games behind the A's. Despite Hooper's fine year, an equally strong performance from Lewis (.298 batting average, ninety RBIs), and another routinely brilliant season for Speaker (.365 batting average, .535 slugging average, ninety-four runs scored, forty-six stolen bases), which placed him fourth in the Chalmers balloting, Boston trailed the league leaders from the opening week of the season and never threatened to finish above .500 until September. Boston's woes were familiar ones—injuries and dissension. Jake Stahl fell victim to both. Replaying an all-too-familiar scene, the manager-first baseman suffered a serious leg injury during spring training that removed his .301 bat and sixty RBIs of the previous season from the lineup for all but two plate appearances in 1913. As injuries and illness claimed Yerkes, Wagner, and Henriksen as well for long stretches in the early going, Stahl's relationship with McAleer deteriorated along with his club's downward slide in the standings.

The crushing blow to whatever hopes the Red Sox entertained of repeating their championship performance also came in the preseason when Joe Wood broke the thumb on his pitching hand as he tried to brace himself after slipping on wet grass while fielding a bunt in a game against Detroit. Languishing in fifth place two-thirds of the way into the season, the club was desperate to get Wood back on the mound again. Before his thumb was completely healed, Smoky Joe returned to the rotation. Remarkably, despite severe shoulder pain which resulted from the adjustments in his pitching motion to compensate for the problems with his hand, Wood recorded eleven victories in sixteen decisions with a team-leading 2.29 ERA. Yet, whereas Joe had pitched 344 innings for the Red Sox in 1912, he appeared on the hill for only 145 this season. Although Collins recovered from his own knee injury of the previous year to post a 19–8 record, the rest of the staff failed to pick up the slack. Bedient, Hall, and O'Brien, 54–30 in 1912, were 23–27 in 1913. The troubled state of the Red Sox pitching was no more clearly in evidence than when Hooper and Lewis were called upon to throw in a game against Washington on October 3. After Boston starter Earl Moseley had been hammered for nine runs on nine hits in five frames, Harry came in to relieve him in the sixth. In his only Major League pitching appearance, Hooper gave up two hits and a walk but allowed no runs in his two innings. Duffy was less effective, surrendering two runs on three hits in the single inning he pitched.

Since the pennant race had long since been decided when Harry and Duffy threw their few frames, the anomaly of the occasion drew no unusual commentary in the press. Another oddity earlier in the Boston season, however, had warranted considerable attention. As the club prepared to depart Boston on the same western swing that would cost Lewis his hair, the Red Sox found something missing in their entourage as well: their manager, Jake Stahl. Frustrated with the team's losing record and upset at a nagging rumor around town that Stahl would soon replace him as the Red Sox president, McAleer informed Jake that it was time to make a change in the field management of the club. The choice to succeed Stahl—twenty-nine-year-old Bill Carrigan—was less a surprise than the unprecedented move of replacing the pilot of a World Series champion in midseason of the very next year.

Aside from the usual anxieties that managerial changes create, the real worry with this one was how the Speaker-Wood-Gardner clique would respond to Carrigan's appointment. Although Speaker and Carrigan had no use for each other personally, Speaker's professionalism and Bill's tough-minded fairness ensured a respectful working relationship between the two. Wood's own desire to discount any tension between the pro-Stahl group and Carrigan may have contributed to the arm problems that would ever after plague his pitching career. His premature return to the mound was as much a gesture of support for the new manager as it was a signal that the team was not going to forfeit the entire season while it worked to get its house in order.

The brave work of Wood and the return to the lineup of Wagner and Yerkes helped Carrigan post a winning record the rest of the way (40–30) as the Red Sox occasionally showed flashes of their championship form in the final weeks of the campaign. The team's best run, however, fell far short of what it required to catch the A's. Hooper provided hints of the soured season in his letters to Esther. "We struggled through a doubleheader today," he reported from Detroit in mid-July, a commentary on how the team was playing on the field as well as what it was experiencing in the clubhouse.[31]

Like the moves both on and off the field after Boston's disappointing finish two years ago, the winter months following the 1913 season brought a flurry of activity designed to breathe new life back into the Red Sox. Foremost among these was the arrival of a new part owner in town. Encouraged by Ban Johnson, who was not pleased with Stahl's removal, the Taylors arranged for the sale of the shares in the club held by McAleer and McRoy. Although the Taylors wished to purchase those interests themselves, Johnson rejected their offer of $220,000 for a slightly smaller one from Joseph J. Lannin.[32] The Canadian-born Lannin, who had risen from a bellhop in Boston to a real estate mogul in New York and Massachusetts, was an avid baseball fan who had failed in an earlier attempt to buy a piece of the Philadelphia Phillies. Johnson appreciated Lannin's business success and honest reputation, but, more important, saw an opportunity in his ready funds to depose McAleer without increasing the Taylors' control.

Lannin immediately put his properties and money to good use for the club. A few members of the team, Carrigan among them, benefited from the new owner's generosity when he made available to them apartments in some of his residential complexes at very low rents. Lannin's major influence on the club, however, stemmed from his financial assistance to several minor league clubs, most notably, the Baltimore Orioles and Providence Grays of the International League. In the season about to start, both clubs would be hard pressed to cover their expenses because of revenues lost to the new Federal League. Jack Dunn, owner of the Orioles, resorted to selling off his players in order to remain solvent, if not competitive, in their loss. He felt particularly obligated to Lannin for his previous help. The principal mark of his gratitude would be a three-player deal with an eight-thousand-dollar price tag. The players included catcher Ben Egan and two pitchers, Ernie Shore, a six-foot-four, 220-pound right-hander from North Carolina, and a local boy almost as big, a left-hander who impressed with his arm and his bat, George Herman Ruth.

Although the challenge of the Federal League provided an opportunity to acquire player talent at bargain prices from such financially strapped clubs as the Orioles, it also required Lannin to dig more deeply than he had imagined into his own pockets to keep his team intact. If the Federal League did not have a certain future, it seemed at least to have a plentiful bankroll with which to dangle attractive salary offers before the players of the AL and NL. For the most part, the owners of the older leagues prevented any significant defections from their rosters, although the price of holding certain players was high.[33] The Red Sox renegotiated Speaker's contract, for example, increasing his $9,000 salary of 1913 to a new two-year package worth $36,000. Otherwise, Spoke might have jumped to the Federal League, whose Buffalo entry supposedly offered him $50,000 to manage and play there. The entire Boston payroll for 1914 was slightly over $100,000, a 25 percent increase over the previous year, when the other premium salaries on the club belonged to Hooper ($5,000), Wood ($7,500), Wagner ($6,500), Gardner ($6,000), Lewis ($5,000), and Carrigan ($4,500). Stahl drew $10,000.

As the deal with the Orioles demonstrated, Lannin spent his money not only to ward off the overtures of the Federal League but also to strengthen Boston's roster. He reached out to Saint Paul of the American Association to obtain Everett Scott, a smooth-fielding country boy from Indiana who immediately proved Wagner's equal with a glove at short. Looking to fill the utility slot vacated by Engle, Lannin purchased Del Gainer from Detroit. He spent most of the 1914 season on the disabled list but would prove to be a valuable reserve with Boston for years. Perhaps the most pleasant surprise of Lannin's shopping spree was first baseman Dick Hoblitzell. Obtained, like Gainer, for the waiver price, Hoblitzell had been with Cincinnati since 1908, where he had batted consistently around .290 for mainly a second-division team. Although he had played poorly in the first half of the 1914 season, hitting only .210, Hoblitzell had impressed Carrigan with his fielding and bat in previous years. The Red Sox hoped to get a good year or two out of Hoblitzell, but, more immediately, they were desperate for someone to play first with Stahl and Engle no longer around and Gainer injured. The manager also liked the veteran's savvy and thought he would be a good influence on some of the younger players whom the club was acquiring simultaneously. One of them, of course, was Ruth, and Hoblitzell drew the assignment of rooming with the Babe during part of the time he was with the Red Sox in 1914. He survived that experience and gave Boston nearly four full years handling chores around the initial sack.

As all these roster changes suggested, it took awhile for the Red Sox to jell as a unit in 1914. The sorting process was not helped when appendicitis sidelined Wood for three months, contributing to his woes in staging a comeback from the problems of the previous year. Moreover, Wagner's rheumatism flared up so severely that he was forced to sit out the entire season. From Boston's perspective, the new season had a sadly similar look to the disappointing start in 1913. The standings confirmed the apprehension. On May 1 the Red Sox sat in seventh place, having won only four of their first eleven games. Two months later they had climbed to fifth but were only three games over .500 and trailed the league-leading Athletics by five games.

Boston had stayed as close as it was to this point on the usual stellar play of Speaker; steady performances from Hooper, Lewis, and Gardner; and the extraordinary work of second-year pitcher Hubert ("Dutch") Leonard. Spoke led the club again in most offensive categories, batting .338 and slugging .503 on 193 hits totaling 287 bases. The latter two figures topped both the American and National leagues. His outfield partners combined for a .268 average, highlighted by Harry's 85 runs scored and Duffy's 79 RBIs, both second to Speaker's 100 and 90, respectively. Defensively, the trio continued to uphold their reputation as the best outfield in the Majors. They gunned down 75 runners among them over the season, some of them victims of the 21 double plays in which they participated. By comparison, the Saint Louis outfield of Gus Williams, Burt Shotten, and Tilly Walker, who played in the same number of combined games as the Bostoners (438), managed 69 assists and only 11 double plays.

No one deserved more credit than Leonard, though, in keeping the Red Sox within sight of the Athletics during the first half of the season. The burly five-foot-ten, 185-pound left-hander made the Boston roster in 1913 after spending a brief time with Worcester of the New England League and then compiling a 22–9 record for the Western League champion Denver club in 1912. Ironically, Dutch had actually signed his first contract with one of Connie Mack's agents, who had found him throwing strikes for that place in California where "they raise ball players in the oven"—Saint Mary's College.[34] He came out of Oakland with a reputation as the best pitcher that Agnon's program had ever produced.[35] But the pitching-rich A's did not foresee a future for Leonard with them and gave him his release to sign with Boston. Dutch's reunion with the other former Phoenix at Fenway was an immediate success. In his rookie season, he notched fourteen wins against sixteen defeats, recorded 144 strikeouts, and managed a fine 2.39 ERA. In 1914 he improved on all of these numbers: nineteen victories against only five losses, 174 strikeouts, and the most penurious ERA in the Majors' history for a pitcher throwing at least 150 innings, 1.01. For good measure, Dutch also earned a league-leading four saves.

The arrival of the new players after July 4 and the return to the mound of Rube Foster, who had recovered from a knee injury, rallied the Red Sox to fifty-four victories in the second half of the season. Boston quickly rose from fifth place to second in the standings, passing Chicago, Washington, and Detroit on a 20–9 mark in July. After a slight pause in momentum in early August, the club then won thirty-two of forty-five games over the final weeks of the campaign. The highlight of the surge was a dramatic four-game sweep of the Athletics in late August. Although those victories ensured Boston's winning the season series against Philadelphia, twelve games to nine, it barely cut into the huge lead which the A's had built up over the summer months. Before the set with the Red Sox, the Mackmen had won thirty-nine of their previous forty-five games, including eleven in a row to kick off the streak. While Boston was playing its best ball of the year, the A's were actually increasing their lead over them. The season ended with Philadelphia a comfortable 8½ games ahead of Boston, but the race had not been decided until September 27, the latest a pennant had been clinched since the Tigers edged the A's by 3½ games in 1909.

The emergence of a first-rate pitching rotation around Wood, Foster, Leonard, and Shore, the apparent stabilization of the infield, the continued excellence of the outfield, and the raw potential of Ruth, who spent the latter part of the season helping the Providence Grays to the International League pennant with nine pitching victories and a .300 batting average, gave the club and its fans good reason for optimism in 1915 as Fenway closed for the winter. Several uncertainties accompanied the Red Sox and the other teams of the AL and NL into the off-season, however, not the least of which was the possible effects on professional baseball of the European war which had broken out in the late summer and the nature of the Federal League challenge to the older circuits. The baseball world, like most Americans, was mainly grateful that the United States had not been pulled into the conflagration across the sea and hoped that peace would be restored before too long. The prospect of hyphenated Americans divided against themselves by a war that engulfed their former homelands was a threat to fan loyalty and team harmony. Regardless of the reasons for the war, the club owners could foresee the adverse consequences for their operations if it did not end soon.

No such truce seemed imminent, however, between the established Major Leagues and the Federals. Despite huge financial losses and a sizable long-range debt in the construction of new stadiums, the Federal League prepared for a second season. Its backers had been cheered with the infusion of new capital, most notably from oil millionaires Harry Sinclair and P. J. White, and confidently expected a favorable decision in an antitrust suit they had filed against organized baseball. The league's agents aggressively renewed their efforts to sign established AL and NL stars.

Neither interested in talking to the Federal League nor wanting to stay in Boston for any time after the season, Harry boarded a train for the West Coast on October 9. He had considered driving across the country in his new Stutz, a trip he would make occasionally in subsequent years. But this fall he was particularly anxious to return to Capitola as soon as possible, for awaiting him was Esther, their newborn baby girl, Marie, and a house which they were having built for them high along the cliffs overlooking the Pacific.

7

The Phoenix
at Fenway

Hoop, Hoop, Hooper up for Red Sox,
Hoop, Hoop, Hooper when its dark;
They have shown us they are game,
They will give old Boston fame,
They will bring the flag right home to Fenway Park.

—Chorus of "Hoop, Hoop, Hooper Up for Red Sox,"
Daniel J. Hanifen, lyrics; Bernard H. Smith, music, 1915

Just as the promise of the Red Sox in 1909 had been deferred for a couple of years, the triumph of 1912 had been tempered with two successive years of disappointment. If the pattern persisted, the new season, Harry's sixth with the club, anticipated another flag for Fenway. What 1915 signaled, in fact, was the emergence of a new dynasty in the American League, one whose reign in the middle years of the decade was as convincing and confident as the fall from grace of the former champion was swift and shocking.

Like trains passing in the night, Boston and Philadelphia scarcely noticed each other in their rush to different but once familiar destinations. After a sixth-place finish in 1908, the Athletics had captured four pennants and three World Series over the next six years. They had failed to challenge for the AL title in only one of those years, 1912, when they finished third, fifteen games behind the Red Sox. It was a remarkable run, unmatched even by McGraw's great Giant teams, which had managed three pennants and three second-place finishes between 1908 and 1914 but had come up short in each of their October appearances. In 1915, however, their ranks decimated by retirements, trades, and defections to the Federal League, the A's began a long residency in the cellar of their league from which they would not emerge for seven seasons. Their successor at the top was Boston, whose own years of plenty yielded an even richer fall harvest than that of Philadelphia.

For the period 1915–18, the Red Sox played the best and most consistent baseball in the Majors. Winning ninety or more games in each of the first three years of this stretch, they were on a course to do the same in 1918, but the American involvement in World War I caused that season to be shortened, capping their victories at seventy-five on September 1. Their success on the field translated into three league titles and a second-place finish to Chicago, despite ninety wins, in 1917, the only year their play did not earn them a trip to the World Series. In contrast, no other club in the NL as well won more than one pennant during these years.

Engaged in close races in each of the championship seasons, their largest margin of victory being 2½ games over Detroit in 1915 and Cleveland in 1918, Boston collected its wins and flags on outstanding pitching and solid defense. Remarkably, none of these Red Sox teams had more than one .300 hitter in their regular lineup and the player with the highest average, Tris Speaker with .322 in 1915, left the club after that season. Gardner (.308), Lewis (.302), and Ruth (.300) succeeded as the team's hitting leaders in the three years after Spoke's departure. Boston's team batting averages in 1916 and 1918, for example, .248 and .249, respectively, were the lowest of any pennant winner throughout the decade, except for the Phillies' .247 in 1915.

If the Red Sox did not strike terror into their opponents with their bats, they confounded them with awesome pitching and tenacious defense. "With the best pitching staff and the best defensive outfield" in baseball, Harry explained of those teams, "we played for one run—tried to get on the scoreboard first and then increase our lead."[1] Often one run was all Boston needed to gain victory. Eighty-four times during this four-year period the Red Sox pitchers tossed shutouts. The Phillies staff recorded the second-most whitewashings (78), but Pete Alexander with thirty-six had nearly half of them himself. Matters were more democratic on the Boston hill. Eight pitchers, led by Ruth (17), Leonard (15), and Carl Mays (12), contributed three or more shutouts to the team's total. Similarly, in terms of wins and ERAs, the strength and depth of the Boston pitching was evident in the distribution of outstanding performances. Foster and Shore led the club in wins with nineteen apiece in 1915, but three others—Ruth (18), Leonard (15), and Wood (15)—won at least fifteen games each. Smoky Joe, in his final season with Boston, turned in the lowest ERA on the team and in the league, 1.49. In 1916 and 1917, Ruth led the Red Sox staff with wins, notching twenty-three and twenty-four, respectively. His 1.75 ERA in 1916 was the best in the AL. Trailing the Babe in victories for these two years were Mays (40), Leonard (34), and Shore (29). Mays's twenty-two victories in 1917 were achieved with a team-best 1.74 ERA. In the truncated 1918 season, Mays still managed twenty-one wins, although Bush took team ERA honors with 2.11.

As simple as the formula for victory that Hooper described and as effective its application that the team's record suggested, Boston's seasons in the sun were anything but routine. The Federal League had as dramatic an effect on the pennant races and financial affairs of the AL and NL in 1915 as World War I did in 1918. Both diluted team rosters as players switched uniforms for the Feds' flannels in one case and the military's general issue in the other. Both threatened the clubs' profits, the former in a costly bidding war for players' services, the latter in the unseen revenues of reduced attendance and an abbreviated season. Both effected more wariness between club owners and players as the salaries won in the open competition for talent that the third league fostered were lost when the Federal franchises collapsed and wartime conditions intruded. Boston's success on the field during these years reflected the ability of the club to weather these storms better than its rivals. Yet the strategic keys to victory—pitching and defense—were only as valid as the quality of the players who took up those tasks. One man, Babe Ruth, emerged as the dominant player on the club after Speaker's departure, but no group of players meant more to Boston's execution of its winning formula than the former Phoenix of Saint Mary's College—Hooper, Lewis, and Leonard.

Although he certainly did not know it at the time, with six years behind him as the 1915 season began, Hooper was halfway through his career with the Red Sox. At this point he had established the bases for a personal and professional reputation in and out of the park that was beginning to be appreciated for its complementary qualities. Yet, like all of his teammates, Harry stood in the shadow of Speaker when attention focused on Boston. Spoke's brilliance may have denied Hooper his share of publicity, but it certainly did not obscure the record he was compiling on the field and the intense dedication to his work that largely accounted for it.

By 1915, Harry had emerged as both the premier leadoff-hitting outfielder and defensive right fielder of his day. Among the former group, including Davy Jones of the Tigers, Amos Strunk of the A's, Shano Collins of the White Sox, the Cubs' Solly Hofman, and Brooklyn's Hy Myers, Hooper consistently batted for a higher average, reached base more often, hit with greater power, stole more bases, and scored more runs. The right fielders with whom Hooper was matched included Sam Crawford of the Tigers, Eddie and Danny Murphy of the Athletics, Wildfire Schulte of the Cubs, the Giants' Red

Murray, Philadelphia's Gavvy Cravath, and Cleveland's Elmer Flick. Only Crawford and Flick (whose thirteen-year career in the Majors was ending as Harry's was beginning), however, provided truly comparable records. Wahoo Sam, in particular, whose rigorous physical conditioning, like Hooper's, contributed to his fielding range and effectiveness, had set the standard for right-field play in the American League since he joined the Tigers in 1903. Three years from retirement as the 1915 season began, Crawford already held most of the league's all-time right-field fielding records, including games played (1,072), putouts (1,561), and assists (143).[2] Harry was on a course to surpass all of these marks.

Hooper's value to his team, however, was measured in ways that went beyond the numbers. It particularly focused on the manifestation in his play of certain aspects of his character and manner that made him an ideal leadoff man. Described by one writer as "the most persevering and hard-working man on the Red Sox squad," Harry drew praise for his "every effort to help the team."[3] "His sole ambition seems to be always to do his best," observed another, who especially noted the ways in which Harry's interests "centered on what seems most needful to score his teammates."[4] Admitting that "it would be hard to say just what he lacks of the stellar quality," the writer explained that "it is not uncommon for a valuable player on a club to pass comparatively unnoticed beside the pretenses of some of his more favored associates." Yet stars of Hooper's kind—"unostentatious, but marvelously efficient"[5]—"are far more valuable than any records can show."[6] As the new season approached, Hooper's fans agreed that "a little limelight now is no more than his due."[7]

Harry's abilities and motivational value were no secret to his fellow ballplayers. Although his batting average had been erratic, increasing, for example, from .267 in 1910 to .311 in 1911 and then falling to .242 in 1912, he had either led the club or been one of the team leaders every season after his rookie year in games played, at bats, triples, walks, stolen bases, and runs scored. Moreover, as his play in the 1912 World Series had demonstrated, he often saved his best for when it counted the most. The respect which he earned from McGraw in the Series, echoed in the assessments of his teammates, was no more simply or eloquently expressed than by Walter Johnson, against whom he dueled his entire career. "Hooper," said the Big Train, "was the toughest of them all in a pinch."[8]

Herb Pennock felt the heat of Hooper's fire in the first game of the 1915 season. With two down in the top of the ninth, Pennock needed only to retire Hooper in order to cap a no-hitter. Harry refused to concede the out, beating out a scratch single to foil the masterpiece. A few years later, Hooper faced Johnson himself in a similar encounter. In the previous season, the great Washington pitcher had surpassed Mathewson to become the Majors' career leader in shutouts. But on July 1, 1920, Johnson had a chance to accomplish something which he had not previously managed to do—throw a no-hitter. Like Pennock before him, he had only to get by Hooper to claim it. With neither Boston nor Washington a pennant contender this season, the only drama of the day focused on Johnson's bid. As Hooper took his stance in the batter's box, the Nats' catcher, Val Picinich, suggested that Harry take it easy against Johnson. Hooper muttered, "No way," and lined a shot into right field—but into the waiting glove of Braggo Roth. On the toughest out he faced, Johnson had his no-hitter, the only one of his career.

After five years with the Red Sox, Lewis was at the midpoint of his own Major League career. He had settled into the cleanup spot in the batting order, following Speaker. His smooth stroke providing reliable contact and occasional power at the plate, Duffy benefited from the ability of the players in the lineup ahead of him to get on base and led the club with 432 RBIs from 1910 to 1914. Speaker had the next-highest total on the club during this period with 414. The two reversed positions in batting average, Tris hitting .351 and Duffy .290, over these seasons.

Defensively, of course, Lewis upheld the claim of the Boston outfield as the best in the business. Although he did not play as shallow as Speaker or Hooper, he could go back on a ball as well as either of them. Harry, in fact, judged Lewis to be "the best at making the back hand running catch at balls hit over his head."[9] Duffy also had a powerful throwing style, more like Harry's than Spoke's, in that the ball traveled on a low, straight trajectory to its target. Duffy's long-distance throws to home, for example, usually arrived on one hop, while Speaker's came on a sweeping arc from his sidearm release. Their personal differences notwithstanding, Lewis and Speaker communicated effectively in the field and respected each other's work at the plate. Although Duffy's play in the 1912 Series had been disappointing—he hit a poor .156 with just two RBIs and committed a key error late in game 2 that may have prevented a Boston victory in regular innings—he enjoyed a solid reputation as a clutch hitter. If they teased Duffy for his lack of hair and dapperness of dress, Speaker and his teammates had little reason to criticize his batting.

The youngest of the former Phoenix, twenty-three-year-old Dutch Leonard, had become a mainstay of the Boston pitching staff after only two seasons in the Majors. The southpaw had overcome a particularly erratic rookie year before settling into a championship groove. In 1913, Dutch had issued the third-highest number of walks in his league (94), but he also recorded 144 strikeouts, seventh most in the AL and a total he would exceed just once in his eleven-year career. His glistening 1.01 ERA in 1914 would also help him forget a particularly embarrassing June afternoon from the previous season when, with the score tied 5–5 in the fifteenth inning against Cleveland, three Naps stole home in succession on him. As the Red Sox assembled in Hot Springs in the first week of March 1915, Leonard anticipated sharing the left-handed responsibilities on the staff with veterans Ray Collins and Vean Gregg, the latter coming over from Cleveland in late 1914 after posting three consecutive seasons of twenty wins or more from 1911 to 1913. Waiting to challenge Dutch and the others for a permanent spot in the starting rotation was the Babe.

Like his brief stint with the big club in 1914, when he split two decisions in four games, Ruth had a hard time initially convincing Carrigan that he deserved a place among the regulars. The kid's athletic ability was as impressive as his muscular six-foot two-inch, 195-pound frame, but, as was the case in his personal habits, he sorely lacked self-discipline on the mound. His imposing presence, an effective sinking fastball, and a mean curve had accounted for the Babe's success in the minors.[10] But the Majors required more, and until Ruth refined his skills, balancing finesse and power, mastering the pace and purpose of his pitches, he would likely play a secondary role on the Boston staff. As camp broke for the start of the season, Carrigan intended to use Ruth sparingly until he developed more satisfactorily. Besides, what the manager felt the club most needed in the pitching department was right-handed depth and he was particularly impressed with a gaunt, submarine ball–throwing rookie who had won twenty-five games for Providence in 1914, Carl Mays. It did not help Ruth's case that Mays was as sober and articulate as Babe was brash and crude.[11] Moreover, Carrigan liked Mays's combative attitude and the meanness which characterized his work on the mound. He was less sure how tough the talented man-child from Baltimore really was.

Another patented slow start for the Red Sox, punctuated with key injuries and poor performances by the vaunted staff, soon gave Ruth a chance to claim a spot in the rotation. The usual wet Arkansas spring had curtailed even further the already shortened preseason work which Carrigan had scheduled. The championship season began with neither Leonard nor Wood ready to take their regular turns on the mound and many of the hitters struggling to find their rhythm. Although Heinie Wagner, for example, was back with the club, his illness had certainly taken its toll and now, at age thirty-four, the senior man on the club, he had clearly lost range afield and effectiveness at the plate. Gardner, Hoblitzell, and Gainer, too, had all been hampered in getting into shape with minor injuries and spring colds. The biggest blow in the early going, though, befell Mays. Impressive in two relief appearances in the season's first week, one following a terrible outing by Ruth, Mays earned a start against Walter Johnson and the Nats a few days later. Blanking Washington through four innings, Mays had contributed to the offense as well, coming around to score one of Boston's two runs after reaching base on a single. But it was a costly tally. Sliding home, Mays twisted his ankle badly and left the game an inning later. He would be sidelined for nearly three weeks. Worse for Carl, the injury relegated him to the role of reliever and spot starter once he returned to duty.

The principal beneficiary of these developments was Ruth. Thrust into the starting rotation, Babe pitched erratically but well enough at times for Carrigan to stick with him. A month into the season, Ruth had recorded only one victory in five decisions, but the club was not doing much better. Returning home after a losing swing through the western reaches of the league, one which had begun so promisingly with a three-game sweep of Detroit, the Red Sox sat in fourth place in the standings, a loss under the .500 mark. Boston's troubles took a new twist when Lannin suspended Leonard on May 27 for failing "to get in condition and stay in condition."[12] The suspension prompted an angry outcry from Dutch, who publicly berated the Red Sox owner in the press for his apparent interference with the way the club was being managed on the field. This, in turn, brought a rebuttal from Lannin, who dismissed Leonard's story as "absurd and false" and branded the pitcher as "a spoiled, sore-headed kid." A struggling club scarcely needed additional distractions from the work at hand, but the Leonard-Lannin exchange seemed to have a salutary effect on the team. It cleared the air on several issues, namely, the owner's expectations of his well-paid club and the players' frustrations with their own performances that had prevented the team from living up to its preseason billing as the pennant favorite. "Perhaps," commented Mitchell of *The Sporting News*, the Leonard episode will "put a little ginger in the tea." When the Red Sox returned to Fenway for a long home stand in June, he predicted that "what they accomplish here will tell the tale."

It was a tale worth telling. Beginning with a sweep of New York that moved them into third place, the Red Sox started to play like they had been expected to perform. Slowly, steadily, the injuries healed, the arms strengthened, the bats quickened, and the wins accumulated. The purchase of Jack Barry from the Athletics for eight thousand dollars on July 2 was a key to the Sox success. The A's shortstop had become available when Connie Mack abandoned his plan to try to build a pennant contender around several promising, but untested, younger players and a small nucleus of veterans who had resisted the overtures of the Federal League or the attractions of their own retirement. Lured to the Feds, for example, were Plank and Bender, while Frank Baker, whose long-standing disaffection with Mack had reached a breaking point, decided to sit out the entire season and devote more time to his farm in Maryland.[13] Trying to keep his club afloat financially in the face of the bull market for player talent that the third league had generated and a decline in attendance at A's games that poor play and war anxieties were causing, Mack also unloaded the high-salaried veterans Collins and Murphy. The team he had left, however, was a pale version of the previous occupants of Shibe Park. Halfway through the 1915 season, his club mired in last place, Mack decided to rebuild the Athletics completely. Barry, like the others, no longer fit in Mack's plans, but he satisfied Boston's need for someone who could spell Wagner. With Scott coming into his own at shortstop, Barry converted to second base where he played the latter half of the season, batting .262 for his new club.

With Barry providing the last piece in their team puzzle, Boston captured the league lead on July 18 and never relinquished it. After their slow 14–15 start, the Red Sox collected eighty-seven wins against only thirty-five defeats the rest of the way. As impressive and sustained as this .713 stretch and its 101 victories were, the Red Sox did not secure the pennant until the last week of the season. Battling both Detroit and Chicago as each team regularly mounted charges at them, the Red Sox proved their mettle in head-to-head play with their principal challengers. Winning the season series against all the AL teams, Boston's victories over the Tigers, fourteen to eight, were particularly sweet because they told the difference in the final standings. Reminiscing with Ruth about the season many years later, Cobb complimented Boston's play and the frustration it generally caused their opposition. "You guys would get off to a lead," Cobb told the Babe, "and hold on like grim death. Time after time we'd think we had a rally going in the late innings only to have Scottie or Gardner come up with great stops. Or Spoke, Duffy, or Hooper pull one of their circus catches in the outfield."[14]

As Ty's comments suggested, Boston's victory, one which surprised "seven-eighths of the Base Ball population in America," according to one observer,[15] was a true team affair. Unlike 1912, when Wood carried the pitching staff and Speaker the offense, the new pennant was the sum of balance and production throughout the roster. Two performances did stand out, however, one for the heart it displayed, the other for the awe it inspired.

That Smoky Joe was never the same after his broken thumb in 1913 was no secret. That he would still be throwing through the pain three years later was a measure of the man. That he would still be so effective was a mark of his talent. Needing to rest his arm almost a week after each outing, Wood appeared in only twenty-five games in 1915. But completing ten of the sixteen games he started and recording three of the club's nineteen shutouts and two of its sixteen saves, Joe led the team and the league in winning percentage (15–5, .750) and earned run average (1.49). There were many pitchers in the league now who could throw as hard as Wood. Indeed, observed Grantland Rice, "the smokeball appellation has been canned."[16] But the columnist found two more enduring qualities "that carried him through—brains and courage." He was still, said Cobb, "one of the best pitchers I ever faced throughout my entire career."[17] His friend Harry Hooper regarded his work in 1915 as one of the "bravest" performances he had witnessed in baseball. Wood's fifteenth win, coming in the final week of Boston's regular season, was for Smoky Joe, at age twenty-five, the last pitching victory of his career.

The other special story on the 1915 Red Sox was Ruth, whose fabled years in the Major Leagues were just beginning. "Not so very different from a lot of other nineteen-year-old would-be ballplayers" when he first joined the club, Hooper recalled, the Babe was exceptional in two ways: "he could eat more than anyone else, and he could hit a ball farther."[18] The former amused his teammates, the latter amazed them. Getting his licks at the plate only on days when he pitched, Ruth behaved in a most unorthodox manner with a bat in his hand. Not only did he refuse to concede an automatic out from the ninth spot in the batting order, he had a swing to match his attitude. In only ninety-two at bats Ruth collected twenty-nine hits. Only Speaker had a higher average than the Babe's .319. Not even Tris, however, matched Ruth's rate for accumulating bases. His hits included ten doubles, one triple, and four home runs for a slugging percentage of .576. The Majors' leader in this category in 1915 among the regular roster players was Cravath of the Phillies with a .510 mark.

In an era when home runs were neither common nor accorded a particularly reputable place in the game, Ruth's shots drew attention because of their source and effect. He was, after all, a pitcher, and seventeen wins in his last twenty-one decisions of the 1915 campaign indicated that he was a very good one. The conventional wisdom of the game, though, dictated that pitchers should stick to their business on the mound and leave the hitting to the others. Ruth had already caused a stir on the club when he insisted on taking batting practice with the regulars. Actually out hitting them only complicated matters. Hitting the way he did confounded everyone. His initial circuit clouts, though, had less an effect on the outcome of the games in which they were hit than in the memory of those who witnessed them. His home runs created indelible impressions for their sheer majesty. Each one traveled distances rarely imagined, much less reached: the upper right-field stands in the Polo Grounds, the right-center-field bleachers in Fenway, completely out of the ballpark in Saint Louis. Searching for an explanation of such power, a New York sportswriter suggested, "All lefthanders are peculiar and Ruth is no exception, because he can also bat."[19]

Others, though, recognized that Ruth was indeed someone special, not just another representative of an alleged strange breed of pitcher who threw from the port side. The attention his first home run received, a solo blast off New York's Jack Warhop on May 6, 1915, signaled an early appreciation of his extraordinariness. Focusing on his nickname and position, Damon Runyon of the *New York American* observed that "fanning this Ruth is not as easy as the name and occupation might indicate."[20] Fred Lieb of the *New York Press* described Ruth as "the sensational kid who set the International League afire last season."[21] Referring to the high praise for Ruth's hitting ability which Boston sportswriter Paul Shannon had been sharing with his colleagues in the press box, Lieb noted how Babe had "illustrated Paul's remarks by lifting the pill far up in the upstairs section of the rightfield stand for a merry-go-round trip." Wilmot Giffin of another New York daily referred to Babe as "Ruthless Ruth" and lauded his versatility as a pitcher and hitter.[22] "In these days of efficiency," Giffin continued, "he is an ideal player," although his home run was a distinctly "unclubby" thing to do to a fellow pitcher. Runyon agreed that Ruth was "quite a demon pitcher and demon hitter—when he connects."[23] That he connected as frequently and eloquently as he did facilitated Babe's transformation,

Hooper explained, "from a human being into something close to a god."[24]

Not yet assigned a divine mantle, or role, Ruth had very little to do in the 1915 World Series. Coming to the plate only once, an unsuccessful pinch-hitting appearance for Shore in the ninth inning of the Series opener, Babe was not used on the mound at all against the predominantly right-handed hitters of the Philadelphia Phillies. Yet his absence from the lineup was not felt. The Red Sox had no shortage of heroes this October, none performing more impressively than the trio of former Phoenix.

Harry Hooper set the tone for the Series with a single off Grover Cleveland Alexander in his first at bat. His hit marked the sixth time in nine Series games that he had reached base safely to start Boston's first inning. By the end of the five-game Series, Harry had added six more hits, including another leadoff single, for a championship average of .350. Two of his blows were home runs, doubling his regular season output in this department. Both round-trippers came in the final game of the Series, marking only the second time in Series history that a player had hit two in one game.[25] His second homer of the game, like the first, a line drive on one bounce into the temporary field boxes in center field, came with one out in the ninth inning. It broke a 4–4 tie and won the game and the Series—for Boston when Foster retired the Phillies in order in the bottom half of the inning. Harry's ninth-inning four-bagger was the first time a Series game had been won with a homer. The run he tallied on it was his fourth of the Series; no other player on either team had more than two.

Although Harry's ground-rule home runs were perfectly valid and would be until 1931, when a rule change relegated such hits to doubles, Fred Lieb sought to discredit them. Perhaps surprised at Hooper's power at the plate or upset that Philly owner Bill Baker, like Taylor and McAleer at Fenway in 1912, had shortened the dimensions of his park by installing extra seats on the field to accommodate a few hundred more spectators, the writer derisively labeled the hits "Chinese homers."[26]

It was an odd charge. Although Baker Bowl was an intimate park, a throwback even in 1915 to an earlier time when the fans sat very close to the action on the field, its playing space compared favorably with that of most Major League diamonds. Measuring 341 and 272 feet down the left- and right-field foul lines, respectively, and 408 feet to the 35-foot-high stone-and-mortar wall of the clubhouse in center field, Baker Bowl was small in terms of the number of spectators it could hold, about 20,000, and in comparison with the vast reaches of Braves Field, which the Red Sox had borrowed for their home games this Series, and the 7,000 more ticket buyers than Fenway it could hold. That decision paid off in a big way when 42,300 spectators poured into the park for game 3, the first of the Series in Boston, and established a new single-game attendance record.

With twice the seating capacity of Baker, Boston's National League park also had the largest playing surface in the Majors. Its foul poles stood 402 feet from home plate, center field 550. Until 1928, when the fences were brought in considerably, only seven balls had ever been hit for home runs over them.[27] Only seven others went for ground-rule homers. Harry's shots would not have carried out of Braves Field, but his speed and the distance the balls rolled might have resulted in inside-the-park home runs, a fairly common occurrence there. In Baker Bowl, such four-baggers were rare, but the kind of drives Harry hit would very likely have bounced into the stands in several parks, including Fenway. Since the temporary seating section shortened the distance to the center-field wall by only fifteen feet, Harry's duplicate hits both traveled over 380 feet before hopping the short wall. They were hardly cheap shots.

What Harry did not do at the plate, Duffy Lewis did. Batting fifth in the order behind Hoblitzell, Lewis rapped out eight hits in eighteen at bats for a Series best .444 average among the regulars. His offensive numbers included the only other Red Sox home run, a long blast into the left-center-field bleachers just to the side of the clubhouse wall, five runs batted in, and game-winning hits against Alexander in the bottom of the ninth of the third game and George Chalmers in game 4. He was the only player on either team to hit safely in all five Series games. Together, Lewis and Hooper drove in eight and scored five of Boston's twelve Series runs. They excelled in the field as well. Throughout the Series they accepted eighteen chances flawlessly, including six putouts by Duffy alone in game 4, although a bad bounce on a throw from Harry to third base in game 5 eluded Gardner and cost him his only error in World Series play. The "all-around work of the modest Californian never has been equalled in a big Series," wrote Tim Murnane of the *Globe* about Lewis, but he could just as easily have directed this praise at Harry.[28]

Dutch Leonard's contribution to the Boston victory was a masterful three-hit shutout in game 3. Going the distance in his only Series appearance, the left-hander struck out six, walked none, and set down twenty Phils in a row from the third inning on to post the victory over the "great Aleck," Pete Alexander. Fittingly for this

Phoenix October, one of the hits off him was a single by the Philadelphia catcher, Ed Burns. Thrust into a starting role for the Series when an arm injury sidelined Reindeer Bill Killefer, the Phils' regular backstop, Burns brought to four the number of former Saint Mary's players to participate in the Series. Graduating from the college in 1911, Ed played minor league ball at Sacramento, Tacoma, and Montreal before joining the Phils for spring training in 1913. A highly regarded defensive player—in fact, he was linked with Wally Schang as "the best backstops ever to come out of the International League"[29]—Burns did not have the steady bat to move the veteran Killefer out of the lineup. In the Series, though, Eddie collected three hits, a number exceeded by only two of his teammates. Behind the plate for the entire Series, Burns handled the catching chores well. His only error was a costly one, however, when he fumbled a poorly thrown ball from second baseman Bert Niehoff in a collision with Hooper at the plate in the first inning of game 2.

While Hooper, Lewis, Leonard, and Burns upheld the honor of their alma mater through their play on the field, still another Saint Mary's alumnus had appeared on the roster of one of the Series participants during the regular season. This was Joe Oeschger, a sparsely used right-hander with the Phillies, who had spent most of the 1915 season with Providence in the International League, where he compiled a 21–10 record. Completing an engineering degree at Saint Mary's in 1913, Joe, like Hooper, had opted for a career in professional baseball when Philadelphia made an attractive offer. Although he would not see any action in the 1915 World Series, Oeschger had lasting fame waiting for him five years later with the Boston Braves when he went the distance in the longest game in Major League history, a twenty-six-inning, 1–1 affair between the Braves and the Brooklyn Dodgers on May 1, 1920.

Oeschger's presence on the Phils' roster with Burns and their relationship with their three counterparts on the Red Sox added a special touch to the championship proceedings. With a mixture of hometown pride and baseball hyperbole, the *Oakland Tribune* celebrated the reunion of the former Phoenix in the World Series:

> Five boys from Saint Mary's College, Oakland, in the coming World Series. Can any other institution of learning in the whole wide world equal that record? Can they even tie it? Can they even approach it at a respectful distance? Were we a Saint Mary's College boy, we'd feel amazingly proud of that school. We're not a Saint Mary's College boy, but still we feel amazingly

proud of that institution of learning. We're an Oaklander, and we believe that most Oaklanders feel a bit of pride in an institution that can develop five boys good enough to play in the greatest of all American sporting events, probably the greatest of all sporting events in the world.[30]

While the Bay Area prided itself on the appearance of its own in the World Series, the Red Sox celebrated the Series victory which its share of local talent had largely produced. The games that Hooper's and Lewis's bats or Leonard's arm did not win were secured through the pitching of the best staff in the Majors. Dutch's 2–1 gem in game 3 was bracketed by Foster's three-hitter in the second game and Shore's complete-game, seven-hit victory in the fourth. Both were won with identical 2–1 scores. The final game, which featured Harry's homers, was the highest-scoring affair of the entire Series, 5–4. Twice Boston came from behind to overtake early two-run Philadelphia leads. Foster settled down after the fourth inning and recorded his second victory of the Series when Duffy and Harry played long ball in the eighth and ninth innings.

The series triumph meant a $3,780 payoff to each Boston player and the opportunity to earn more on the winter vaudeville circuit. This had become a popular activity for the country's sporting heroes ever since Jim Corbett first took to the stage to display his form and field questions from the audience after winning the heavyweight boxing championship from John L. Sullivan in 1892. Among the first baseball players to venture on the vaudeville stage was Chicago's Cap Anson. He starred briefly in a production entitled *The Runaway Colt*, which called for him to take a mighty swing at a ball, dash off the stage in one direction, then reappear at the other side before sliding safely into home as the curtain came down.[31] Only Leonard among the Saint Mary's men, however, could be tempted in this direction.[32] While Dutch divided his time on the stage in a baseball uniform feigning a few pitches and in formal wear playing the drums, Hooper and Lewis headed home to California. Capitola turned out to honor their favorite son with a parade and banquet.

For the second time in four years, Harry wore the jeweled pin of a World Series champion. Moreover, the winner's share provided the means to improve his new home and to acquire some farming properties that his father thought would be a good investment.[33] These acres were located in the northern Sacramento Valley near Marysville and promised harvests of peaches and raisin grapes. All this could wait, though, for the extended play in October had cut into the hunting season and Harry was eager to apply his sporting energies to a different field.

8

Captain Harry

The profound regard for the great ability as a ball player of one of Boston's best loved and leading ball players, Harry Hooper, has inspired his friends with a desire to furnish added incentive to better playing, if that be possible. They present him, therefore, with this gift, of which the gold is no purer nor better than his playing, nor the diamond more modest than he, as a token of love, esteem and their very greatest good wishes.

—James M. Curley, July 2, 1917

Meeting in New York's Waldorf-Astoria Hotel on December 22, 1915, the big three of the National Commission—Ban Johnson, August Herrmann, and John Tener—signed an agreement with representatives of the Federal League that officially ended the third circuit's brief challenge of the AL's and NL's Major League monopoly. Principal provisions of the settlement included $5 million in buy-out compensation for the debt-ridden backers of the Federal franchises, the transferral of ownership of several Federal ballparks to organized baseball, and amnesty for all players who had jumped to the new league. Like the National Association of the early 1870s, the Union Association of 1884, the Players League of 1890, and the American Association after the 1891 season, the Federal League collapsed under the limitations of its own financing and the powerful interests arrayed against it. Although Irving Sanborn of the *Spalding Guide* gloated that the Federal League was "the attempt of misguided capitalists to give the American public too much Base Ball," more likely explanations of the league's failure were the unified resistance and deep pockets of its opposition, ambitious and aggressive capitalists in their own right who had the financial and political resources to outwait and outmuscle the challenger.[1] So complete was organized baseball's victory over the Federal insurgency that it effectively discouraged thereafter further entrepreneurial ventures along similar lines. Any expansion of the Major League game in the future would take place under the terms and aegis of organized baseball.

In reestablishing their monopoly, the Major League owners moved quickly to cover the costs of the peace treaty with the Federals. The magnitude of their victory was underscored by the manner with which they dealt with their players. Not only had they eliminated their competition for the consumer dollar, but they had also contained the market for player talent. No longer needing to pay high salaries or to grant concessions to the players on such issues as severance pay, working conditions, and reentry bargaining rights to keep their rosters intact, the owners systematically began to cut payrolls and ignore other player interests.[2] The Baseball Players Fraternity, a union organized in 1912 by former Major League player and Ivy League degree holder Dave Fultz and including Ty Cobb and Christy Mathewson among its officers, collapsed in the wake of the Federal League settlement.[3] Its voice, like that of the Brotherhood of Professional Base Ball Players in the late 1880s and the short-lived Players Protective Association at the turn of the century, echoed the cause of collective bargaining but commanded little attention when the owners were not compelled to listen to it.

Months before the demise of the Federal franchises yielded higher gate receipts and advertising revenues for their clubs, the Major League owners reaped the first harvests of their victory. Supported by the competitive realities of a changed baseball marketplace, they began to trim player salaries and overhaul team rosters. With the number of Major League teams reduced by a third, even discounting the marginal players and postprime veterans who had lasted a year or two in a Federal uniform, a larger number of talented and experienced ballplayers now competed for membership in a sharply restricted fraternity. Major League clubs re-signed many of their former players, most of whom were delighted to continue their baseball careers, if not with their Federal salaries. The clubs vied, too, for such homegrown stars of the third circuit as Bennie Kauff, Edd Roush, and Max Flack, although most of the Federals for whom that league was their only shot at the "bigs" either disappeared into the minor leagues or abandoned altogether their notions of a professional baseball career.[4]

Lannin's main objective with the Red Sox in 1916 was to return to the field the team that had just won the World's Championship. Unlike some of his fellow owners, he showed no interest in either going after the Federal stars or bringing back to the Boston fold those few players who had left the Fens for the Feds. Among the latter, the only one of note in any case was Hugh Bedient, who had jumped to the Buffeds after his disappointing season with the Red Sox in 1914. But his 16–18 record and 3.11 ERA with the Blues warranted neither Lannin's nor anyone else's attention. With all except Wood and Speaker signed before the start of spring training, Lannin ignored the scramble for the few choice crumbs from the Federals' table.

Lannin did not stand apart, however, from the salary reduction efforts of his fellow owners. With only two noteworthy exceptions, again Wood and Speaker, Lannin's strategy in these matters focused less on actually reducing salaries than on not increasing them. Hooper and Lewis, for example, despite their World Series heroics, re-signed for $5,000, the same salary they had drawn in 1914 and 1915. Ruth, in the second year of his initial three-year contract, drew another $3,500.

With Wood and Speaker, however, who at $7,500 and $15,000, respectively, were the highest-paid players on the team, Lannin sought drastic reductions in their salaries. He offered Smoky Joe $5,000 and Tris $9,000 for the new season. Lannin's offers partly reflected his solidarity with the other owners as they attempted to control their payrolls after the inflationary years of the Federal challenge. They also indicated his doubts about Wood's ability to pitch effectively anymore and his disappointment in Spoke's declining batting average, which had dropped from .383 in 1912 to .322 in 1915. Neither took kindly to the offers. Wood refused to report to Hot Springs for such a "measly salary."[5] Speaker did, however, gambling that his appearance in the Red Sox camp would make a favorable impression on Lannin and resolve the salary dispute to his satisfaction. Whatever hopes Tris had that this would happen were dealt a severe blow when, only a few days before the start of the season, Lannin purchased outfielder Tilly Walker from the Browns. The message in the acquisition was obvious: the best center fielder in the Majors was expendable unless he agreed to the owner's terms.

For the first time in many years, the Red Sox had a relatively injury-free and dry spring. Although Wood's absence and Speaker's awkward status created some concern, Boston was the solid favorite to retain the AL crown as opening day approached. Neither wishing to forfeit his opportunity to play for a pennant contender nor to forego the World Series shares that might mean (the winners collected $4,025 in 1912; $3,780 in 1915), Spoke indicated he would consider a salary reduction to twelve thousand dollars for the new season. His bottom line, however, did not match Lannin's, who remained steadfast in his initial offer. On April 12, two days before the start of the season, the Boston owner announced that salary negotiations with Speaker had collapsed and the Grey Eagle had been sold to the Cleveland Indians. The price: fifty thousand dollars and "two obscure players," Sam Jones and Fred Thomas.[6]

Speaker's sale, the largest amount ever paid for a single player to that time, shocked the baseball world. Identified with the Red Sox as closely as Cobb was with Detroit or Mathewson with the Giants, Tris was the heart of the Boston batting order and the centerpiece of its celebrated outfield. No group was more stunned by his departure than his now former teammates. Yet, on the eve of the new season, they had little time to contemplate the gaping hole in their lineup. As surprised and uninformed as anyone regarding the Speaker deal, Carrigan reminded the team that their past success and future prospects went beyond one man. A team did not simply replace a player like Speaker, the manager explained, it relied upon its proven strengths and rallied around other leaders. In 1916, more clearly than ever with Speaker's bat gone, pitching and defense would have to carry the club. So, too, in the matter of team leadership, Spoke's departure created less a crisis than a shift in attention to other styles and exemplary models. For Hooper, the breakup of the Boston outfield thrust not a new role upon him, but a more visible and acknowledged one.

Scoring fewer runs than any of the league's pennant contenders in 1916, Boston pinned its championship hopes on its veteran rotation. Despite the loss of Wood, who found Lannin's contract offer a good reason to sit out the entire season and seek rehabilitation for his arm, the staff performed brilliantly. Led by Ruth's nine shutouts and Leonard's six, the latter including a no-hitter against Saint Louis on August 30, the Boston hurlers whitewashed their opponents a league-leading twenty-four times. Although Foster recorded a no-hitter of his own in June against New York, the clear star of the staff was Ruth. Emerging as the best left-hander in the league, if not in the Majors, the Babe was the workhorse of the Red Sox mound. Leading the team in innings pitched (323), games started (40), wins (23), and ERA (1.75), he played consistently well all season but showed a particular flair for the dramatic. Pitching his best against the toughest opponents—he won four of five games when matched against Walter Johnson, for example, including a thirteen-inning 1–0 victory—Ruth often found himself on the slab when the Sox needed to stop a losing skid or make an important move in the pennant race. Occasionally his bat more than his arm made the difference in a game's outcome. In three successive games in June, once as a pinch hitter, Babe cracked home runs, although these were his only four-baggers of the season. Nevertheless, as in 1915, such clouts and the team-best .419 slugging average they helped build drew considerable attention. The newly appointed team captain of the Red Sox, Harry Hooper, was one of those taking notes on the Babe's bat work for future reference.

The name of the game for the Red Sox in 1916, though, was not Ruthian power at the plate but the familiar struggle for a run or two and the dogged protection of the slim leads they provided. It was Harry's game and his captaincy underscored it. Leading the team in at bats (575), hits (156), walks (80), runs scored (75), and stolen bases (27), Hooper strengthened his claim as the best leadoff man in the business. His on-base average, .361, was his highest since 1911 and trailed only Gardner's .372 on the club. Moreover, Harry raised his batting average to .271, thirty-six points over the previous year.

In the field, he faced the dual challenge of covering more ground now that Speaker was gone and tutoring Spoke's replacements in Boston's defensive system and, especially, Fenway's corners and shadows. Neither the right-handed-hitting Walker nor Chick Shorten, who swung from the left side and platooned with Tilly in center, were particularly noteworthy fielders. Carrigan, in fact, had briefly experimented with both of them in left field, hoping that Duffy's area would be more manageable territory for them. But Lewis felt uneasy in center and Hooper was certainly not going to be moved out of right. Carrigan finally decided to leave them in center but encouraged Harry and Duffy to poach in that direction. Although the new Boston outfield recorded fewer assists and double plays than any of the years of the Hooper-Speaker-Lewis patrol, it committed no more errors. Its performance in that regard helped Boston post the best team fielding percentage in the Majors in 1916, and, with the pitching, relinquish the fewest runs in the AL.

In the most wide-open pennant race in the AL's history, one which saw all but two of the league's teams occupy first place during the season, Boston's veteran poise and pitching depth made the difference. Challenged early in the season by New York and Cleveland, the former, like other teams throughout the Majors, strengthened with key Federal League acquisitions, the Red Sox broke on top of the pack in April but then settled into a pattern of .500 ball for nearly two months. Their mediocre play during this stretch dropped them as far back in the standings as sixth for a one-day stay on June 20. In July, however, the platoon arrangement in center field having been set and the entire starting rotation throwing well, Boston began a steady climb back to the top. The club moved to second place in the standings by mid-July, then seized the lead for the first time since late April on July 29. From then until the end, the Red Sox alternated with the other preseason pennant favorites, Chicago and Detroit, for the lead. As in 1915, Boston's play in crucial series against its chief rivals in late September determined the outcome of the race. On their final western swing of the season, one which began with Lannin's upsetting announcement that Carrigan intended to retire at the end of the year, the Red Sox whipped Chicago on September 17 and 18, swept the Tigers in a three-game set, then took three of four from Cleveland. The victories boosted the Sox back into first, where they remained "to cop the bunting" for the second consecutive time.[7] Their final record of 91–63 gave them a two-game edge over Chicago. The Tigers finished another two games back.

Awaiting Boston in the World Series, having earned their first National League pennant in a hotly contested race with Philadelphia, Boston, and New York, were the surprising Brooklyn Dodgers. Manager Wilbert Robinson's club was an unlikely but well-orchestrated aggregation of castoffs from other teams and a few longtime Brooklyn players. Former Giants Chief Meyers, Rube Marquard, and Fred Merkle headed those in the first group, which also included Mike Mowrey from Pittsburgh, Larry Cheney from the Cubs, Cleveland's Ivan Olson, and former Mackman Jack Coombs. The most prominent among the homegrown veterans were outfielders Zack Wheat, Hy Myers, and Casey Stengel, second baseman George Cutshaw, and pitchers Nap Rucker and Jeff Pfeffer. Although the Dodgers' pitching staff had compiled a Majors best ERA of 2.12 and their hitters had combined for a .261 batting average, highest in the NL, few baseball observers gave Brooklyn much of a chance in the Series. Most felt that the Dodgers had peaked in winning the pennant and that their weaknesses, principally defense and postseason inexperience, would be their undoing in a short series. Rarely have the experts been more correct.

Hoping that Marquard still had some of the magic in his arm, which had baffled the Red Sox twice in 1912, Robinson started Rube against Shore in game 1. It did not take Boston long to set the tone for the championship or for its familiar Series heroes to announce their presence. In the bottom of the third inning, the Red Sox scored first as Lewis lined a two-out double down the left-field line to score Hoblitzell, who had tripled his way on ahead of Duffy. Striking right back, though, Stengel led off the Brooklyn fourth with a single and then scored on Wheat's triple. With a man on third and none out, the Dodgers threatened to grab the lead and, perhaps more importantly, shake Boston's confidence. Coming to the plate was George Cutshaw, one of the toughest men in the Majors to fan and second only on the Brooklyn club to Wheat in RBIs. The likely contact of Cutshaw's bat seemed certain to bring in another run for the National Leaguers.

Cutshaw did his job. He sent Shore's pitch on a high arc toward the right-field corner. Hooper, who had been shading the right-handed hitter to center, broke for the ball the instant it was hit. Racing at full speed toward the right-field line, Harry stretched his glove hand before him as he slid into the descending ball. Popping to his feet with the ball secured, Harry straightened, pivoted counterclockwise a full circle, and fired a bullet toward home. It was perfect. Cady had time to spare in applying the tag on Wheat to complete the double play.

It was a stunning play, brilliantly executed, devastatingly effective. Perhaps even more so than his throw in the ninth inning of game 1 of the 1912 Series or his catch of Doyle's drive in the final game of that Series, the play underscored Hooper's mastery of his craft and his play under pressure. Although occurring earlier in the Series than his 1912 heroics, Harry's play was no less dramatic. It combined the fielding skills of his previous Series work and thwarted a rally on which the underdog Dodgers might otherwise have built a winning momentum. While the sporting press searched for new superlatives for Harry's show—Frank Lane of *Baseball Magazine* labeled it as "one of the most wonderful plays ever seen on a ball field"[8]—the Brooklyn manager described the catch as a "wonder" and the throw as a "heart-breaker."[9]

The rest of game 1, if not the Series, bore out Robinson's assessment. The Red Sox followed Harry's great play with a go-ahead run of their own in the fifth. Hooper again showed the way, leading off the inning with a double and scoring moments later on Walker's RBI single. Harry figured still further in the Boston scoring when he walked in the eighth, advanced to third on Hal Janvrin's single, and came home on a wild throw by Stengel. The unearned run, Brooklyn's third of the game, proved to be decisive as the Dodgers mounted a brave rally in the ninth that came up just short. Mays relieved Shore with two outs and the bases loaded to retire Jake Daubert and preserve Boston's 6–5 victory.

Behind Ruth's dazzling debut on the mound in postseason play, a fourteen-inning 2–1 triumph in game 2, the Red Sox took a 2–0 lead in the Series, an advantage that since 1903 had always ensured an eventual championship. Nineteen sixteen was no exception. Playing their only errorless game of the Series, the Dodgers won game 3, 4–3, before the home crowd at Ebbets Field. But Brooklyn's rally was short lived. Dutch Leonard shut down the Dodgers on five hits the next day despite a shaky first inning when he was victimized by his own wildness and a costly error by Janvrin. Doubles by Hoblitzell and Lewis and a three-run inside-the-park home run by Gardner provided all the runs the Red Sox needed as they coasted to a 6–2 victory. Back in Boston for game 5, Shore scattered three singles, the Dodgers made as many errors, and the Royal Rooters filled the air with a triumphant chorus of "Tessie" once more. Erasing an un-earned Brooklyn run on Lewis's triple in the second, his third extra-base hit of the Series, the Red Sox put runners on base in every inning except the first and seventh. The 4–1 final score belied a game that was never very close. The four-games-to-one margin of victory in the Series was more indicative of Boston's dominance.

In post-Series interviews, many of the Dodgers cited Shore's work in particular and the overall balance of the Boston club as the keys to the Red Sox victory.[10] A few, Robinson and Stengel, for example, had little doubt that Hooper's play had made the difference. Leading all Series players with most hits (7) and runs scored (6), Harry was the only one to hit safely in each of the five games. His .333 batting average (7 for 21), trailed only Lewis (.353, 6 for 17), and Stengel (.364, 4 for 11) among those players with ten or more at bats. Scoring in all but one of the games, Hooper also had Boston's only stolen base in the Series. In the field, of course, his work was flawless. He was the only outfielder on either team with more than one assist, his second occurring in game 2 when he nailed a base runner at third to help Ruth out of a jam. The respect which the Dodgers on the base paths showed for his arm limited his opportunities for more. Asked to comment on his own work, Harry admitted that "naturally a player wants to do his best in the World's Series, but," he added, "I never promise anything out of the ordinary." With typical modesty and forthrightness, he explained: "I had rather let my work speak for me if I can say anything to my credit." A winner's check for $3,910 spoke clearly about Harry's performance in his third World Series appearance and triumph.

Only one incident marred the World Series celebration, a marti-netish ruling of the National Commission that was a prelude to an even more bitter afterglow to come. While Hooper, Gardner, and a few members of the Outing Club headed for the White Mountains of

New Hampshire for a hunting and fishing vacation, several players went south to New Haven to participate in an exhibition game against a local semipro outfit on the Sunday following the Series. Since blue laws in the city of Boston prohibited Major League play on Sundays, the game was a rare opportunity to view the Red Sox for many fans whose work schedules frustrated their attendance at Fenway during the regular season. The Boston players who appeared in the exhibition did so more to thank their loyal followers than to pocket a few extra dollars. After the game, an additional group of Red Sox, including Ruth and his wife, joined the Hooper party in the woods. There they learned that the National Commission had reacted angrily to the Boston players' participation in the exhibition game. Citing a baseball rule prohibiting World Series players from such postseason activities, the commission threatened to withhold distribution of the World Series shares until the matter was investigated.

Led by Fultz in a desperate attempt to revive the moribund Players Fraternity and aided by a sympathetic Boston press who were outraged that their heroes' hard-earned Series bonuses might be forfeited on a technicality, a stream of protest compelled the commission to rethink its position. Lannin shouldered some of the blame for the incident, admitting that he had given his players permission to play in the game although he had not consulted with the commission office beforehand. The commission agreed to release the checks but accompanied that decision with the announcement that the offending players would be fined one hundred dollars for their participation in the exhibition. Moreover, in order to ensure payment of the fines, the commission office said that it would withhold distribution of the commemorative pins it traditionally awarded the World Series winners to any of the Red Sox until all the fines had been paid. The players—not Lannin—eventually anted up the fine money and the pins were released, but the incident was a sharp reminder of the locus of authority in the game and the petty manifestations it could take.

The embarrassment the entire affair caused Lannin may have been the final factor in confirming his own decision to exit the baseball business. Despite the World Series championship, his second in three seasons, 1916 had been a tough year for him. Vilified for the Speaker sale and Wood's loss, humiliated when an ill-tempered criticism of umpires late in the season required him to make a public apology, warned by his doctors to mind a poor heart condition, and saddened by Carrigan's resignation, the Boston owner announced the sale of the Red Sox on November 1 to a three-man group headed by thirty-six-year-old Harry Frazee, a wealthy theatrical man who had made a fortune producing plays for his stages in Chicago and on Broadway. The purchase price was $675,000, less than half in cash, the rest in notes between Frazee and Lannin.

Frazee's arrival and his inability to convince Carrigan to return to the helm meant that for the third time in Hooper's eight-year career with the Red Sox he started spring training under a new owner and manager. Frazee's choice to succeed Rough was thirty-year-old Jack Barry, the former member of the Athletics' "$100,000 infield" who had joined the Red Sox midway through the 1915 season. The appointment pleased Harry because he liked Barry personally, respected his steady if not outstanding play, and felt that the Holy Cross alumnus and veteran of eight seasons in the Majors had the experience and savvy to handle the managerial reins.

That Barry, though only a few months older than he, was an established baseball man particularly appealed to Hooper. Unlike Freddie Lake, Harry's first manager, and Ed Barrow, who would be his last with Boston, Barry had enjoyed success as a player and learned the game's finer points from one of baseball's master strategists, Connie Mack. Key lessons focused on the importance of adjusting defensive alignments to different game situations and the value of on-field communication among the players. Both depended upon conscientious preparation before taking the field and alertness once play had started. Barry declined Mack's intrusive managerial style, particularly reflected in the way the Philadelphian directed the field positions of his charges from the bench with a waving scorecard, for a more laissez-faire manner. This approach acknowledged the familiarity that the experienced Boston players had for each other's habits and abilities and reflected Barry's continuing role as a player, for he was still the Red Sox starting second baseman slated to play 116 games in the new season.

Hooper appreciated Barry's manner because it gave him a freer hand to direct the Boston outfield and to influence other aspects of the team's play. Respecting Hooper's knowledge of the game, Barry often deferred to his right fielder's judgment on matters ranging from the determination of lineups and the order of the pitching rotation to game strategy and even pitch selection. Like most established veterans, Harry enjoyed considerable discretion at the plate within certain broad bounds of what the club intended to accomplish offensively. The Red Sox, for example, had a virtually inviolable rule that their batters take the first pitch. Beyond that, however, and an occasional steal sign which would be flashed from the third-base coach's box, the Boston hitters largely controlled their own conduct at bat. For a contact hitter like Hooper, the hit-and-run play figured prominently in his bat work. With his own set of signals, Harry could alert runners ahead of him of a hit-and-run attempt or, as a base runner himself, he could call for it from the next hitters.[11]

Similarly, when in the field, Harry had the authority to advise certain pitching decisions, which he exercised through another group of signs with the catcher. These rarely dealt with specific pitches to throw—for example a fastball or a curve—but focused instead on pitching strategy at a given point in a ball game. With a good hitter at bat and first base open, Harry might signal one of three options to the catcher: walk the batter intentionally, pitch to him, or pitch around him. Barry could heed or not Harry's input on such matters, for it was purely advisory. But more often than not, the two agreed on how to handle a particular situation, increasing Barry's reliance on Hooper and underscoring Hooper's active captaincy.

The new manager's style and rapport with his players complemented the needs of a veteran club. Returning their entire starting lineup and pitching rotation from the 1916 season, the Red Sox confidently expected to contend for their third consecutive league championship. Despite an unusually cold and wet New England spring, which would take its toll later in the season when Boston had to play several make-up doubleheaders, the Red Sox started well, winning fifteen of their first twenty games. Ruth in particular was most impressive in the early going. He won eight straight decisions to start the season and sported a 10–1 record two months into the campaign. The Red Sox led the league throughout most of this period, occasionally dropping to second place when New York, Cleveland, or Chicago briefly nudged past them. By June, however, it was clear that the American League race would be a two-team affair between Boston and the White Sox. After May 23, in fact, they ran first or second continuously for the rest of the season.

Unlike the new Boston ownership, Chicago's Charlie Comiskey had made some moves during the winter months to strengthen his club. He added Swede Risberg, a shortstop from California, to the roster and the rangy rookie with a powerful arm and short temper immediately earned a spot in the starting lineup. Swede's addition enabled Buck Weaver to move to third base, his preferred position. On the other side of the infield, Comiskey solved the club's long-standing defensive problems at first with the purchase of Chick Gandil from Cleveland for thirty-five hundred dollars. The big man—six feet two inches, 200 pounds—promised a bat no stronger than that of the man he replaced, Jack Fournier, but provided a surer target for one of the league's best infields. In 1917, Chick would lead all regular first basemen in the Majors with a .995 fielding average.

Chicago's acquisitions were decisive in snapping Boston's hold on the AL title. Ironically, the Red Sox actually improved their winning percentage over the previous season (.592 to .591), but the White Sox added eleven more victories to their second-place total in 1916 to finish with a 100–54 record, a comfortable nine games ahead of Hooper's club in the final standings. Although the pitching performances of Leonard, Shore, and Foster did not match their work in the recent championship years, the inability of Boston to win the season series against any of their first-division opponents sealed their pennant hopes. After Chicago moved into first on August 19, the Red Sox gamely stayed on their heels through a steady run of victories over the weaker teams in the league. Boston took thirty-five of forty-eight decisions against Saint Louis and Philadelphia, for example, but the Red Sox could not close on the leaders in head-to-head play. Chicago's rotation of Eddie Cicotte, Lefty Williams, Red Faber, Reb Russell, and Dave Danforth rivaled the 1915 and 1916 Red Sox staff in the numbers they posted, including twenty-two shutouts and a team ERA of 2.16. Only Ruth and Mays performed as well for Boston.

For Harry, notwithstanding his increased role in directing the club on the field, 1917 was a season typical of his nine years with the Red Sox. Although his batting average dropped to .256, only Lewis (.302), Gardner (.265), and Hoblitzell (.257) did better among the regulars on the team. Measured against Boston and AL team averages of .246 and .248, respectively, Hooper's average was certainly creditable, but it only partly reflected his contributions to Boston's offense. Leading the team again in at bats (559), walks (80), stolen bases (21), runs scored (89), and on-base percentage (.355), Hooper had fewer hits (143) than only Duffy (167). In the power categories, Harry led the team with eleven triples and three home runs, one of only three times between 1917 and 1931 when Ruth was not the leader in round-trippers on his own team. The Babe had two in 1917, although he only registered 123 at bats.

Approaching his thirtieth birthday, Harry continued to train rigorously, especially concentrating on leg strength. Consequently, he had lost very little quickness afoot. The statistics suggested that, but, as in the Doc Powers Day field competitions of 1910, a similar occasion late in the 1917 season gave him the opportunity to test his speed directly against some of the best players in the game. The setting was a benefit for the widow and family of longtime Boston sportswriter Tim Murnane, who had died earlier in the year. An exhibition game between the Red Sox and an all-star contingent featuring Rabbit Maranville, Ray Chapman, Ty Cobb, Tris Speaker, Joe Jackson, Buck Weaver, Wally Schang, and Walter Johnson highlighted the afternoon's schedule on September 27. It attracted over seventeen thousand spectators to Fenway and raised more than fourteen thousand dollars for the Murnane family. Before the game, a 2–0 victory for Boston behind a combined three-hitter by Ruth and Foster, the players participated in several skill competitions. Harry entered two timed baserunning events: the bunt and run to first and circling all the bases. In the former, Hooper tied his teammates Mike McNally and Hal Janvrin, plus Cobb and Maranville, in a "world's record" time of 3.15 seconds.[12] In the other event, Harry crossed home plate one-tenth of a second slower than Chapman, who won the dash in fourteen seconds flat. Only Cobb among the contestants in the running events was older than Harry, and Ty by less than a year.

If Harry was not slowing down after a decade of professional ball, organized baseball itself was proceeding cautiously and warily now that the European war had formally pulled the United States to its battlefields. President Woodrow Wilson's address to Congress calling for a declaration of war against Germany came on April 2, a week before the start of the 1917 season. Although mobilization and the dispatch of American troops to the combat zones were months away, club owners, reminded of the "war" with the Federal League, were concerned about keeping their rosters intact. Similarly, the National Commission was nervous about the public's reaction to the notion of able-bodied men playing a game for a living while the nation went warring to make the world safe for democracy.

Believing that America's entry into the war was inevitable and reflecting the preparedness mood in the country prior to the congressional declaration, Ban Johnson directed the club owners in his league to institute close-order military drills for their players during spring training. Led by army drillmasters assigned to each team, players shouldered their bats and marched around the ball fields as part of their daily regimen. The drills continued to be a common feature at games in the early part of the regular season as the players paraded by the spectators before play began. Although the commission's office claimed that these exhibitions enabled baseball "to join hands with the government in arousing the patriotism of its civilians," they also provided the Major Leagues with an explanation of why they chose not to encourage enlistments or curtail the season.[13] The drills technically qualified as "military instruction," and, at least initially, men engaged in occupations that provided it were not subject to the early conscription calls. A couple of months into the season, however, the drill program had lost its novelty and credibility. It was abandoned for other demonstrations of baseball's contributions to the war effort, such as benefit games for military dependents, free admissions for military personnel, and patriotic parades and music. Pregame martial extravaganzas, often involving thousands of marching troops accompanied by several brass bands, reminded spectators of the struggle "over there." These were sights, observed Sanborn of the *Spalding Guide,* that made it "impossible for even the most pronounced pacifist to escape a thrill of patriotism."[14]

Except for a few volunteers, though, rosters were not affected in any significant way by the 1917 summer draft calls. Major League players joined the nearly ten million American males between the ages of twenty-one and thirty-five who registered in the military census of early June, but bureaucratic inefficiency and operational problems with the entire mobilization effort virtually ensured that no players would be called to active duty before the end of the season. With a wife and child and another baby on the way, Hooper was exempt from military service. Although his orchards in the Sacramento Valley were entrusted to a foreman and his father and rarely felt his hand directly in their management, Harry also earned an exemption as a farmer.

There was no celebratory hunting trip in New Hampshire at the close of the 1917 season. Esther, pregnant with their second child, had returned to Capitola in early September after spending the summer in Winthrop, and Harry was anxious to join her. The business of his other military exemption, namely, his agricultural interests, also commanded his attention. His foreman, Harvey Bradley, recognized the increased market for California produce that was likely to develop from America's entry into the war and encouraged Harry to expand his holdings. Bradley suggested to Harry that he not only acquire additional peach orchards in neighboring Yuba City but also diversify his properties. He thought pomegranates and artichokes would be a good investment. Since Bradley's management of the original acres had already realized modest profits, Harry followed his foreman's advice and took out the necessary bank loans to cover the new expenditures.

Hooper's behavior in this matter typified his approach to the investment opportunities and business deals that came his way from individuals who were eager to profit by his name and success. Although he made a good effort to investigate prospective ventures and then to follow his interests carefully, Harry had difficulty sharing his attention with matters that were not as primary to him as baseball and hunting. He generally relied on the advice of others, who, well intentioned though they may have been, sometimes made improvident judgments or overestimated Harry's financial resources to cover their mistakes. Trusting and generous, Harry would suffer setbacks in the years ahead from false starts in such diverse ventures as juice processing, oil drilling, and an insurance agency. Hooper did, though, have a keen eye for coastal property values, and the investments he made in his own and adjacent lots in Capitola would provide one of the bases for his family's security after his retirement from baseball.

In an era before press agents and business consultants (Harry had neither) and the marketing bonanza for sports heroes that began in the 1920s, Hooper nevertheless had some experience with promotional advertising. He lent his name to a few products, Ground Gripper shoes and Draper-Maynard gloves, for example, and usually received a gift of the advertised item, not financial remuneration, for his endorsement. He did earn $50, though, for promoting a vitamin supplement called Nuxated Iron on the heels of his 1915 World Series performance. Pointing out that "in the World's Series games every player is put on his mettle . . . to play equally hard in the ninth and the first innings," Harry testified that with Nuxated Iron a part of his regular training, he had found himself "possessed of strength, power and stamina to meet the most severe strains." For "real stay-there endurance," Harry urged, "take Nuxated Iron for the extra spurt that wins."[15] Harry was similarly thanked by the Stutz Motor Car Company for sitting in one of its roadsters with Larry Gardner for an ad that proclaimed "Three Sturdy Winners, Gardner-Stutz-Hooper, Speed Boys in a Speedy Car." Although a gift of that particular product was not forthcoming, Hooper did apply the Stutz check toward a new "driving machine" of his own, a $900, four-cylinder Ford, something a bit less costly and grand than the six-cylinder, sixty-horsepower vehicle for $2,250 in which he and Larry posed.[16]

Through the winter months of 1917–18, it became more obvious from the news overseas that the American entrance into the war was not in itself going to bring about a quick end to the fighting. The overthrow of the czar in Russia in March 1917 and the successful

Bolshevik Revolution several months later set in motion steps that eventually led to a Russian armistice with Germany by the end of the year. This allowed Germany to shift massive numbers of troops from Eastern Europe to the Western Front, where they prepared to assault the Allied forces before they were significantly reinforced with the Americans. Aiming to split the British and French armies and capture Paris, Germany launched the first of five great offensives during the spring and summer of 1918 against the Allied lines at Amiens in March. By then, the American Expeditionary Force in Europe numbered 80,000 men. Nearly 250,000 more were destined to arrive each month thereafter while the war continued.

The effects of the war first reached the Red Sox when Jack Barry announced at the end of the season that he would not be returning to manage the club in 1918. He had decided to enlist in the naval reserve. With another round of draft calls scheduled, several players, including Del Gainer, Hal Janvrin, Duffy Lewis, Mike McNally, Herb Pennock, Chick Shorten, Fred Thomas, and Jimmy Walsh, followed suit. At home in California awaiting the birth of his first son, Hooper kept abreast of these developments. The anxiety of familial matters and apprehension of what lay ahead for Major League baseball led him, for the first time in his career, to contemplate a change in his professional direction. Several clubs in the Pacific Coast League were eager for Harry's services, and the attractions of playing ball on the West Coast in a league which many thought was the equal of the American and National were considerable. Frazee's appeals to Harry's sense of duty and loyalty to the club, however, backed up with a slight salary increase while the owner made payroll cuts elsewhere, kept Hooper in a Red Sox uniform. Likewise, Esther assured Harry that she could manage with two children as easily as one in his absence. Harry signed his contract in late January, wondering who his third manager in three years would be and what shape the Boston lineup would take in the uncertain season to come.

The sheet music cover of "Hoop, Hoop, Hooper Up for Red-Sox," a ragtime piece written in Harry's honor as Boston prepared to face Philadelphia in the 1915 World Series. (National Baseball Library, Cooperstown, N.Y.)

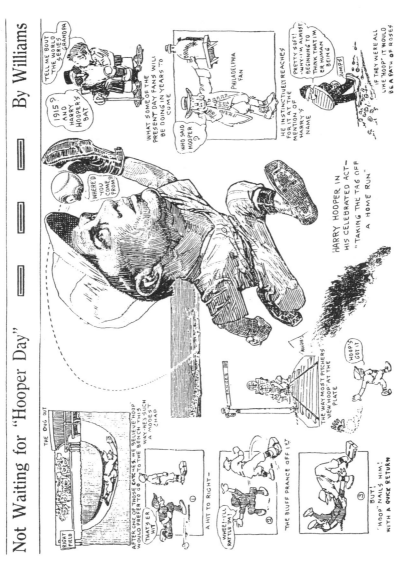

A cartoon from the *Boston Traveler*, May 30, 1916, commenting on many of Harry's traits and abilities: modesty, integrity, clutch play, and so on. (National Baseball Library, Cooperstown, N.Y.)

Harry leading off for Boston in the bottom of the first inning in game 1 of the 1916 World Series against Brooklyn. (National Baseball Library, Cooperstown, N.Y.)

Harry toward the end of his career with the Chicago White Sox, 1924. (National Baseball Library, Cooperstown, N.Y.)

Harry, honored at Fenway Park upon his return as a member of the Chicago White Sox, shakes the hand of former Boston mayor John Fitzgerald, 1921. (National Baseball Library, Cooperstown, N.Y.)

A cartoon from the *San Francisco Chronicle*, June 26, 1923, includes John McGraw's and Walter Johnson's appreciations of Harry. *(San Francisco Chronicle)*

Duffy Lewis, Tris Speaker, and Harry at an Old Timers game, 1930. (National Baseball Library, Cooperstown, N.Y.)

Harry, Esther, and their three children, Harry, Jr., Marie, and John, in Denver, Colorado, 1924. (Courtesy of John Hooper)

Harry, wearing a White Sox jacket and a Princeton cap, as the Princeton baseball coach, 1932. (Princeton University Archives, Princeton, N.J.)

Harry serving as postmaster in Capitola, California, mid-1930s. (AP/Wide World Photos; Courtesy of John Hooper)

Hall of Fame inductees and members, 1971. Harry is in the first row, third from the right. He is flanked by fellow inductees Chick Hafey (to his right) and Rube Marquard. Next to Marquard is Roy Campanella. Directly behind Harry is Bob Feller. Not bad company. Eighty-three-year-old Harry was the oldest living member of the Hall at the time. (National Baseball Library, Cooperstown, N.Y.)

9

Bitter Victory

Who was the greatest fielding outfielder? Harry Hooper of the old Red Sox. No doubt about it. He could do anything any other outfielder could and on top of that he was a great position player. His instinct for knowing where the ball was going to be hit was uncanny. I'm sure, too, that he made more diving catches than any other outfielder in history. With most outfielders the diving catch is half luck; with Hooper it was a masterpiece of business.

—Babe Ruth, 1936

The Major Leagues had come through the first year of the country's formal participation in the World War in relatively good shape. Attendance had fallen off nearly 1.3 million from 1916, but rosters generally held as few players were affected by either the summer draft calls or the voluntary spirit to military service. The game had effectively deflected any charges of "slackerism" and even earned praise from friends in the government for its contributions to the national morale. Nineteen eighteen, however, was a different matter entirely. There was no mistaking the signs that these were not normal times. Seeking to reduce club expenditures, the owners agreed to shorten the spring training season and to use sites closer to home. They also decided to limit the regular season schedule to 140 games, hoping that fewer games would save on travel and operational costs yet ensure higher attendance at those which were played. Nevertheless, the owners anticipated a lean year at the gate. To cover their expected losses somewhat, they resorted to the familiar tactic of cutting salaries.

The Red Sox who had followed Jack Barry into the armed services were among the more than two hundred Major Leaguers from the 1917 rosters in military uniform when the preseason camps opened in mid-March.[1] Many more would join them in the months ahead. Back in Hot Springs, Hooper found the piney surroundings more familiar than the men who shared the practice fields with him. In-

stead of Walker and Lewis, Harry looked across the outfield grass at
Amos Strunk in center and George Whiteman in left. Strunk, a member of Connie Mack's championship clubs in the early teens, was a
fleet-footed, sure-handed veteran of ten years in the Majors. When
Mack cut his salary after the 1917 season, Strunk complained so
bitterly that Mack promptly put him on the trading block. Frazee
dangled sixty thousand dollars before the financially strapped A's
owner, threw in three seldom-used reserves, and came away with
Strunk, catcher Wally Schang, and pitcher Joe Bush. It was the kind
of deal that won pennants. Both Schang and Bush, he of a no-hitter in
1916, were solid players whose best years still lay ahead of them.
The thirty-five-year-old Whiteman, who had labored in baseball's
hinterlands for years around two brief appearances in the Majors
with Boston in 1907 and the Highlanders in 1913, arrived from Toronto of the International League.

Except for Everett Scott, there were strangers in Red Sox uniforms
throughout the infield as well. Dave Shean was a journeyman second
baseman who had spent time with five Major League clubs before
coming over from Cincinnati in a trade for Rube Foster. With Hoblitzell awaiting a commission in the army, Frazee went shopping again
in Philadelphia for his eventual replacement. This time the price was
dearer. Acquiring Stuffy McInnis, the lone remaining veteran from
Connie Mack's last championship teams, Boston had to give up
Gardner, Walker, and reserve catcher Forrest Cady. McInnis, a line-
drive hitter who batted consistently around .300, was also one of the
surest-fielding first basemen in the business. He was a solid addition
to the club. Hooper and many others, though, were saddened to see
the inclusion of Gardner in the deal. Harry lost his roommate and
closest friend on the team and the Boston press lamented the departure of "one of the best 'money' players in the league."[2] Only Harry
(and coach Heinie Wagner) now remained on the team from the
1909 Huntington Avenue Speed Boys who had first challenged the
perennial hold of the Athletics and the Tigers on the American
League pennant. Larry's successors at third were two rookies, Fred
Thomas and George Cochran, whose mediocre play only made Boston miss Gardner more.

The least-known newcomer to Hooper and the other Boston veterans in the Red Sox camp appeared on the field in street clothes and a
straw hat. This was Ed Barrow, the former president of the International League who had quit that position in February when the
league's club owners, many of whom detested Barrow's heavy-
handed manner in running their affairs, voted to cut his salary dras-

tically. Anticipating this development and wary of the prospects for his league during wartime, Barrow had let Frazee know that he might be interested in changing jobs. Despite less than two years of managerial experience on the Major League level with Detroit in 1903–4, although his involvement in organized baseball reached back to the 1890s, when he handled concessions with Harry Stevens in the Pittsburgh Pirates' park, Barrow was now Boston's third manager in three seasons.

It was an appointment that did not initially thrill Hooper. Although Harry appreciated the new manager's reputation as an intense competitor, he doubted Barrow's credentials to lead the club on the field. For unlike Carrigan and Barry, Barrow had no experience as a player, no knowledge, Hooper observed, "of the finer points of the game."[3] Instead, Harry recalled, Barrow tried to intimidate those around him and bluff his way through the job. Barrow initially hoped that he could rely on his coaches, Johnny Evers and Dan Howley, for advice on the bench. But Evers fell out of favor with Barrow during spring training for the ill effects his driven personality had on team morale, and Howley, a veteran of only one year in the Majors with the Phillies in 1913 before becoming manager of the International League's Montreal club, commanded little respect among the Red Sox veterans. Barrow dismissed Evers before the season began and Howley departed shortly thereafter for Toronto, where he managed the club to the IL pennant in 1918. As self-assured as he acted, Barrow had sense enough to realize that he needed help to run the club. He turned to Captain Hooper.

Sitting on the bench near Barrow when the Red Sox were not in the field or signaling directions from his post in right, Harry advised the new manager on every aspect of the business, from lineup selection to game strategy. The arrangement served them both—and the club—well. Barrow respected Harry's experience and knowledge of the game and the league but particularly appreciated his disinterest in seeking credit for the larger role he had assumed in guiding the club. Hooper was pleased with the increased influence he had on team matters, since it served both his short- and long-term interests. For the future, his role as shadow manager afforded him the opportunity to exert managerial authority and to learn more about this job without much risk. His input was strictly advisory. If Barrow followed it, he was the one responsible for both the successes and the miscalls. More immediately, Barrow's dependence on him gave Hooper the opening to advance a few notions about the use of the team's personnel. The key to Harry's thinking was Ruth.

Like most of the Red Sox and their journalistic entourage who had watched the Babe perform on a regular basis since his first full season with the club in 1915, Harry had always been impressed with Ruth's "natural faculty for hitting and for being a ballplayer."[4] He "had all the earmarks of being a great hitter," Hooper remembered, "slim waisted, big biceps, in perfect shape when he came up, a wonderful specimen!" Moreover, as a pitcher, Ruth faced no expectations about his hitting, thus giving him the freedom to experiment at the plate. He had no conscience as a hitter in the early years. He could, observed Cobb, "take that big swing. If he missed, it didn't matter."[5] As Ruth learned to control his swing, his batting average improved without any diminution of his power stroke.

Although few in the Boston organization questioned the Babe's ability to do damage to a baseball when he connected, his strikeout frequency of nearly 20 percent during his career so far and the conventional wisdom of the game to rest pitchers on days when they did not throw kept his bat out of the regular lineup. Occasionally Ruth appeared as a pinch hitter, but a .162 average in this role before the 1918 season seemed to confirm that he should get his licks only when he pitched and then only from the ninth spot in the batting order. In any event, with the possible positions where Ruth could have played, namely, the outfield, first, and third, set with a solid veteran cast, there was no need—or room—for him anywhere else except on the mound. Despite leading the Red Sox in slugging percentage in each of his three full seasons with the club, including Speaker's last year in 1915, Ruth expected that he would get no more swings under Barrow than he had with Carrigan and Barry.

Hooper had other thoughts about this matter. Ever since Babe had hammered out fifteen extra-base hits, including four home runs, in ninety-two at bats in 1916, Harry had entertained the notion of playing Ruth occasionally on days when he did not pitch. As he considered the power drain from the Boston lineup with the losses of Lewis, Walker, and Gardner and the imminent departure of Hoblitzell, the Red Sox captain figured it was time to explore a new role for Ruth. Approaching Barrow during spring training, Harry argued that Ruth would be more valuable to the team playing every day instead of every fourth day in the pitching rotation. Barrow did not leap at the suggestion. Claiming that "they'd have had him investigated if he moved the best left-handed pitcher in the game into the outfield," the manager informed Hooper that his plans were to keep Ruth on the mound.[6] That was where he was when the 1918 season began.

But Harry had not exhausted his arguments on Ruth's behalf and developments early in the new season supported them. Pointing out the increased attendance figures on the days when Ruth pitched, Hooper suggested that the crowds turned out as much to see his bat in motion as his arm. He reminded Barrow that the manager's sixty-thousand-dollar investment in the club was only as sound as Boston's ability to draw fans to the park. Why not give them one of the game's top gate attractions on a more regular basis? An injury to the slumping Hoblitzell gave Barrow the excuse he needed to act on Harry's advice. He assigned Ruth to replace Hoblitzell at first on May 6 against New York. It marked the first time Ruth appeared in the starting lineup for a Major League game in a position other than pitcher. The Babe signaled his delight with a home run, his second in two days. The next day, batting fourth in the lineup, he hit another. Trying now to accommodate Ruth's bat, Barrow juggled his lineup still further, moving McInnis from third to first and the Babe to left field. Assigning Hooper the responsibility of developing Ruth's skills as an outfielder, Barrow asked Harry to play center occasionally whenever the Babe was in left. For fifty-nine regular season games in 1918, Harry had his "experiment" roaming the distant grasses with him.

It was a touchy assignment for Hooper. Principally responsible for Ruth's being in the lineup, Harry was now held largely accountable for his performance by Barrow. Reflecting his initial doubts about the move, Barrow had predicted to Harry that upon Ruth's first slump "he'll be down on his knees begging me to pitch."[7] The Babe, however, had responded to his new daily role with a display of hitting not seen in Boston since Speaker's best streaks. A month into the season, Ruth was hitting almost .500, half of his hits during these weeks, as they would the entire year, going for extra bases. It was an average he could not possibly sustain, but it raised the question of how the Red Sox lineup could afford not to have Ruth's bat in it.

Finding a place for him in the field, however, was a different matter. Preferring to play first base when he was not pitching, Ruth was a reluctant outfielder initially. But since his glove work was not the equal of McInnis, Babe really had no other choice than the outfield if he was to play regularly. Barrow, of course, felt that moving Harry to center would help hide Ruth's defensive deficiencies and put the Babe in more proximate contact with his tutor. The manager's expectations that Hooper would bring Ruth along as an outfielder placed an additional burden on Harry, but he patiently turned to the task of making the Babe at least respectable in this aspect of the game. After years of sharing the outfield with the likes of Tris

Speaker, Duffy Lewis, and Tilly Walker, Hooper could scarcely believe what sometimes went on around him now. Standing in center between Ruth in left and George Whiteman, Frank Gilhooley, or Braggo Roth in right during the 1918–19 seasons, Harry witnessed the antics of "wild men, hollering all the time, running after every ball."[8] Hooper eventually persuaded Barrow to play Ruth in center so that he could return to right and avoid "being killed." Nevertheless, the Babe proved to be a willing student under Harry, blending his physical skills with some fundamental pointers to become a fine defensive player.

Pounding out his base hits in the early going, Ruth had little interest in limiting his playing time to the pitching rotation. Particularly after he slammed four home runs in as many games during the first week in June, he became increasingly disinterested in pitching at all. Helping Barrow oblige the Babe's interests in these matters was the emergence of Joe Bush and Sam Jones as dependable starters, along with the veterans Mays and Leonard. Although Dutch departed for the navy shortly after tossing a no-hitter against Detroit on June 5, taking with him an 8–6 record and a 2.72 ERA, the others upheld the pitching equation in the club's decade-long formula of success. Mays (21–13, 2.21 ERA) and Bush (15–15, 2.11 ERA) were the mainstays of the staff, appearing in thirty-five and thirty-six games, respectively. Jones posted the highest winning percentage of the lot (.762), with sixteen victories in twenty-one decisions. Ruth, the only left-hander of note on the team after Leonard left, contributed a 13–7 record and 2.22 ERA in twenty appearances, less than half the number of games in which he had appeared in each of the two previous seasons. His reduced activity on the mound signaled that the most important corner in his playing career had been turned.

Notwithstanding Ruth's problems in adjusting to the outfield, which his .950 fielding average, the poorest on the club, underscored, the Red Sox continued to rely on excellent defense to complement their pitching. In 1918, Boston committed the fewest errors (149) and compiled the best fielding average (.971) of any team in the Majors. McInnis at first, Scott at short, and Strunk in center led all players for fielding in their positions. The Red Sox allowed their regular season opponents only 380 runs, 32 fewer than the next stingiest record of the Washington Senators, whose 2.14 team ERA, paced as usual by Walter Johnson with a league-leading 1.27, bettered Boston's 2.31.

At the plate, the Red Sox managed a team batting average of only .249, a mark surpassed by every other club in the American League except the last-place Athletics (.243). Ruth led the club in batting average (.300) and supplied most of the team's power. Appearing in just over 70 percent of Boston's games, Babe accounted for eleven of the club's fifteen home runs to lead the Majors with Tilly Walker of the A's, who had ninety-seven more at bats than Ruth. His slugging percentage of .555, built on twenty-six doubles (second in the AL), eleven triples (fourth), and the round-trippers, topped Cobb's runner-up performance in this category by forty points. No one else in either league produced a slugging average close to .500.

The other offensive star for the Red Sox in 1918 was the team captain. Not content merely to tutor Ruth in the field or to assist Barrow on the bench, Hooper underscored his veteran leadership with the best hitting performance of his ten-year Major League career. Batting .289 and slugging .405, both averages surpassed only by Ruth, Harry led Boston again in several key areas—at bats (474), hits (137), doubles (26, second to Speaker in the AL with Ruth), triples (13, second with Bobby Veach of the Tigers behind Cobb), walks (75, third behind Ray Chapman of Cleveland and Detroit's Donie Bush), runs scored (81, third in the AL, trailing Chapman and Cobb), and stolen bases (24). The war-depleted rosters of his American League opponents certainly gave the experienced Hooper an advantage over less-effective replacements and accounted somewhat for his outstanding year. Gone to military service for all or part of the 1918 season were, for example, such fine hurlers as Ed Klepfer of Cleveland, Bob Shawkey of New York, Ernie Koob of the Browns, Jim Scott of the White Sox, and Detroit's Howard Ehmke and George Cunningham. When placed in the context of his entire career, though, it seems that 1918 marked Hooper's arrival on a new plateau of individual performance that would characterize his play for several seasons to come. Assuming a larger role in the offense of this and future teams, clubs which lacked the hitting talent and balance of the Red Sox between 1909 and 1916, Harry began to hit for a higher average and more power. Prior to 1918, Harry's career batting average was a modest .267. For the next seven years, he hit at a .301 clip, including a career-best .328 in 1924. Moreover, he would post his best offensive numbers in every important category except stolen bases and walks during this period.

Hooper's greater output at the plate, particularly after 1920, came at a time when some fundamental changes were occurring in the chemistry of the game. Technical, legal, and strategic factors were at work in moving baseball into a new era that emphasized run production rather than crafty pitching and stingy defense. Higher-quality yarns and more uniformly manufactured baseballs, rules outlawing the spitball and other trick pitches, and approval of the home run and the "swing from the heels" batting style it encouraged created a permissiveness at the plate that had not been seen since the pitching distance was lengthened in 1893. What is noteworthy about Hooper's loftier offensive numbers is that he began to produce them before the age of "the lively ball" and that he sustained them in the final years of his career.

What made some of his numbers particularly impressive in 1918 was that they were achieved in only 126 games, the fewest games in which Harry had played since his rookie year. These were, in fact, all the regular season games that Boston played in 1918, for contrary to the owners' plans for a 140-game schedule, the season ended on September 2. The baseball year had lasted that long only because of a temporary dispensation for Major League players from Provost Marshal Enoch Crowder's notice of May 23 ordering all draft-eligible men to find work deemed essential for the war effort or face induction. Another two-week waiver of the order applied to those players who were on the Labor Day leaders in each league so they could participate in the World Series. Atop the AL after play concluded on Labor Day, two and a half games ahead of Cleveland and four up on Washington, were the Red Sox.

With the roster of the preseason favorite White Sox decimated by the departure of Red Faber, Happy Felsch, Joe Jackson, Swede Risberg, Lefty Williams, and others to the draft and war-related work, the American League pennant race promised to be a wide-open affair. During the first two months of the season it was, as Cleveland, New York, Washington, and Boston vied for the league lead. Playing exceptional ball in Fenway, however, where the war-shortened season favored their home schedule, and making the most of Frazee's purchases and trades, the Red Sox gained first place on July 6 and never relinquished it. Hard pressed by the Indians heading into the final week of the campaign, Boston may have owed its fourth pennant of the decade to the man largely responsible for its first two—Tris Speaker. With his club trailing the Red Sox by only two games with a week left in the season, Spoke took a swing at umpire Tom Connolly after being called out on a close play at the plate in a losing effort against Philadelphia on August 28. Typically rushing to the protection of his umpires, Ban Johnson suspended the Cleveland star for the remainder of the season. When Mays pitched—and won—both ends of a doubleheader against the A's on August 30, Boston claimed the AL pennant once more. Pitching, defense, Ruth, and

Hooper, "a star as usual," sent the Red Sox in quest of their fifth World Series title in as many tries since 1903.[9]

Awaiting Boston in the almost-fall Series were the Chicago Cubs, winners of their first National League pennant since 1910, when, as this year, they finished comfortably ahead of the second-place Giants of John McGraw. Featuring only one .300 hitter in their lineup, rookie shortstop Charlie Hollocher, the Cubs mirrored Boston in their reliance on veteran acquisitions from other clubs and outstanding pitching. First baseman Fred Merkle, catcher Bill Killefer, and outfielder Dode Paskert, for example, each of whom had been in the Majors for at least ten years, counted less than four years among them in a Cubs uniform. Behind Hippo Vaughn (22–10, 1.74 ERA), Lefty Tyler (19–9, 2.00 ERA), and Claude Hendrix (19–7, 2.78 ERA), the Chicago pitching staff had compiled the lowest team ERA in the National League (2.18) and had tossed twenty-five shutouts, one fewer than Boston's total. Not since the Giants of Mathewson, Marquard, and Tesreau had the Red Sox faced such formidable arms in a World Series.

In the latter half of the season, Barrow had rarely called on Ruth to pitch except to help out in doubleheaders or to give his three principal starters an occasional extra day's rest. Prior to the start of the Series, the manager had announced that Ruth would play left field and was unlikely to see any action on the hill. But as play began for game 1 in Chicago on September 5, Barrow pulled a surprising switch and started the Babe instead of Bush. He responded magnificently. Scattering six singles, Ruth shut out the Cubs, 1–0, extending his streak of scoreless innings in World Series play to twenty-two. His teammates played errorless ball in the field behind him, highlighted by defensive gems by Scott and Shean. The latter's leadoff walk in the Boston fourth, pushed around on singles by Whiteman and McInnis, accounted for the game's only run. Vaughn, the big Texan who was coming off his fourth season in five years of at least twenty wins, allowed only three other Boston singles, retired fourteen consecutive Red Sox in one stretch, but suffered the tough loss.

Games 2 and 3, both played in Chicago because of wartime travel restrictions, confirmed that this would be another pitchers' Series. Although Hooper, Strunk, and Ruth were the only left-handed hitters in the Boston lineup, Chicago manager Fred Mitchell decided to pitch his lefty aces, Vaughn and Tyler, throughout the championship. In his first Series appearance since a ten-inning, no-decision effort for the Boston Braves in game 2 of the 1914 championship, Tyler rallied the Cubs with a sparkling six-hitter of his own in the next game. The only damage came on back-to-back triples by Strunk and Whiteman in the top of the ninth with none out. Lefty quietly retired the side after those blows to secure the win. The Cubs managed only seven hits themselves off Joe Bush, but four of them, including Tyler's only hit of the Series, a single scoring two runs, came in the second, when Chicago tallied all three of its runs in the game. Bush settled down after that to complete the game, but the Series was now squared at a game apiece.

In a matchup of very contrasting styles, Vaughn was back on the mound for the Cubs in game 3 and Carl Mays got the nod for Boston. The Chicago veteran was a pure power pitcher whose six-foot four-inch, 215-pound frame made his fastball even more intimidating. There were no tricks to Vaughn's success. He threw strikes and challenged hitters directly. Mays, on the other hand, relied for his advantage on an exaggerated sidearm delivery that released a rising fastball and sharp curve. Often scraping the knuckles of his pitching hand on the mound as he fired the ball toward home, Mays particularly threatened right-handed batters who crowded the plate. Many—a league-leading fourteen hit batsmen in 1917 and eleven more in 1918—felt the sting of his pitches. This record and his own sour disposition led Mays to be branded as a beanballer, a label he vigorously denied but never overcame. Even among his own teammates, who generally respected his competitive spirit, Mays was distrusted and shunned. He was, said Hooper, "an odd bird."[10] But unshakably self-confident under even the most stressful circumstances, Mays answered his critics with a steady, often brilliant, record on the mound and a suspicious, reclusive manner away from it. In game 3 he was at the top of his game, his submarine throws effectively keeping the Cub batters off balance and his head-hunting reputation playing on their minds. Yielding only one run, Mays outdueled the hard luck Chicago ace, 2–1, and sent the Series east to Fenway with the Red Sox leading two games to one.

Both clubs rode the same overnight train to Boston, their separately chartered Pullmans coupled on either end of the dining cars. Except for two teams riding the rails to the same destination and the occasion for their travel, the trip was a familiar ritual to the players. For many, the long hours on the train provided much-needed rest, a chance to relax over a game of cards, to write home, or to catch up on one's sleep to the soothing clickety-clack of wheels on rails. Hooper often played bridge to pass the time and attracted a small fan club among the players and sportswriters for his skill in the game. Sometimes playing for as much as a dollar a point, Harry rarely left the table poorer or disappointed those who bet on him. For others, the trains offered an opportunity to mingle with nonbaseball people as players wandered throughout the cars striking up conversations with whomever they met. The outgoing Ruth, for example, particularly enjoyed roaming the train and talking to strangers.

For most, though, train travel was a time for conversation among teammates. Stories about off-season hunting and fishing trips, analyses of current events, joke telling, and tales of sexual conquests filled the hours, but mostly the players talked baseball. The shared wisdom of veterans mingled freely with the tentative opinions of rookies. The exchanges underscored the camaraderie of the profession, cementing friendships that would last a lifetime and instilling greater unity in the team at the moment. As rolling clubhouses, the trains encouraged fraternity and provided sanctuary.

In this season of uncertainty, one whose very beginning had been called into question, whose progress constantly provoked debate about its appropriateness and purpose, and whose ending signaled a sigh of relief rather than a sense of celebration, the talk on this trip particularly went beyond the games just played and those to come. The course of the season had been accompanied with unsettling rumors—pay cuts and canceled contracts, abbreviated schedules and unexpected trades, forfeited bonuses and unstable franchises. In matters of salary and security, the players were well aware that threatening rumors and signs had a nasty habit of becoming reality. Three games into the earliest-starting World Series ever, the rumor mill ground out news of further setbacks to the players' interests.

The players did not have to invent a case to support their concerns. It was there in the cold reality of reduced attendance figures throughout the regular season, a pattern which continued into the World Series. Major League games drew barely three million fans to the parks in the truncated campaign, more than two million less than the previous year and worse than any season since the National Agreement of 1903 went into effect. Any hopes the owners and players might have had of a World Series revenue bonanza were dashed when only 19,274 showed up for the first game. This turnout was particularly disappointing because the owners had decided to keep ticket prices at regular season levels to attract a good gate. Moreover, the Cubs had agreed to host their games in the White Sox's Comiskey Park, which could accommodate 32,000 patrons, twice more than the National League champions' own Weeghman Field. The turnout for games 2 and 3 were only slightly better: 20,040 and 27,054, respectively.

The prospects for significantly stronger attendance figures and buoyed receipts were not much better in Boston. For, unlike both 1915 and 1916, the Red Sox would be hosting their games in their own ballpark, rather than Braves Field, which they had borrowed on their two most recent trips to the Series. His theatrical senses alerting him to the low draw of this championship, Frazee saw no need to vacate Fenway for the five thousand additional seats across town.

The players were particularly concerned with the low attendance because for the first time since 1903 their own receipts pool would be divided differently. In an agreement among the owners of both leagues at their 1918 winter meeting, the old system of allocating the players' share (60 percent of all receipts of the first four games of the Series to the two teams actually in the Series) was abandoned for an arrangement that reserved a percentage of the players' receipts for distribution among the members of the top four finishers in each league for the regular season.[11]

Although this plan anticipated that the players' shares for the Series champions would be no less than $2,000 each ($1,400 minimum for the losers), it based this amount on a players' fund of at least $152,894 derived from total revenues for the first four games of $254,823. It is unlikely anyone calculated the exact cost of each empty seat at Comiskey, but for those players who were aware of the new distribution system, the modest crowds were not a good sign. Little did the players realize at the time just how poor their situation was. Receipts for the three Chicago games totaled only $100,463.[12] Even a capacity house at Fenway for game 4 would leave the players' pool far short of the amount necessary to ensure the payoff targets.

On the train to Boston, players from both teams met together to discuss their situation.[13] Although they were unhappy about the new distribution system, the reduced ticket revenues, and, of course, the disappointing crowds, the players had no real authority in these matters and few avenues open for them to express their disgruntlement. Not consulted on the new revenue-sharing arrangement, restricted in their ability to bring their views to the public by an owner-coddling press, and wary of the fine line between fair compensation and greed, especially in wartime, they decided to select a delegation to meet with Johnson and his fellow commissioners, August Herrmann and John Heydler, to state their concerns. The players' committee, consisting of Hooper and Shean of the Red Sox and Les Mann and Killefer of the Cubs, sought out the commissioners on the morning of the fourth game of the Series. Johnson and the others flatly rejected the request for a meeting. The disappointed players agreed not to press the matter at this point and returned to their respective teams with news of the unsuccessful attempt at a meeting. The players agreed to seek out the commissioners again before game 5.

When the teams took the field on September 9 to resume the Series, they encountered a familiar sight—one in five of Fenway's twenty-seven thousand seats sat empty. This meant that barely seventeen thousand dollars more would be added to the players' pool. If the players were disheartened by the financial direction of the Series, they did not show it in their play. The fans who did show up witnessed the most exciting game of the Series, a 3–2 Red Sox win which was not secured until the ninth inning when Bush, the team leader in saves, relieved Ruth with two on and none out and retired the Cubs without any damage. The last outs came on a Scott to Shean to McInnis double play, Boston's third of the game, and gave the home team a 3–1 edge in the Series.

With the Red Sox moving closer to the championship, the players' attention returned to their Series participation shares. As agreed upon the day before, the four-man players' delegation sought out the commissioners again on Tuesday, September 10. Just before noon they cornered Herrmann and Heydler at the ballpark. Johnson had been delayed in arriving because of a generous and largely liquid lunch with friends at the Copley Plaza Hotel.

Neither Herrmann nor Heydler was particularly eager to meet with the players, much less to do so without Johnson present. As a result, the brief meeting was little more than an exchange of viewpoints, with Hooper stating the players' position and Herrmann that of the owners and commissioners. Harry acknowledged the disappointing attendance for the four games so far and the effect this and the reduced ticket prices had on Series revenues. Nevertheless, he argued that the players had been assured before the Series began of winners' and losers' shares of $2,000 and $1,400, respectively, even though these amounts were significantly less than previous Series payoffs and had been determined by the new distribution plan which reflected neither player consultation nor approval. Herrmann emphasized that the Series receipts, more specifically those representing the players' portion, were indeed lower than expected. The players, like everyone else, he said, would just have to suffer the consequences.

Hooper was not willing to let the matter drop with that and pressed Herrmann on the distribution plan. This was a delicate issue and Harry had to be careful. Challenging the owners on the management of the Series receipts raised, in effect, basic questions regarding their authority and conduct. The business of baseball, reflected in such practices as the reserve clause, market monopolies, and revenue sharing of regular season gate receipts, underscored the power of the owners and their effectiveness in maintaining control of their enterprise. The National Commission, if not "the owners' Kangaroo Court," was certainly the owners' creature.[14] Although it had occasionally demonstrated an interest in protecting players' "rights," the commission limited its concern to individual cases, where a fine imposed on the player's club was typically the severest action taken against management. What the players raised now in the umpires' room beneath Fenway Park suggested interests and an agenda that were critical and collective.

Hooper first asked that the commissioners, in recognition of the poor receipts so far and the fairness of the players' concerns, postpone implementation of the new distribution system until after the war. Herrmann refused to budge. Hooper countered. Unless a satisfactory decision was reached on the players' request, they would refuse to complete the Series. Moreover, they would donate their entire share of the receipts to the Red Cross, not just the 10 percent they had pledged before the Series began. Hooper emphasized this latter point as further evidence that equity, not greed, motivated the players.

Herrmann and Heydler insisted that they could promise nothing to the players and that in any event they were powerless to act without Johnson. Hooper informed them that he and the other members of the players' delegation would wait for Johnson to arrive before carrying out their threat not to play. The commissioners adjourned to find and brief Johnson. The players had meetings with their teammates to keep them abreast of the status of the talks, then gathered again in the umpires' room with several reporters to await Johnson and the others.

Shortly before the two-thirty scheduled start of the game, an inebriated Ban Johnson entered the room with his two fellow commissioners. Herrmann, who may have sought some bracing spirits of his own in the interregnum, opened the meeting with a rambling discourse on how much he had done for baseball. Johnson then threatened to take up the beat. Interrupting Herrmann after only a minute or two, he seemed about to launch his own monologue when he suddenly stopped and began to cry. With tears streaming down his face, Johnson threw his arm around Hooper's neck and implored, "Harry, go out and play the game. Harry, you know I love you. Harry, go out and play. For the honor and glory of the American League, go out and play the game."

Harry, though, was not swayed by the commissioner's appeal. Neither was he convinced that much progress was going to be made with Johnson in his condition, Herrmann quite possibly sharing the same, and Heydler a virtual nonentity in the whole affair. He turned to the newspapermen and said, "It's apparent that these men are not in a condition to hear our argument." Hooper conferred briefly with the other players and decided they needed to meet with the rest of their teammates before responding to the situation as it now stood.

The two teams gathered in the Red Sox dressing room for the briefing. As Fred Thomas, a utility infielder for Boston, and Charles Spink, founder of *The Sporting News* and one of the reporters present in the room with the commissioners and the players, later recalled, Harry's counsel and leadership were decisive in bringing the strike threat to its conclusion.[15]

Pointing out the difficulties that the players had always had in currying fan support for higher salaries, Hooper argued that the players' quest for the financial recognition they were seeking in the World Series was unlikely to gain public support. Notwithstanding the distortion of their viewpoint which a press sympathetic to ownership might present, the players risked alienating those fans who had relied upon baseball to help them through the trials of wartime. A strike, Hooper reasoned, would particularly hurt "the very people who supported us by attending games day after day." Finally, Hooper reminded the players how fortunate they were compared to the thousands of men their own age who were serving in the military. The presence at the game that day of scores of wounded servicemen emphasized this point.

Little discussion followed Hooper's presentation. The players quickly and unanimously agreed that they would play, but with one important proviso. They wanted a guarantee from the commissioners that no action would be taken against any of the players for the strike threat.

Hooper and Mann returned to the umpires' room to report the players' decision and to seek an assurance against reprisal. Johnson was happy to comply. Once more throwing his arm around Hooper, the commissioner gushed, "Go out and play, Harry. Everything will be all right." The meeting immediately broke up in confusion, too confused, Hooper later recalled, for him to insist that Johnson put his guarantee of no reprisal in writing.[16]

An hour after the scheduled start of the game, the players finally took the field. Their entrance was preceded with an announcement read by former Mayor Honey Fitzgerald, who had been present during the discussions in the umpires' room. Johnson had agreed to allow the players to make a public statement, which Hooper hastily composed for Honey Fitz to read. The somewhat vague remarks informed those in attendance that the players would be playing the game "not because we think we are getting a fair deal, because we are not," but for the fans who have "always given us . . . loyal support, and for the wounded soldiers and sailors who are in the grandstand waiting for us."[17] Although few in attendance had any idea of the substance of the meetings which had taken place over the last twenty-four hours, many were aware of the players' concerns for their Series paychecks from comments in the press. As Hooper had suspected and as a scattering of boos throughout the park confirmed, the players were unwise to assume that the fans would necessarily embrace their position.

The Red Sox quickly discovered that any assumptions they may have had of their own regarding an imminent Series championship were also not shared—by the Cubs. Hippo Vaughn finally notched the win which had eluded him in games 1 and 3. Scattering five hits, allowing only two runners to advance as far as second base, and assisted by three double plays in the field behind him, Vaughn shut down the home team 3–0. The effort lowered his ERA in the three complete games he pitched to 1.00. No pitcher with as much work in a World Series has had a losing record and a better ERA.

Lefty Tyler was on the mound again for the Cubs in game 6, while Mays returned for Boston. An unseasonable cold snap dropped temperatures to forty degrees at game time. The weather and, as many in the press speculated, rumors about another strike threat affected attendance. Only 15,238, the smallest crowd of the entire Series and the sparsest attendance at a Series game since 1909, when only 10,535 watched Detroit edge Pittsburgh 5–4 in the sixth game of their championship matchup, turned out to see whether the Sox could maintain their unblemished record in World Series play.

Mays tossed another gem. Allowing only one runner to reach second base, he scattered three Chicago singles and set them down in order in six of the nine innings. The only Cub run came in the fourth when Merkle drove in Flack, who had worked his way around to third on a single, a fielder's choice, and a stolen base. Tyler pitched almost as well. Four infield hits and a Texas Leaguer were all the offense the Red Sox bats could manage. But Tyler, like Jones in game 5, hurt his own cause with free passes to five Red Sox. Two of these came in the third and led directly to Boston runs. Mays walked on four pitches to start the inning and moved to second on Hooper's sacrifice. Shean worked Tyler for a walk to put two men on. They moved up ninety feet on Strunk's groundout. Then the decisive play of the game. Whiteman waited on a Tyler curve and drove it hard into right. Flack, who had hesitated a split second at the crack of the bat, then dashed forward to snag the liner. The ball ricocheted off the heel of his glove for a two-base error. Mays and Shean scampered home with the two unearned runs. They stood up the rest of the way.

The Red Sox batted only .186 as a team in the Series, compared to the Cubs' barely more impressive .210. Boston's pitchers allowed only ten earned runs in the six games for a team ERA of 1.70. Chicago's staff—Vaughn and Tyler, that is, with an inning each of relief from Hendrix and Phil Douglas—compiled a team ERA of 1.04, the lowest ever in a six-game Series. The Sox committed only one error in the field, a harmless muff by Whiteman in game 2, while three of the five Cub miscues led to Boston runs. Ed Barrow clearly recognized what had spelled the margin of victory for his club: "There have been greater World's Champions," he acknowledged, "but none that fielded a tighter game. When one looks at the scores by which we won, he can appreciate what a few errors at the wrong time could have done to us."[18]

For their winning performance, the Red Sox players each earned shares of $1,103. The Cubs received $671 apiece. Both payoffs were the lowest in World Series history and bore out the fears of the players which had precipitated the strike threat. Hooper's additional concerns about the sporting press's reaction to the players' point of view and the trustworthiness of Johnson's promise against any reprisals proved equally well founded.

With few exceptions among them, the baseball writers placed blame for the "unpleasant protest" on the "mercenary-minded" players. Taylor Spink, one of the official scorers for the Series, reporting for *The Sporting News,* described the encounter between the players and the commissioners as "a nasty situation."[19] "Their [the players] judgment in pulling a strike at such a time was more than deplorable," he concluded, "it was downright stupid." Covering the Series for the *Spalding Guide,* John Foster characterized the players' action as "devoid of reason."[20] Since the World Series "was not originated as a co-partnership affair in which the players were to be governors as well as governed," Foster explained, the players' argument was "without warrant." *Baseball Magazine* editor William Phe-

lon joined many who explained the poor turnout for the final game
as a direct reaction to the threatened strike. "Interest in Boston
seemed to evaporate after the players' strike," he observed. "The
fans didn't seem to be with the noble athletes, apparently taking the
view that they were dead lucky to get any post-season money at
all."[21]

Although the players' judgment in threatening a strike drew virtually unanimous criticism from the baseball press, their integrity on
the field once the matter was settled was above question. The press
exuberantly tossed bouquets their way. "Whatever the shortcomings
of the players may be," observed Richter of the *Reach Guide,* "their
honesty in the playing of the game is incontestable."[22] "They gained
every reputation for admirable and honest play," chimed Foster of
the *Spalding Guide.* "After the argument was ended, they walked to
the diamond and played one of the best games of the series with all
the courage, honesty, and grit which the ball player has surrounded
himself for years."[23]

Similarly, Hooper drew praise for his behavior in the whole affair.
The *Boston Globe* assured its readers that Harry "was not a ring-
leader in the trouble, but that he had been selected to present the
case of the ball players."[24] This "trouble," wrote Charles Spink to
Hooper, "would have been more than an incident if you and Les
Mann had not shown the consideration you did."[25] Years later, Taylor Spink recalled Hooper's effective handling of the situation "after
Mr. Johnson (slightly under the weather) put his arm around you
and told you to go out and play for the honor of the American
League."[26] Spink appreciated Hooper's ability to recognize the commissioner's condition and to avert an ugly scene.

The day after the World Series ended, the Boston players assembled at Fenway to pick up their winner's shares and to pack their
belongings for the off-season. They also received their final paychecks of the shortened regular season. In a maneuver to cut their
losses, the Major League owners had agreed among themselves to
withhold the balance of the players' salaries due after Labor Day by
"releasing" them from their contracts. They further agreed not to
invade each other's rosters. This latter move negated the free-agency
status of the players which contract releases normally provided. It
was a callous reminder of the owners' power and the effectiveness of
their collusion.

With their Series bonuses, the Red Sox players were in better
shape than most financially as they looked at the months ahead.
They fared no differently, however, from any other players in the

Majors regarding their temporarily deferred wartime obligations. Many of them immediately departed for military service or war-related employment. Fred Thomas, for example, who had been granted a furlough from the navy to participate in the Series, headed back to Great Lakes Naval Station. Wally Mayer planned a brief visit to his home in Cincinnati before reporting to Camp Jackson at Columbia, South Carolina. Bill Pertica, anticipating a call from the navy, registered the day before and was awaiting his assignment. Mays expected induction into the army any day. Others, like Strunk, Bush, Agnew, Ruth, Wagner, and Walt Kinney, had offers from shipyards and munitions works. With his wife and two children awaiting him, Hooper left for his home in California.[27]

Three months after the Series, Hooper and his Boston teammates again felt the heavy hand of the baseball establishment. This time it affected them in a more galling and lasting manner than the diminishment of their paychecks. Shortly before Christmas, they received a letter from Heydman, who was serving his term as president of the National Commission. Hooper's worst fear about Johnson's "guarantee" against reprisals for the players' abortive challenge was realized. "Owing to the disgraceful conduct of the players in the strike during the series," Heydler declared, the Boston players "would be fined the World Series emblems" that were traditionally awarded the winners.[28]

Angered that baseball had broken its word and saddened for those players for whom 1918 was their first and perhaps only World Series appearance, Hooper began a lifelong campaign to try to get the emblems (actually lapel pins) for those who had earned them. At stake, Hooper explained, were not only the restoration of the symbols of the Red Sox victory "in a hard-fought Series," but also the removal from all the players' records of a stigma "caused by the Commissioners who were intoxicated and tried to cover up their own disgraceful actions by deliberately breaking a promise."[29] He initiated a lengthy and persistent correspondence with every baseball commissioner from Kennesaw Mountain Landis to Bowie Kuhn. Although Landis assured Hooper in 1922 that he would look into the matter, he never replied to Hooper's inquiry and a detailed report of the affair which he had asked Harry to prepare for him.[30] Only Kuhn ever directly responded to Hooper, and then it was simply to inform him "that there is nothing I can do at this late date."[31] Kuhn expressed sympathy for Hooper's cause but declined to reverse "a decision made more than a half century ago, [for it] undoubtedly would lead others to request a review of decisions made in the long ago past." When he died in 1974, Hooper was no closer to securing the emblems (rumored to be locked in a safe in the commissioner's office with a letter from Johnson ordering them never to be awarded[32]) than he was in 1918.[33]

Harry's own performance on the playing field during the Series did not match his record in his three previous appearances in postseason play. Coming into the 1918 championship, Hooper had compiled a World Series batting average of .319, including seven extra-base hits, thirteen runs scored, six RBIs, and three stolen bases. Against the Cubs, Hooper managed only four singles in twenty official at bats for a .200 average. Although he had a couple of sacrifices at critical times for the Red Sox, he was otherwise not a factor with a bat, shut out in all of the important offensive categories.

In Harry's own assessment, two factors probably accounted for his poor bat work.[34] First, in Vaughn and Tyler he faced two of the Majors' best left-handers throughout the Series. Considering that Boston's only other left-handed-hitting regular, Amos Strunk, fared worse than Hooper (.174), that no Red Sox player except Wally Schang (four for nine, .444) hit better than .250, and that only two teammates had more hits (McInnis and Whiteman each had five), Harry's effort can be put in more favorable perspective. Second, as team captain and the players' spokesman in the negotiations with the commissioners and relations with the press, Harry had other matters on his mind besides the games to be played. These responsibilities no doubt took a toll on his mental preparation for the games and hampered his performance at the plate.

Not diminished in any sense by his disappointing work at the plate was the high regard with which Hooper was held by players, management, and the press. His role in the strike threat and single-handed effort afterward to secure the winners' emblems won him lasting admiration from those players who applauded his principled representation of their interests. Others, notably Charles and Taylor Spink, Judge Landis, and Ellery Clark, appreciated his honest manner and reasoned presentations. Ironically, as Hooper's star rose as a result of the unsuccessful strike threat, that of his main antagonist in the affair, Ban Johnson, sank significantly. Again the establishment-friendly press was careful in its criticism of the commissioners. Richter of the *Reach Guide,* for example, suggested that the players' protest against the new distribution plan for the Series receipts "was not altogether without merit."[35] But no one directly censured Johnson for his tardiness in getting to the ballpark for the fifth game and the condition he was in upon arrival. This came later, and it primarily took the form of opposition to the three-man commission and advocacy of a strong one-man administration to replace it. John Heydler, who had uttered few words throughout the negotiations between the commissioners and the players, later said that "the spectacle in the umpires' room" had convinced him and others of the outmoded character of the National Commission and the need for more effective government of the game.[36] If that leadership could act in a more dignified manner, as the players had demonstrated they were capable of doing, so much the better.

Hooper's performance and Johnson's demise hardly ushered in a new era of respect and power for the players. The writers' criticism of the players' position and the subsequent decision to withhold the Series emblems typified a pattern of "condemnations and penalties . . . contrived to disgrace them [the players] into submission."[37] Still generally publicized and treated as "dumb plowboys and muscle bound characters who were incapable of thinking," the players had little reason to expect that their efforts to protect their interests would be viewed as serious, responsible behavior.[38] Hooper's individual example, though, and the qualities which supposedly shaped it—his college education, personal integrity, work ethic, strong devotion to family—increased his stock and appeal, if not that of the fraternity for which he was a spokesman. Transcending the negative stereotype of professional ballplayers that persisted throughout his era, Harry represented a new breed that had yet to establish itself.

10

Changing Sox

I will deal any player except Harry Hooper.
—Harry Frazee, December 27, 1919

A nation at peace, a championship for the home team. Amid the celebration of the Red Sox's fourth World Series victory of the decade and the armistice of November 11, 1918, few in Boston, or elsewhere, could have imagined how illusory the promise of both triumphs were. Just as the arrival of American troops on the battlefields of Europe had proved decisive for the Allies, the presence of President Woodrow Wilson at the head of the American delegation to the Paris Peace Conference in January 1919 announced the intention of the United States to influence the shape of the postwar world. At the height of his prestige, Wilson carried the hopes of both his countrymen and the exhausted Europeans for the millennium that he said was possible. It quickly became apparent at the conference, however, that Wilson's abstract idealism did not appeal to the Allied representatives, who dealt in balance-of-power politics and demanded harsh terms for Germany. Wilson returned to the United States with a treaty that shocked the progressive elements of both the Democratic and Republican parties for its severity, angered Irish-Americans for failing to achieve self-rule for Ireland, and divided the nation in a debate about its role and responsibilities in world affairs.

While winners and losers emerged from the divided spoils of Versailles, pent-up frustrations with wartime shortages and inconveniences and impatience with the reconversion process to a peacetime economy and social order revived old tensions and revealed new antagonisms at home. Nearly five million Americans went to war, but many found no jobs waiting for them when they returned. Often they found their old jobs filled by southern blacks, who had migrated northward to find work in urban factories, or immigrants, who were unaffected by the draft. The curtailment of government contracts produced massive layoffs in war-production industries and added to the workers' troubles. Those who had jobs faced lower wages and rising prices at the market. The bitterness of jobless veterans turned to violence throughout the country. Ugly race riots in Arkansas, Texas, and several northern cities dramatized the anger of white workers toward their new competitors in the labor market. Shocking the nation as much as these incidents was the wave of strikes that rolled across the land in 1919. Over twenty-six hundred strikes involving more than four million workers underscored labor's unrest and seemed an ominous portent for the peaceful future Wilson had promised.[1]

Much of the blame for these developments focused on political dissidents in the United States who rallied to the flag of bolshevism. Creation of the Communists' Third International in March 1919 inspired uprisings in Eastern Europe and aroused fears that a red revolution would soon engulf the Western world. The discovery of dozens of mail bombs in April and bomb explosions in eight American cities on the evening of June 2 convinced many in the United States that the revolution had begun. With Attorney General A. Mitchell Palmer sounding the alarm of the so-called Red Scare, nativist and patriotic groups carried their wartime animosity toward nonconformists and dissenters forward in a new campaign against radicals and aliens.[2]

Fear and hatred of foreigners particularly influenced a movement throughout the country to affirm the virtues of "one hundred percent Americanism." Various patriotic organizations, such as the Loyal American League, the Association for Constitutional Government, and the Sons of the American Revolution, attracted large memberships united in their desire to promote and protect "American" values and institutions. Echoing the observation of Nicholas Murray Butler, the president of Columbia University, that the nation would be "saved . . . by those who look with respect and reverence upon the great series of happenings extending from the voyage of the *Mayflower*," these and similar groups voiced strong nationalistic sentiments.[3] The symbols of the American spirit—historical landmarks, the Constitution, the flag—became special objects of veneration. Although some, like the resurgent Ku Klux Klan, pursued the concept of a homogenous Americanism to violent extremes, most focused on more comfortable and less threatening ways to celebrate their national pride and identity. No place, suggested an editorial in *The Sporting News*, offered Americans greater prospect "to keep a lot of us out of trouble" during these "ticklish times" than the ballpark.[4]

Although the doughboys had returned from Europe and the ball-players among them were back in the camps of their clubs before their war service, the Major League owners initially planned for another lean year in 1919. They agreed to keep their training schedules within the self-imposed wartime limits of the previous season, restrict the new campaign to 140 games, limit club payrolls, and reduce rosters from twenty-five to twenty-one players. It quickly became apparent in the crowds that turned out for games in the early going, though, that baseball was in for a prosperous year. Spectators were filling the parks in numbers that had not been seen since before the Federal League challenge. Even "the most pronounced optimist," observed Sanborn of the *Spalding Guide,* could not fail "to be surprised by the quick recovery in popular estimation made by professional Base Ball in 1919."[5]

The restored rosters and the excitement of competitive pennant races certainly contributed to the revolving turnstiles. And turn they did, as six and a half million fans, more than double the previous year's number, poured into Major League parks. But more than watching baseball's best perform again, the postwar crowds appreciated the reassuring patterns and rituals of the national game and the momentary escape it provided from the crises of the daily headlines. In the aftermath of a horrible war and the questions it raised about the blessings of progress and the promise of modern times, baseball offered a nostalgic link to a simpler past. Its alleged native origins provided a framework for the attribution of such ideals and images to its agency as ethnic assimilation, individualism, rags-to-riches opportunism, and primitive pastoralism. In a society grown increasingly more bureaucratic, systematic, and complicated, the game's heroes assumed a "compensatory cultural function" for many who despaired at "the passing of the traditional dream of success, the erosion of Victorian values, and feelings of individual powerlessness."[6] Although baseball's appeal rested fundamentally upon the pleasure of its play and observation, its meaning transcended the nature of the game with its sensitive balance of physical skill, problem solving, and chance, and reflected wider social contexts.[7]

Whatever role the game played in individual lives or the national culture, it had a basic obligation to provide honest competition and engender public trust. Yet despite the attempts of baseball magnates and publicists to keep the game above reproach, it frequently failed to uphold the reputation they claimed. Gambling, bribery, and game-fixing scandals plagued the professional game from its beginnings. A Buffalo writer in the 1860s observed that "any professional ball club will 'throw' a game if there is money in it. A horse race is a pretty safe thing to speculate on, in comparison with an average ball match."[8] A corrupt foursome for the Louisville Grays earned a lifetime banishment from the game for their role in dumping games that cost their club the National League pennant in 1877. Umpire Richard Higham suffered a similar fate when an investigation revealed that he had placed bets on teams which he favored with his calls in the 1882 NL season. Undoubtedly, the most unsavory ballplayer after the turn of the century was Hal Chase. Until his ultimate suspension from the game while playing for the New York Giants in 1919, Prince Hal displayed a penchant for crookedness as impressive as his glove work around first base. Betting on games in which he played, conspiring with teammates to throw games, and bribing opponents, Chase cavorted through fifteen Major League seasons while the baseball establishment largely looked the other way at his indiscretions. Fittingly, the season of his departure signaled how wide the gap had grown between the rhetorical representation of the game's innocence and the actual corruptibility of the playing fields.

Hal Chase's lingering presence was one element of a gathering storm in the Major Leagues in 1919. The bitter conclusion to the 1918 World Series and the owners' collusion to cap salaries in the new season were others. But a nation struggling to return to normalcy was little interested in front-office matters or jurisdictional debates between the owners and the National Commission. Fans bought their tickets for the entertainment of the professional diamonds, not the unseen machinations away from them. As the season progressed, however, weaknesses within the game's governance structure that often confused lines of authority and frustrated effective policing efforts brought the storm closer to the field of play. The fury of its outbreak was particularly felt in Boston and Chicago. Its aftermath profoundly affected the direction of Harry Hooper's final years in the Majors and the roles he assumed in completing his playing career.

Despite the likely rise of the caliber of competition in the Major Leagues in 1919 to prewar levels, Hooper anticipated that the Red Sox would again contend for the pennant in the new season. "The 1918 team," he felt, "was as good as any that ever played baseball," and the return of those who had left for military service promised to strengthen the club.[9] As Harry had already learned in the news regarding the withholding of the World Series pins, though, the December mail brought more than holiday greetings. It now delivered a letter to the team captain from Ed Barrow informing him that the club had traded Duffy Lewis, Ernie Shore, and Dutch Leonard to the Yankees.

Frazee's decision to unload the Boston veterans made little base-ball sense, but then no one ever accused the Red Sox owner of having too much of it. "He had no business in baseball," Hooper stated, remembering the "evil genie from Peoria's" first moves in the ruination of the club.[10] What Boston received in the trade was scarcely worth the trouble: Frank Gilhooley, a light-hitting outfielder in the twilight of his career; Al Walters, an even more feeble-hitting second-string catcher; and two pitchers, Slim Love and Ray Caldwell, the former never pitching a game for the Red Sox before being traded to Detroit and the latter going 7–4 for Boston before heading to Cleveland in a cash deal.

Frazee tried to explain the trade as a consequence of a defending world champion team not having any room on its roster or seeing any reason to make room. His explanation fooled no one. The real reason for the trade—and the subsequent sale of Caldwell—was evi-dent in the low gate receipts of the 1918 season and World Series and the poor ticket sales at his theaters. Frazee had overextended himself in acquiring Bush, McInnis, Schang, Shean, and Strunk for his base-ball club and backing losers for his stages. He needed funds desper-ately. The deal with New York relieved the Boston payroll of several high-salaried players and netted Frazee fifty thousand dollars. He parceled it out in small pieces. Only Hooper at nine thousand dollars and Ruth with a new three-year contract worth ten thousand dollars a season received salary increases. The others remained where they had been in 1918 or accepted reductions.

Despite the trade, the Red Sox started well, winning four of their first five and leading the AL through the first week of the new sea-son. It was the high point of their year. Over the next month, Boston began to slip steadily in the standings, finally dropping out of the first division on May 22. Except for one day in June, the club did not move above fifth place the rest of the way. The Red Sox finished the season in sixth tied with Saint Louis 20½ games behind Chicago. Their 1917 championship roster completely restored after the war, the White Sox combined the best hitting in the Majors with an effective pitch-ing staff led by former Red Sox Ed Cicotte and nipped Cleveland in a race that went down to the final week of the season. Boston's 66–71 record was the club's worst since 1907 and marked the first time in Hooper's career that he had played for a losing team.

That the Red Sox failed to keep the AL pennant was less a surprise than how completely their championship form unraveled and how far they fell. The strong play of Chicago and the other teams ahead of them in the standings certainly affected their descent, but it only partly explained it. The principal factor in the club's collapse was the breakdown of its pitching, the perennial key to Boston's success over the last decade along with strong defense. For the first time since 1906, the staff produced an ERA above 3.00 (3.30) and recorded the fewest number of strikeouts in the league. Out with a sore arm for all but two starts of the entire season was Joe Bush. The casualty list mounted behind him. Pennock pitched only once during the first month and a half of the season, Jones missed three weeks with a tired arm midway through it, and even Ruth, pressed into the rotation occasionally, passed up a few starts with a nagging knee injury.

The most damaging blow to Boston's pitching came on July 13 when Carl Mays, his club trailing the White Sox 4–0 in Comiskey, stormed off the mound after the second inning and announced that he was through throwing for the Red Sox. With only five wins in sixteen decisions at the time, Mays was frustrated with his teammates' lack of run production behind him. In June, for example, Boston scored only eight runs in the seven games that Mays pitched. The two that he won that month were by scores of 2–0 and 2–1. Although his 2.48 ERA was the lowest on the club, his losses were the most. Mays was fuming at his misfortune and looking for someone to blame. When Wally Schang's low throw to second to thwart an attempted steal clipped Mays on the side of his head, the surly pitcher had had enough. Slamming his glove down in the dugout, Mays stomped off to the clubhouse. When Barrow sent Jones to retrieve him, Mays snarled, "Tell Barrow I've gone fishing."[11]

Ordinarily, Mays's walkout would have earned him a suspension from the club and a hefty fine. But these were not ordinary times for the financially strapped Frazee and he saw an opportunity to realize more than a few days' salary savings from his pitcher's action. Directing Barrow not to suspend Mays, Frazee contacted the Yankee co-owners, Cols. Jacob Ruppert and Tillingham Huston, to see if they were interested in striking another deal with his club. They were eager to talk. Ignoring an order to the league's teams from Ban Johnson not to negotiate with the Red Sox for Mays until the pitcher had been disciplined and returned to the Boston club in good standing, the colonels concluded the deal on July 29, sending pitchers Allan Russell and Bob McGraw and forty thousand dollars to Boston for the temperamental, but talented, right-hander.[12] Johnson immediately suspended Mays and ordered the AL umpires not to allow him to pitch in a game in a Yankee uniform, but the New York owners countered with a court injunction against Johnson that permitted Mays to take the mound for their club. In his new surroundings, Mays found the wins coming his way again. For the last two months of the season, he posted nine victories in twelve decisions and a team-best 1.65 ERA. His work helped the Yankees to a third place finish in the standings with an 80–59 record, their strongest season in thirteen years. It was evident that Mays's new club was a rising force in the American League. The move that would secure the Yankees' surge to the top waited in the wings.

For only the second time in his career after his rookie season, Hooper failed to lead the club in either at bats or any of the principal offensive categories other than stolen bases. Hampered at the outset of the season with a case of Spanish influenza, part of a pandemic sweeping the United States in late 1918 and the early spring months of 1919, Harry found his energies further sapped in the attention he had to give to restructuring the Boston outfield and trying to understand Frazee's player transactions. As frustrating as the defensive orchestration of Ruth, Roth, Gilhooley, and the others was, Hooper was particularly disheartened with the circumstances—and consequences—of his teammates' departures. They constituted a simple, sad equation: "To get money, Frazee sold players. He tore our team to pieces."[13]

The most shocking rending of the Boston roster came a few months after the season ended. On January 5, 1920, the club announced the sale of Babe Ruth to the Yankees. In a straight financial deal, the New York colonels paid $125,000 for the Babe and added a $350,000 loan to Frazee in the form of a mortgage on Fenway Park. The sale price alone was more than twice that paid previously for any single player. Ironically, that man, too, was a Red Sox: Tris Speaker.

Like Spoke's departure, the news of Ruth's sale produced an outcry of protest among the Boston faithful. Signs quickly appeared on Faneuil Hall, the Boston Public Library, and other historic landmarks in the city derisively announcing that these civic treasures were also "For Sale." Frazee's latest play, a failed comedy entitled *My Lady Friends,* collected graffiti on its billboards declaring: "Those are the only friends he has left." Frazee did have a few in the Boston press, however, who dutifully reported the owner's line. Blaming Ruth for the club's lowly finish in 1919, Frazee claimed that the Babe "had become simply impossible, and the Boston club could no longer put up with his eccentricities."[14] Apparently, Ruth's record-breaking twenty-nine home runs were among the undesirable oddities of his performance for Frazee dismissed them as "more spectacular than useful."[15] Suggesting that Ruth would never again be the player he had been in the last season, some sportswriters echoed the owner's contention that the club would be improved without him.

That was hard to figure. In his first full season as an everyday player in the Boston lineup, Ruth had fulfilled the enormous promise of his hitting which Hooper had first observed in 1915. Leading the club in batting with a .322 average, Babe posted the best numbers in the Majors in all of the power categories—slugging average (.657), home runs (29), total bases (284), and runs batted in (114). Underscoring the completeness of his play were Babe's league-leading on-base percentage (.456), runs scored (103), and fielding average (.992). The latter particularly pleased Harry as his pupil's work even surpassed his own. To see all this talent heading to New York, though, made Hooper "sick to my stomach."[16] Convinced that Ruth's departure "had spoiled whatever chances the club had of getting in the Series again," Harry had concluded that it was time for him to move on to a new club as well.[17]

Such plans, however, were easier made than met. Since the collapse of both the Federal League and the Players Fraternity, the Major League owners had reestablished their tight grip on the game. Controlling club expenses principally by reducing rosters and payrolls and curbing the negotiating power of the players in the absence of a competing professional market, the magnates faced few checks on their business. Moreover, their power had been strengthened in their ability to withstand serious legal challenges, of which the most important was a suit filed by the owners of the Baltimore Federal club alleging that the Major Leagues had conspired with other Federal League officials to ban them from the game's top business level in direct violation of antitrust laws.[18] Six years of litigation later, the case reached the U.S. Supreme Court. Speaking for the Court, Justice Oliver Wendell Holmes upheld the 1921 judgment of the District of Columbia Court of Appeals that professional baseball deserved an exemption from antitrust laws because it was not interstate commerce.[19] The ruling not only affirmed the game as "sport, not trade," but supported the broad authority of the owners to conduct their affairs as they saw fit. In particular, Holmes upheld the legality of the reserve clause "to protect the rights of clubs operating under that agreement to retain the services of sufficient players." The ruling was a complete victory for the owners, leaving the players little to negotiate with management except the threat of retirement or actual departure from the game.

Hooper briefly considered both options while he debated whether to sign his contract for the 1920 season. Despite his modest performance in 1919, Harry felt that he still had several good years of Major League ball left in him. He knew, though, that he had to prove it to others to enhance his market value. He concluded that sitting out the season would do more harm to his chances to sign on with a new club than having a solid season with the Red Sox. If Frazee stayed true to form, he would likely be interested in unloading Hooper and his relatively high salary if Harry commanded some interest around the league. Frazee helped Harry's decision somewhat with a new contract offer of ten thousand dollars making him the highest-paid player on the club. Notwithstanding the owner's respect for Hooper, the salary increase reflected Frazee's recognition that any further diminution of the Red Sox roster would shatter whatever hopes the team had for a decent showing in the new season. As the only member of the 1912 championship team still with the club and, along with Everett Scott and Mike McNally, one of the few remaining from the great 1915 team, Harry provided a link to the glory years that Frazee was not yet prepared to sever.

The Ruthless Red Sox, however, reminded few in the AL of the Boston teams which had dominated the league over the last decade. Slipping even deeper in the standings, the Red Sox finished 25½ games behind Speaker's Indians with a 72–81 record. While the Babe launched pitch after pitch into the outer reaches of the league's parks on his way to fifty-four home runs, 137 RBIs, and a .376 batting average, Boston's hitters managed just a .269 team average and twenty-two home runs on the season. Only last-place Philadelphia had a lower average; no club hit fewer homers. Even the reputable pitching staff of Jones, Bush, Pennock, and second-year man Waite Hoyt seemed to get caught up in the despair of a failing franchise. Their combined record of 50–50 and 4.06 ERA hardly compensated for the team's lack of offense.

It did not help matters in Boston to notice how well the team's other expatriate, Carl Mays, was throwing for the Yankees. Leading the league with six shutouts, he had become the ace of his new team. He was on the mound for the Yankees against Cleveland on August 16 when a win could have pushed New York ahead of the Indians into a first place tie with Chicago. Cleveland held off a ninth-inning rally to beat Mays, 4–3, that day, but the victory was no consolation for the terrible tragedy that occurred earlier in the game. For in the fifth inning, one of Mays's high, hard fastballs crashed against the left temple of Ray Chapman as he crouched at bat for the pitch. The popular Indian shortstop died less than twenty-four hours later. As remarkable as Cleveland's pennant under the pall of Chapman's death was the work of Mays the rest of the season. He finished the year with twenty-six wins against eleven defeats, second only to Jim Bagby of the Indians in victories and winning percentage. A year later, no pitcher in either league had a better record than Mays. He went 27–9 as the Yankees won their first pennant. The other outstanding pitcher on the Yankee staff that championship season was Waite Hoyt. Frazee had sent him to New York in an eight-player deal shortly after the conclusion of the 1920 season.[20] Hoyt found the new surroundings to his liking and launched a nine-year career with the Yankees during which he averaged over seventeen wins a season.

Intent on bolstering his trade value as much as providing needed punch in the lineup with Ruth's departure, Hooper fashioned the best season yet of his Major League career at the plate. Posting new marks in batting average (.312), on-base percentage (.411), slugging average (.470), hits (167), doubles (30), triples (17), home runs (7), and RBIs (53), Harry replaced the Babe as the team leader in all of these categories, including walks (88) and runs scored (91). The only important offensive area in which he did not pace the club was stolen bases. Mike Menosky, an aggressive outfielder acquired from Washington over the winter, pilfered twenty-three to Harry's sixteen. This total was Hooper's lowest since his rookie year and gave perhaps the first indication that eleven years with the Red Sox were beginning to take its toll on his legs. Eleven errors in the field, too, a number exceeded in his career only once previously, suggested that he had lost a step or two in the outfield as well.

While Hooper was enjoying his fine season in Boston, the dramatic epilogue to the 1919 World Series was being played out in Chicago. Claiming that he had "lived a thousand years in the last twelve months" harboring his guilt and fending off accusations about his play in the championship loss to Cincinnati, Eddie Cicotte confessed to the Grand Jury of Cook County, Illinois, on September 28 what the baseball world had long suspected yet dreaded to have confirmed.[21] "I don't know why I did it," began the ace of the Chicago pitching staff as he launched a lurid tale of corruption and deceit about how eight members of the heavily favored White Sox had thrown the Series. A few hours later, Joe Jackson confirmed Cicotte's story in his own appearance before the jury. Emerging from the hearing, Shoeless Joe managed a smile and remarked "I got a big load off my chest. I'm feeling better."[22]

The Old Roman, Charlie Comiskey, found nothing in his ballplayers' confessions to make him smile. He immediately issued a telegram to Cicotte, Jackson, and the others notifying them of their indefinite suspension from the club.[23] "If you are innocent of any wrongdoing," Comiskey informed them, "you and each of you will be reinstated; if you are guilty, you will be retired from Organized Baseball for the rest of your lives if I can accomplish it."[24] Releasing the telegram to the press, Comiskey reaffirmed the vow he first made when rumors of a fix surfaced during the Series to root out any crookedness on his team. His quick action on the players' testimony also sought to upstage Ban Johnson, whose contempt for Comiskey had clouded his judgment in not taking the initial rumors seriously. Johnson had dismissed Comiskey's concerns about a fix as "the whelp of a beaten cur."[25] Yet Johnson, stung by criticisms of his handling of the threatened players' strike in the 1918 Series and the Mays' case, could ignore neither the mounting evidence his own investigation had gathered against the White Sox nor the opportunity to embarrass Comiskey. Supplying Justice Charles MacDonald of the Cook County Criminal Courts Division with the names of dozens of individuals who could shed some light on the alleged fix, Johnson provided the grand jury with the ammunition it needed to subpoena Cicotte and Jackson.

On October 22, having completed its investigation, the grand jury returned indictments for fraud against the eight White Sox and five others, including Hal Chase, for their roles in arranging the fix. Although the testimony of the indicted players and news of the formal charges against them shocked those who believed in the incorruptibility of the playing fields, others closer to the game were less surprised to learn what the Chicagoans had allegedly done. Hooper attributed the players' action to their sense of aggrievement regarding their low salaries and the penurious ways of Comiskey. Citing the comparatively low wages of such established stars as Cicotte ($5,500), Jackson ($6,000), Weaver ($6,000), and Gandil ($4,000) with others of similar records and experience, for example, Heinie Groh ($8,000), Jake Daubert ($9,000), and Edd Roush ($10,000) of the Reds, Harry saw "these fellows up there winning pennants and not getting nothing and I guess they just figured that here came along something they could have."[26]

Comiskey's tightness with the club's money irritated his players in other ways as well. He allowed them only three dollars a day for meals, for example, while the league norm was four. Commie did not hesitate, however, to entertain the press and friends with lavish buffets and flowing bars. The way he had deprived Cicotte of a

$10,000 bonus in 1917 still rankled the pitcher and his teammates. Promising his star right-hander the handsome bonus if he won thirty games that season, Comiskey ordered the Chicago manager, Pants Rowland, to bench him after he reached twenty-eight wins. Comiskey explained the decision as a strategic move to rest Cicotte for the World Series, but most saw it as a betrayal to keep the club's purse strings knotted. "They had a wonderful team there," Hooper summarized, but a stingy owner and a few "crooks" in the game proved their downfall.[27]

Regarding the latter, Hooper had two particularly in mind, Chase and Gandil. When Harry learned that Chase was one of the indicted parties, he was hardly surprised. Familiar with Prince Hal since his days at Saint Mary's when the New York first baseman helped coach the Phoenix in the off-season, Harry had always felt that Chase "just wasn't all there."[28] Hooper could never reconcile Chase's superb baseball skills, especially his fielding, with his addiction to petty thievery and unsportsmanlike conduct. Recalling the fights which Chase frequently instigated while he played for Bay Area teams between Major League campaigns and his perverse pride in stealing cigars and other small items, Harry had concluded that Chase "just wasn't straight shooting."[29] As for Gandil, who, like Chase, was frequently seen in the company of known gamblers, Harry considered him to be "the crook of the bunch" among the indicted players.[30] Indeed, Gandil's longtime association with sports gambler and bookmaker Joseph ("Sport") Sullivan was the key connection in launching the Series fix.

Despite the indictments, the trial of the Black Sox did not open until June 27, 1921. It had been delayed because of the necessity of drawing up a second set of indictments against the players when the initial charges were dismissed for lack of evidence. The main problem with the prosecution's case was the mysterious disappearance of the grand jury's papers, including the players' confessions. The entire case against the players had to be rebuilt. This time, however, the players repudiated their confessions, leaving the Cook County jury with little hard evidence of the "conspiracy to commit an illegal act" with which the eight had been charged.[31] On August 2 the jury returned a verdict of not guilty.

The decision of the jury, however, was not the judgment of organized baseball. The very next day, Kenesaw Mountain Landis, barely nine months in office as the game's first commissioner after the collapse of the three-man National Commission in the wake of the Series scandal, issued his opinion in the matter. "Regardless of the verdict of juries," Landis explained in a statement to the press, "no player who throws a ball game, no player that undertakes or promises to throw a ball game, no player that sits in a conference with a bunch of crooked players and gamblers where the ways and means of throwing a game are discussed and does not promptly tell his club about it, will ever play professional baseball."[32] Hired to convince the country that the integrity of the national pastime had been restored beyond a doubt, Landis destroyed the players' hopes that their acquittal would return them to the field of play.

The commissioner's decision also permanently deprived Comiskey and the White Sox of the services of tens of thousands of dollars' worth of player talent. Despite the suspensions he had ordered for the eight in September 1920, Comiskey had continued to hold open the possibility of their return to the club if they were cleared of all charges. He had even drawn up their contracts for the 1921 season, including hefty pay increases and bonuses for several of them.[33] But Comiskey knew that he could not field a team on the uncertain outcome of the court's proceedings. Moreover, even if his players were acquitted, Comiskey wondered how their contempt of him would affect their trustworthiness in the future and whether the Chicago fans would forgive the tainted players and return to the ballpark to see them perform. Seeking roster insurance for the 1921 season and a way to restore the public trust in his club, Comiskey immediately started looking for players who could fill the gaping holes in his lineup and clean up the team's image. No player interested him more in both regards than Harry Hooper.

Chicago's needs exactly complemented Hooper's plans to leave Boston. But Harry still had to win his gamble that Frazee would rather trade him than pay him. If Harry had any hesitation about calling the owner's bluff, it was lost when the club announced in December that Hugh Duffy would succeed Barrow as the new manager of the team. Although Hooper had typically not pressed for the job, it had long been speculated in the Boston sporting press that he would be the club's next manager whenever Barrow stepped down.[34] When Frazee appointed Duffy, a hitting hero of the Boston Braves in the 1890s and an experienced Major League manager with brief stints at the helm for the Philadelphia Nationals and the White Sox before becoming the Red Sox head scout, Hooper was disappointed that he had not been given a chance to accept or refuse the management. He resolved to make things as difficult as he could for Frazee in his contract demands for 1921, even if he risked not playing at all.

Considering the season he had just had, however, Hooper knew that Frazee could ignore neither his value to the Red Sox nor his appeal to other clubs, most notably Chicago. In January, Harry informed Frazee that the owner's initial offer of another ten-thousand-dollar contract for the 1921 season was unsatisfactory. He told Frazee that he would not sign for less than fifteen thousand dollars, an amount representing a 50 percent pay raise for himself and nearly double what the next-highest-paid player on the Red Sox received. For several weeks the two corresponded on the matter, Frazee gradually increasing his offer, Harry holding firm. Hooper's holdout, the only one of his career, attracted the attention of the press, but Duffy denied there was any "serious trouble" in signing him. If the manager had any doubts regarding Hooper's joining the club, a reporter observed, "his views would not be as cheerful as they apparently are."[35] But Frazee's patience—and pockets—had worn out in negotiating with Harry. He reached his limit at $13,500 and wired Hooper for an immediate response.[36] When Harry refused to budge, the Boston owner announced less than twenty-four hours later that he had dealt the senior member of his ball club to Chicago for two outfielders, Shano Collins and Nemo Leibold.

The news shocked the Hub City. "Loved by the fans of Boston," ran the lead story in *The Sporting News,* Harry's trade provided them with "a fresh grievance" against Frazee.[37] "Now that Harry's traded Harry," noted a fan, "he's batting 1.000 as a wrecker."[38] Citing Hooper's link to the great Red Sox teams of the 1910s, his strong performance in 1920, and his enormous popularity, the baseball writers who were not beholden to Frazee cut to the quick in their analysis of the deal. Focusing on Frazee's statement that "sentiment does not win ball games," the press challenged the owner's contention that Hooper was an unreliable investment for the future because "he will play not more than one year longer."[39] Duffy echoed this line in telling the Boston writers that "Harry's letters from the coast have sounded as if he were not especially eager to play ball and intended within a short time to devote his entire attention to his plantation in the West."[40] Arguing instead that "Hooper has plenty more baseball in him," the national sporting press concluded that Frazee "let him out in order to have as cheap a ball club as possible."[41]

There was no controversy in Chicago about the nature of the trade. Although the White Sox lost two established players, neither commanded the kind of respect that Hooper did nor matched his numbers year after year. In marked contrast to the news of the trade in Boston, Chicago fans learned that their team had been "strengthened considerably" with the acquisition of "one of the world's greatest outfielders for years."[42] The White Sox manager, Kid Gleason, was especially pleased to land Harry. "Say, fellows," he explained to the press, "you don't know how happy I am to get Hooper on my ball club. He's a veteran, but he's got a lot of baseball left in him and he's a smart player, too."[43] Smiling broadly for the writers as he boarded a train in Chicago bound for spring training in Waxahachie, Texas, Gleason announced his intention to play Hooper in right and bat him in his familiar leadoff spot in the lineup. "He's a champion," proclaimed Gleason as he set off to reknit the Sox around Hooper and returning veterans Eddie Collins, Ray Schalk, Amos Strunk, Red Faber, and Dickie Kerr.

Amid the euphoria of Hooper's acquisition in Chicago, there was still the matter of his contract to settle. Although he was now the property of the White Sox, whether he actually took the field for them depended on his salary negotiations with Comiskey. Despite speculation in the press that Harry "would not change the color of his hose without considerable coaxing," he quickly came to terms with his new club.[44] Assuming that he would "be doing business with Mr. Comiskey for some years," Harry was willing to split the difference between his holdout figure of $15,000 and Comiskey's first offer of $12,000, even though he felt he could have received the higher figure if he pressed the matter.[45] Hooper, however, wanted something in exchange for dropping his demand–a three-year contract at the compromise figure of $13,750 a season. Comiskey agreed. Harry affixed his signature to the only multiyear contract of his career and reported to the Chicago camp on March 21. His salary placed him second only to Eddie Collins as the highest-paid player on the club.

For the first time in twelve years, Harry was a newcomer again in spring training. He displayed a rookie's enthusiasm and a veteran's presence. Joining the White Sox, as he did Boston after the long winters, "in good trim," Hooper "galloped around rightfield like a streak in addition to spanking the ball in lusty fashion."[46] "The swarthy Californian" impressed all who watched him, lending "a spirit of loyalty and aggressiveness" to the proceedings.[47] Gleason declared the outfield "quite acceptable" with Hooper's procurement and predicted Harry would instill "harmony and confidence" in its play. As for the team's prospects in general, the Chicago analysts concluded that would depend largely upon the club's pitching. "One thing is certain," observed a writer, "if the White Sox lose a game this year it will be a loss on the square, and it is much more worthy to have tried and lost than to never have tried at all."[48] With that stirring prologue, the clean Sox embarked on the redemption of the franchise.

The 1921 season demonstrated how difficult that task would be. Stumbling from the outset, the White Sox never challenged for the pennant. They spent the entire season mired in the second division of the league and finished 36½ games behind the Yankees, who captured their first pennant on the hitting and pitching of the former Boston stars Ruth (59 home runs, 171 RBIs, .378 batting average), Schang (.316 batting average), Mays (27–9, 3.05 ERA), and Hoyt (19–13, 3.09 ERA). Only the hapless Athletics, one of two teams the White Sox bested in their season series, trailed Chicago in the final standings. Remarkably, the other team was second-place Cleveland as Chicago took thirteen of its twenty-two games against Speaker's club, probably preventing the Indians from repeating as league champions in the process.

The record against Cleveland indicated that the White Sox were capable of playing good ball at times. Usually this occurred when either Faber or Kerr was on the mound. One of nine American League pitchers who were allowed to continue to throw the spitball after the pitch was outlawed in 1920, Faber specialized in control and a balanced repertoire. Like Walter Johnson, Red labored his entire career with a single club that had more losing seasons than winning ones. Nineteen twenty-one was a typical year for him and the postscandal White Sox. Leading the AL in complete games (32) and earned run average (2.48), the steady right-hander notched twenty-five wins for a team that won only sixty-two. Dickie Kerr recorded most of the others. The only pitching star of the club in the 1919 Series, when, as a rookie, he won both of his starts with outstanding complete-game efforts, the diminutive left-hander claimed nineteen wins in 1921. Yet Kerr's seventeen losses and high 4.72 ERA suggested his vulnerability on days when either his control or curve was not sharp. The club's remaining eighteen wins were scattered among an ineffectual lot, including Roy Wilkinson, Shovel Hodge, and Doug McWeeney, whose combined numbers (13–34, 5.91 ERA) contributed to the highest earned run average of any staff in the Majors (4.94).

Despite the insurmountable problems with their pitching, the White Sox were "a scrappy team" that played good defense and presented a respectable, if not formidable, starting lineup.[49] Future Hall of Famers Collins at second and Schalk behind the plate led their positions in fielding as the team compiled the second-best fielding average in the AL (.969 compared to Boston's .975). Eddie also led the team in batting with a .337 mark, one of six .300-plus hitters on the team. In the high-scoring world of the postwar era, though, when Major League batting averages soared from a .248 mean in

1916 to .292 in 1925, the Chicago bat work was more modest than exceptional. The team's .283 batting average trailed four other clubs in the league which hit .300 or better and reflected too many weak spots in the regular lineup and on the bench. Schalk, for example, hit only .252, and Harvey McClellan, the club's most versatile reserve, was a classic "good field, no hit" man with a poor .179 average in sixty-three games.

Among the times McClellan appeared in the starting lineup were those days when he replaced Hooper. Late in the season, Harry took a pitch on his right hand that fractured a bone and kept him out of action for several weeks. He played only 108 games, the fewest since his rookie year. If the injury suggested that Hooper's service to the club was not worth the salary Comiskey was paying him, his record for the year quickly dispelled such a notion. Finding agreeable both the club's East Texas spring training site and the attention he received in camp, Harry had a strong preseason that carried into the regular campaign. For the first time in his career, he improved his batting average in consecutive years, raising the .312 mark of his Boston finale to .327, a new personal high for him. Although fewer at bats in 1921 reduced his overall extra-base hits, his eight home runs trailed only Earl Sheely's eleven on the club and contributed to a .470 slugging average, the same he achieved in 1920. Reflecting his diminished speed afoot, Harry managed only five triples and thirteen stolen bases, but drove in fifty-eight runs, five more than his previous best in this category.

Amid the satisfaction of his own work and the frustrations of the team's sour season, surely the most poignant moment of Harry's first year in Chicago was his return to Fenway in a uniform other than that of a Red Sox. On Saturday, June 11, with both teams already dismissed as pennant contenders, the White Sox opened a series against Boston. A fair number in the crowd of more than twelve thousand showed up to watch Chicago's rookie pitcher, Dominick Mulrenan, throw. A native of nearby Woburn, Massachusetts, Mulrenan received a diamond ring in a pregame presentation from his hometown's mayor, who headed a delegation of about five hundred to cheer their local hero. Most, however, were there to see Harry.

The Boston press had played up Harry's return for several days. The *Globe* predicted that the opportunity to see Hooper, "one of the great outfielders of all time," would draw "many of the stay-away fans out of their spells" and even cause them "to put off week-end excursions."[50] Running a quarter-page cartoon on game day announcing "Here He Is—the Ball Player You've Been Waiting to See," the morning paper proclaimed the return "to the campus" of "the most popular Red Sox alumnus." Noting that he "has been playing like a house afire for the White Sox," the paper recalled some of Harry's great moments in Boston and assured all who attended the game that they would be in for "a treat."

No treat was sweeter, though, than the one Hooper himself received from the Boston faithful. "Never in the recent history of Boston baseball," reported the *Herald,* "has a player been given the spontaneous ovation which Harry Hooper, former Red Sox star, received when he came to bat."[51] Approaching the plate for his first swings, Harry was showered with the kind of sustained applause "with which delegates greet the nomination of a top notcher for President on the Republican or Democratic ticket." For over two minutes, the fans paid their "mighty tribute to a great player, a clean sportsman and one of the most popular athletes who ever wore Boston big league regalia." With tears streaming down his face, "too proud to wipe them away," Harry waited for the ovation to subside before taking his stance in the batter's box.[52] A sweeping curve from Pennock caught Harry off balance and he popped weakly to Scott at short, but what he did at bat was irrelevant to the moment. As he returned to the dugout, another "tidal wave of applause swept over the crowd." The touching scene was particularly memorable for its spontaneity. Although Hooper enjoyed an official "day" later in the season when former Mayor Fitzgerald presented him with several gifts from his old teammates and the Boston fans, the homage on June 11 came "all from the heart." After his first at bat, Harry responded in a way that no doubt pleased and anguished his Red Sox admirers. He collected five hits, including three doubles, in twelve more trips to the plate as his new Sox took the series two games to one.

The next two years of Hooper's extended contract with the White Sox closely resembled his first for both himself and the club. Fully recovered from his hand injury and anxious to quiet any rumors that the end of his career was imminent, Harry appeared in 152 of Chicago's full schedule of games in 1922, one fewer than his most active previous season back in 1910. Although his batting average dropped to .304, the lowest of three consecutive seasons above the .300 mark, he tallied 111 runs and drove in 80, both career highs and team-leading totals. He also established new career marks in at bats (602), hits (183), and home runs (11).

His "splendid work" completely overshadowed that of Leibold and Collins in Boston.[53] Outhitting his counterparts in the trade by a wide margin, Harry surpassed their combined totals in runs scored, RBIs, and homers, further discrediting Frazee, whose club slumped to last place in the league.[54] "Four years' despoliation by the New York club," including Joe Bush, Sam Jones, and Everett Scott after the 1921 season, had taken their inevitable toll on the team's fortunes.[55] Finishing at the bottom of the standings for the first time in the AL's history, the once proud Red Sox showed "every prospect of remaining in that undesireable position indefinitely." Indeed, only twice in the next ten years did Boston emerge from the cellar. Its miserable performances included six consecutive last-place finishes from 1925 to 1930, during which time it averaged more than a hundred losses a season.

Furnishing "the chief surprise of the 1922 season," the White Sox barely missed finishing in the first division, losing out to Cleveland for fourth place on the last day of the season. Still, the club's 77–77 record marked a significant improvement over the rebuilding year of the previous season and suggested what the team could do with better pitching. Although Kerr had not returned to the club, preferring instead to play for an independent team outside the realm of organized baseball when Comiskey refused to give him a five-hundred-dollar raise, the staff lowered its ERA by a full run from 1921 and seemed to have the makings of a respectable rotation with Faber, Charlie Robertson, Dixie Leverett, and Ted Blankenship. Faber had another outstanding year, fashioning his third consecutive twenty-plus win season (21–17) and leading the Majors in ERA (2.80) and innings pitched (353). His principal supporting trio on the Chicago mound compiled a 35–35 record and 3.59 ERA. Hidden within these numbers was that rarest of all baseball feats. Pitching against Detroit on April 30 in only the third start of his career for the White Sox, Robertson retired in order the twenty-seven Tigers he faced that afternoon for a 2–0 victory. His performance constituted only the sixth perfect game in Major League history, the fourth since the turn of the century. Hooper had played in two of them, the other being Ernie Shore's perfect effort against Washington on June 23, 1917, when he relieved Ruth in the first inning with none out.

Unfortunately for Robertson and the White Sox, such brilliance was illusory. The Texas right-hander developed arm trouble a year later and never lived up to the expectations of that glorious day in April. He struggled through six more seasons in the Majors, never winning more games than he lost or pitching as many innings as he did in 1922. Slipping to 13–18 (3.81 ERA) in 1923 and 4–10 (4.99 ERA) in 1924, yet still holding a spot in the club's starting rotation, Robertson mirrored the desperate straits of Chicago's pitching and the lowly finishes in the standings for which it largely accounted. The White Sox fell back to seventh in 1923 and landed in the cellar the next year, temporarily elevating Boston and saving the Red Sox the embarrassment of nine consecutive last-place finishes.

These years were among the most frustrating of Hooper's career. Playing along side four future Hall of Famers (Collins, Schalk, Faber, and Ted Lyons, who joined the club in 1923) and enjoying many of the best individual seasons of his own Major League career, Harry found little consolation in his own numbers for the club's poor showing. Remarkably, his best year at the plate, 1924, when he set personal career marks in batting average (.328), on-base percentage (.413), and slugging average (.481), was the club's worst during his tenure with them. Again, hitting was not Chicago's problem. With five .300-plus hitters in the regular lineup, led by Collins (.349) and Bibb Falk (.352), and two others in reserve, the White Sox posted a .288 club batting average, the highest for any team on which Harry had played. Yet with only Faber and a stylish curveballer despite his nickname, Sloppy Thurston, managing decent earned run averages, the pitching staff compiled the league's worst ERA again, 4.75.

Always the consummate team player, Hooper was little impressed with individual performances unless they translated into success for the club. Although he proved he could hit for average and power as the situation warranted, and certainly with their inadequate pitching the White Sox demanded run production from their lineup to stay competitive, Harry preferred the more scientific game of his Boston years. He found it particularly frustrating that those who excelled at this game—men like Larry Gardner, Duffy Lewis, and Joe Wood— were often not as highly regarded for their own abilities and contributions to team play as those who accumulated gaudy statistics for clubs which never jelled as a championship unit. Observing that only three players from the great Red Sox teams of the teens had been elected to the Baseball Hall of Fame compared to five on the 1920s Chicago clubs, none of which finished higher than fifth place, Harry wondered whether "there must be a better way to select the men best qualified" for Cooperstown.[56] But enshrinement in the hall was not on Hooper's mind in 1923 and 1924; fair compensation for his services was.

Although Harry's batting average had slipped to .288 in 1923, he led the team with ten home runs and trailed only two others in doubles (32), walks (68), runs (87), and on-base percentage (.370). Moreover, his slugging average exceeded .400 for the fourth consecutive season, and the sixty-eight runs he batted in constituted the second-most-productive output in this category in his career. Hooper's performance hardly compared with Collins's remarkable .360 batting average in the eighteenth season of his distinguished career or distracted attention from the club's exciting rookie third baseman, Willie Kamm, whom Comiskey had purchased from San Francisco of the Pacific Coast League for one hundred thousand dollars, a record outlay for a minor league player. Yet Harry had no reason to expect the low offer he initially received from Comiskey for his services in 1924. Apparently convinced that his veteran right-fielder had permanently faded beneath the value of his three-year contract, Commie chose not to renew it, offering Harry instead only seven thousand dollars for the next season.

Angered and insulted, Hooper refused to report to the Chicago camp in the spring. Claiming that a case of the flu had laid him low, Harry used his feigned illness as an excuse to stay away from the club until Comiskey proposed more acceptable terms for his play. Hooper's ally in this gambit was the team's new manager, Frank Chance. Replacing Gleason, who had moved to Philadelphia to accept a coaching position with Connie Mack's Athletics, Chance had been wooed out of retirement in California to manage the Red Sox in 1923 but had quickly despaired of the prospect of trying to rebuild that decimated club. Comiskey offered him a similar but more promising challenge in the city where he had led the National League Cubs to four pennants as their player-manager between 1905 and 1912. Although Chance appreciated the young talents of Kamm, Falk, and Hooper's potential successors in the White Sox outfield, Bill Barrett and Maurice Archdeacon, he wanted Harry's veteran experience in the lineup and steadying influence on the club.[57] Telling Comiskey that it was essential that the club re-sign Hooper, Chance elicited a new offer of ten thousand dollars for his rightfielder.[58] Chance then convinced Hooper to accept the offer with the promise that he would fight hard for a salary increase for him the following year if Harry had a good season in 1924.

As he had done in 1920 when he also faced the need for a solid season to improve his bargaining position for the following year, Harry rose to the occasion. This time, however, the best batting campaign of his career failed to achieve the end he sought. Too many circumstances—some wholly unanticipated, others more predictable—conspired against Harry and set in motion the final steps to his retirement.

The first blow to Harry's plans came shortly after he had signed his contract and reported to spring training. Chance left the club before camp broke with a severe case of pneumonia. The illness would claim the life of the forty-seven-year-old once "Peerless Leader" of the Cubs within a few months. Comiskey tagged Johnny Evers, Chance's former teammate and currently in his second year with the White Sox as a coach, to succeed the stricken manager. Before the end of the season, both Eddie Collins and Ed Walsh, the workhorse of Chicago's pitching staff during most of his active career and now also a coach with the club, would try their hand at the helm. The loss of Chance and the subsequent disarray of the managerial situation certainly contributed to the team's disappointing performance in the pennant race. For Harry, these developments also undermined his contractual understandings with the club, for none of the men who succeeded Chance had been a party to them. Moreover, in light of the team's miserable season, Comiskey was not particularly inclined to reward any of his players with salary increases, no matter how successful their individual years may have been.

The White Sox owner had reverted to old habits in his handling of the club's finances that worked against Hooper's interests as well. Prepared to lay out considerable funds for the remodeling of Comiskey Park and the acquisition of such new players as Kamm, Roy Elsh, Buck Crouse, and Spencer Harris, Commie attempted to hold down the team's payroll in order to contain overall costs. Although a few players occasionally benefited from demonstrations of generosity on his part, only Collins enjoyed consistent salary increases during his years with the club.[59] Comiskey named him player-manager for the 1925 season at a salary of forty thousand dollars, far outdistancing anyone else on the team. Hooper's reward for his fine season in 1924, another contract for ten thousand dollars, still placed him among the highest paid players on the roster but did not match his expectations. He was particularly disappointed that his friend Eddie Collins had not been able to intercede successfully on his behalf with Comiskey and he wondered how hard Collins had tried.

There were other distracting matters on Harry's mind as he reported to the team's 1925 spring training headquarters at the Youree Hotel in Shreveport, Louisiana, in early March. Although his salary was still relatively high by league standards, its 27 percent reduction for two consecutive seasons from that which he had earned during his initial three years with the White Sox revealed how thin the margin of financial stability was for someone in his circumstances. With a wife and three children—his second son, John, having been born in June 1921—and a permanent West Coast home, Hooper faced increasing expenses in supporting them there in addition to his own room and board in Chicago and whatever arrangements he made to bring his family east to spend some time with him during the season. Continuing the practice he had established in Boston, Harry had brought Esther and the children to Chicago for most of each of the previous four summers. But money was tighter now and Esther was finding the annual uprooting more tedious and difficult to manage. They agreed not to rent a home this summer, but to rely on occasional visits by Esther alone. These more modest plans, however, also had their share of problems.

Acknowledging a letter from Harry with the White Sox season schedule enclosed, Esther wrote, "I certainly don't know what to do about going east. I haven't the faintest idea who I could get to stay with Harry and Marie or all of them."[60] Concerned with the costs of a trip, the growing unsuitability of Harry's aging parents to mind the children, and the complications of school calendars and home maintenance, Esther could foresee little possibility for a trip until July.[61] This news did not please Harry and he urged her to reconsider.[62]

Esther, however, held firm. In a series of letters to her husband in April and May, she shared both her irritation at the pressure he was putting on her and frustration with him for not fully comprehending her view of their separation. "It's terrible to think of being away out here all that time," she wrote about the time and distance between them. "I don't know if I could stand the pressure." But, she reiterated, "I can't leave the children." "Can you plan anything I can't?" she asked, hoping that Harry had a solution to their dilemma.[63]

But he did not. With dentist's bills accumulating for her and the children, the housemaid demanding more money, her bank account overdrawn, and Harry continuing to press for some decision on a trip east, Esther finally unloaded on him. Informing him that she had to cash several Liberty Bonds, she threatened to "put a tent in the back yard or keep the downstairs bedroom and rent the rest of the bedrooms or house" to make ends meet. "This way of living is a joke," she wrote bitterly. "There isn't one pleasure here for me, not one." Complaining about Harry's "touring around" with his teammates, she noticed how he could "have a beautiful time, see things, and then go enjoy everything" while she could not even have a male friend and neighbor over to the house to "play the banjo with her . . . [because] they would say I was sleeping with him." "Sometimes," Esther confessed, "I just don't care."[64]

Writing Harry three or four times a week during this stretch,

Esther desperately tried to convey her unhappiness without unduly burdening him with the troubles at home. Often her letters reflected an undeserved sense of guilt for the tales of woe she transmitted. She quieted her angry observations with loving reassurances. "I am awfully sorry you feel toward me like as though I didn't want to come east," she wrote in response to another entreaty from him. "You have me all wrong. There isn't anything I would have liked better to have been alone with you in Chicago. No one but ourselves. It seems ages since I have been with you." Dropping a few lines before bed on a late April night "as cold as winter," Esther told Harry that "I wish you were where I could crawl in beside you—wouldn't that be fine."[65]

Harry undoubtedly thought that would be quite fine and a far preferable way to spend his time than what most of the month of May had in store for him after a game on the second. Standing in against Garland Buckeye of the Indians, a 260-pound left-hander with a reputation for wildness and a four-year career as a guard with the Saint Louis football Cardinals behind him, Hooper took a pitch on his right shin that nearly toppled him at the plate. Although Harry attempted to stay in the game, the pain of the blow did not subside and he left the field for the usual treatment in such instances, an ice pack. However, the injury was more serious than Harry or the team trainer imagined. A blood clot developed in the leg, sending Harry to the hospital, where surgery to remove it was contemplated. Although his doctors eventually decided against such a measure, it was clear that Harry would be out of the White Sox lineup for quite some time while he healed.

The first indication that Esther had about the injury came, typically, not from Harry but from secondhand accounts. Noticing in the newspaper box scores that her husband's name had suddenly disappeared from the Chicago roster, she wrote him asking "what is the matter with Eddie [Collins] that he don't have you in the game." Complaining "that's the worst dealing with you have ever gotten," Esther wondered whether Collins was jealous that Harry's strong performance in the early weeks of the season had received more credit for the team's first-division play than the manager's own handling of the club.[66]

Before Harry could respond, however, Esther received much more disturbing news from the papers. "I got quite a scare today," she wrote three days after his injury. Reporting that a neighbor had called to inquire about his condition after reading that he had been operated upon, Esther worried that "maybe your leg had gone bad with blood poisoning or something." Although her friends assured her that Harry would have wired a message if an operation was necessary, Esther began to make arrangements in earnest for a trip east.[67]

The next day Harry's letters arrived in Capitola with details about the injury and reassurances that his leg did not require surgery.[68] Writing Esther and his parents, Harry reported that he "would be laid up some time" but that he expected to be back in the lineup "as good as new" after that. His father expressed relief at hearing from Harry for he "was wondering what was keeping you out of the game. I just thought they were breaking in some of the young lads."[69] Although wishing his son a speedy recovery and assuring him that his younger teammates "have nothing on you yet," Joe suggested that this kind of injury "makes a man think he is getting old."

In addition to the favorable report on his leg, the best news in Hooper's letter to Esther was his schedule for the next several weeks. Left behind in Chicago while the team embarked on its first extended road trip of the season, Harry expected to be at his apartment in the Cooper Carlton Hotel for nearly a month without interruption. It seemed an ideal time for a visit. "The world seemed to have brightened up since I got word from you," wrote Esther about this prospect.[70] Forgetting for the moment the troubles she was having getting the house painted, recovering a stolen cigarette holder from one of the painters, trying to sell their Cleveland sedan, tending to the children's cuts and bruises, and treating her own case of poison oak, Esther could "feel fine now when I think of coming on." Telling Harry that his leg must "pain like a tooth ache," she promised "ever so many loving kisses" to distract his attention from it. Leaving the children in the shared care of Harry's parents and friends, Esther joined her husband in Chicago for nearly three weeks together before he was well enough to take the field again. Watching him struggle after his return to the lineup, though, Esther sensed that he especially needed her and his family near him this summer. Despite their earlier plans and the tight finances, they agreed to rent for two months later in the summer the same house on Blackstone Avenue where they had stayed the previous four years.

Although Hooper did not play particularly well on his immediate return to the lineup, his club surprised the league with its showing in the first half of the season. Led by the pitching of Lyons, Blankenship, and Faber and the steady bats of Collins, Falk, and Mostil, the White Sox occupied third place behind Washington and Philadelphia from mid-May until late July. By the time Esther and the children joined Harry, however, the team was beginning a slide toward its eventual fifth-place finish. Lack of pitching depth behind the three principal starters and a string of late-season misfortunes that side-lined Collins (infection in a leg ligament), Archdeacon (tonsillitis), and McClellan (gallstone operation) frustrated the team's first-division aspirations. Nevertheless, Chicago ended its season above .500 (79–75) for the first time in six years.

Appearing in 127 games, Hooper batted only .265, well below the .310 average with Chicago that he had carried into the season. Con-sidering his strong performance the year before and another charac-teristically quick start at the plate in 1925, where he had been hitting nearly .400 before Buckeye's damaging pitch, Hooper's batting record disappointed and embarrassed him. Banging out only 117 hits, the fewest since his rookie season, Harry trailed every regular in the lineup in batting average except shortstop Ike Davis, who managed a lowly .240. Moreover, for only the third time in his ca-reer, his individual average did not surpass the team's combined mark. Yet Harry's six home runs were the second-highest total on the club. One of them came on August 11 against the Yankees when Hooper accompanied the round-tripper with four singles for the only five-hit game of his Major League career. "The good Harry is im-proving with age," the press reported, but Hooper and others knew differently.[71]

Although speculation about Harry's retirement had been raised briefly before in conjunction with his trade to Chicago, it had sub-sided during his first two seasons with the White Sox. When his average fell off to .288 in 1923 after three consecutive seasons above .300, doubts about the continuation of his career surfaced again. Christy Walsh, for example, suggested that Harry's declining number of stolen bases in recent years and less-impressive play in the field emphasized his aging legs, "the ballplayers' warning" that the end might be near.[72] Now, as the 1925 season wore down, Hooper's fu-ture was the object of discussion once more in the press and other baseball circles.

Reporting the "prevailing indications of the veterans" that Harry's playing career "is fast coming to an end," a Chicago sports columnist disagreed with Walsh's earlier analysis and focused on Hooper's hit-ting.[73] "Sad to relate," the writer continued, Hooper's likely retire-ment "is not because he can no longer field. The veteran is actually spectacular in the outer garden and has slowed up only slightly on the bases, but his success with the bat has fallen off miserably and it is more because of that than anything else that Harry believes the end has come." Noting Hooper's interests in managing, the reporter suggested that "there is something in the wind at Boston" which may draw Harry back to his original team. If that failed to develop, it seemed likely that Hooper would "close the door on baseball forever." Assuming that Harry's thrifty ways and clean living translated into financial well-being, other reports carried the Boston story further and announced that he could become the sole owner of the Red Sox if he so desired.[74]

Along the latter lines, J. H. Stephens, president of the Merchants National Bank of Sacramento, had written Harry to inquire about his interest in purchasing the local franchise in the Pacific Coast League. Stephens had initially contacted Walter Johnson with the proposition that he and Hooper could form "a splendid combination to take over this club."[75] Offering financial assistance for the purchase price of approximately three hundred thousand dollars, Stephens outlined the club's assets, including specific players and an eleven-thousand-seat grandstand, "second to none on the coast." Johnson, however, declined the offer, explaining that he planned to spend the winter in Florida and then return to the Senators for at least another season in 1926.[76] He did assure Stephens, though, that "Harry Hooper would be a valuable man connected with the Club there." Writing Harry soon after receiving Johnson's reply, Stephens argued that "with you in charge of the management . . . [the club] would be a money-getter."[77] To the banker's disappointment, however, Harry wrote that his own plans were too unsettled at the moment to make such a commitment.[78] Like Johnson, Hooper was not prepared to put his playing days completely behind him yet.

If they were to continue, however, they would not be on the groomed fields of the Major Leagues. As expected, Comiskey drastically slashed Harry's salary, offering him only seven thousand dollars for 1926. Confident that he could still push back the years and demonstrate his worth as he had done in 1920 and 1924, Hooper considered accepting the offer, provided Commie guaranteed him more than a one-year contract. But convinced that Barrett and Harris were ready to replace Hooper permanently in the lineup, the Old Roman was not interested in Harry's terms. Informing his right fielder that "he had never heard of anyone getting a guarantee of anything in this business," Comiskey wired Hooper his release from the club.[79] Harry did not seek an invitation to another club's spring training, and none came his way.

Considering the heavy speculation about his retirement at the end of the 1925 season, the news that he would not be returning to the

White Sox was not surprising. Collins issued perfunctory statements about the quality of Harry's play and character and admitted that he would be missed. The press rehearsed old rumors about his managerial prospects and listed his "civilian" interests. But in a game bound as no other to seasonal images of renewal and expectation, Harry's absence quickly faded as a story worth examining.

In Hooper's last game for the White Sox on October 3, 1925, he collected two hits, including the seventy-fifth home run of his career, in three at bats. It was a performance remarkably like his debut seventeen years earlier for the Sox of another color when he also ripped two base hits and drove in a run. Similarly, his desire to hang on for another season at age thirty-eight reflected the other end of the continuum that had first introduced the West Coast rookie to a competitive stage where he needed to prove he belonged. Although seeming to accept Comiskey's low salary offer to play the game of his youth on middle-age legs, Hooper's insistence on a multiyear contract, a condition which he knew Commie would not likely meet, provided an explanation for his retirement in terms of external circumstances rather than his own declining abilities. Indeed, sympathetic accounts in the sporting press supported Harry's denial in suggesting that his retirement was premature. But assuring their readers that Harry "will be a success at any thing he undertakes," his admirers among the baseball writers ushered him gently off their pages.[80] On October 11, after the completion of the annual "Chicago Championship Series" between the White Sox and the Cubs, Harry headed home to the village on the central California coast from which he had ventured almost two decades, four World Series championships, and over twenty-four hundred Major League hits earlier.

Epilogue

He never seems to strive for the commendation of the crowd, but his
sole ambition seems to be always to do his best.
—*Baseball Magazine*, 1916

Many years after their playing careers had ended, Joe Wood wrote
his former Red Sox teammate Harry Hooper. "I am so glad to note
that you are O.K. financially," Smoky Joe observed. "So many of the
old-timers are really up against it."[1] Wood's characterization of
Hooper's status and that of many of their Major League contemporaries accurately depicted the retirement circumstances of ballplayers from their era. Emerging from a professional career which
typically lasted less than eight years for a regular roster player (the
average was half that if all players who wore a Major League uniform, no matter how briefly, are counted), these men were often ill
prepared, both psychologically and vocationally, for the sudden loss
of status and income that termination of their playing days brought.
Rarely older than their mid-thirties, former ballplayers faced an unfamiliar and uncertain future. A high suicide rate among them and
sad tales of indigency and desperation provided sober commentary
on the failure of many to deal with their fading glory.[2] Most, however, adjusted satisfactorily, and some, like Hooper and Wood, managed the transition both smoothly and successfully.

Returning to Capitola and the real estate agency he had started
several years earlier, Harry initially settled in to the kind of low
white-collar profession that engaged most former Major Leaguers of
his day. Often capitalizing on their fame for their first "retirement"
occupation, these men commonly found themselves in sales, public
relations, and small businesses, where their visibility attracted trade
and helped reestablish themselves in their local communities. Those
who aspired to higher-status white-collar positions found that their
baseball fame, particularly as it receded from the public eye, counted

much less in facilitating mobility than such factors as educational and social background. Over 90 percent of former ballplayers who had some collegiate experience, for example, became white-collar workers, compared with just two-thirds of those who did not. Similarly, about 85 percent of Hooper's fellows whose fathers were employed in nonmanual areas secured white-collar employment, while this was true for less than 60 percent of the sons of manual laborers.[3]

Attempting to maintain the middle-class status they had acquired through professional ball, a significant proportion of former Major Leaguers sought to stay in the game and apply their sporting experience directly to earning a living. Seeking positions as managers, coaches, scouts, umpires, and front-office personnel, they were assisted in these interests by the steady expansion of both professional and amateur play throughout the country in the 1920s. With baseball achieving new heights of popularity and respectability, the lure of the diamond and the discomfort in leaving it persuaded hundreds of former players to remain connected with the game in some active capacity. Considering the confidence he still had in his playing abilities and speculation about his managerial aspirations, Hooper seemed unlikely to restrict his baseball involvement to reading the sports pages. It therefore came as little surprise when Bill McCarthy, owner of the San Francisco Mission Bells of the Pacific Coast League, announced on April 30, 1927, that Harry had signed a two-year contract at five thousand dollars a season to become the club's new player-manager.

The announcement drew an unusually enthusiastic response from the San Francisco sporting press, which had generally treated the Missions with indifference. The franchise had moved to the Bay Area only the year before from Vernon in Southern California, where it had operated for eleven seasons, winning three consecutive PCL pennants, 1918–20. Although the Bells had finished third in the PCL in 1926 with a 106–94 record, the only other team besides pennant-winning Los Angeles and runner-up Oakland to finish above the .500 mark, their performance in the eight-club circuit had recently been undistinguished. Since its last championship in Vernon, the club had finished above sixth place only once, while their Bay Area competitors, the more familiar San Francisco Seals and Oakland Oaks, perennially finished higher in the standings and earned the most attention and support from local fans and writers. Many of the club's problems were attributed to the interfering ways of owner McCarthy, who had hired and fired three managers just in the eighteen months before Harry's appointment. Hooper's immediate predecessor, Bill

Leard, was dismissed barely two weeks into the 1927 campaign. But assuring the press that McCarthy "had given him full assurance that he is to be the boss without restrictions," Hooper prepared to take the helm.[4]

Despite a painful stomach disorder which caused some speculation that an operation might be necessary, Harry worked himself and his new charges hard immediately upon joining them in Seattle for his managerial debut on May 3. The club responded well to his enthusiasm and example. "On their toes, playing smart baseball," the Missions perfectly executed two sacrifices that Hooper had ordered and rallied from a run down in the ninth inning to defeat the Indians for his first PCL victory.[5] Although his abdominal pains prevented him from appearing in the lineup, Harry reported that he expected to be ready to play within a week or two. Promising to be the only Pacific Coast manager to play on a regular basis, Hooper explained that "I'm more inclined to think one can accomplish more as a manager by staying in the lineup. You're right in the game, and you know what's going on. You can size up the situation better."[6]

Harry was doing quite well from the dugout and the first-base coach's box he preferred when his boys were at bat, though, even before he took his familiar place in right field for the club. Winning eleven of their first seventeen games under their new manager, the Missions had climbed from sixth place to second in the league standings by the end of May. Once in the lineup, Hooper gave his young players more than a glimpse of the skills that had carried him through seventeen Major League seasons. Although slowed a step or two from the days when, as Doc Strub of the Seals said, "he could get to first base quicker than any man in baseball," the bronzed and trim Hooper had lost none of his zest for the game or resolve to win.[7] Stroking two doubles against the Los Angeles Angels on May 22 in his first appearance in the Missions' starting lineup, Harry drew "numerous cheers from the Sunday gathering that remembered the Hooper who graced the Red Sox great outfield."[8] Demonstrating that "he may be just the man to get results from the Mission team," Hooper paced the club at bat as well with a gaudy .429 average during his first month in the lineup.[9] Thereafter, the hits came less frequently, but Harry turned in a playing performance remarkably like that of his rookie year with the Red Sox in 1909. In seventy-eight games for the Missions, Hooper batted .284, with nineteen RBIs and thirty-five runs scored. Almost two decades earlier with Boston, he had hit .282, with sixteen RBIs and twenty-nine runs scored in eighty-one games in his first Major League season.

Even Harry's bat, "strong will and well-grounded baseball theories," however, could not overcome some glaring handicaps under which he worked to keep the Missions in the hunt for the PCL pennant.[10] Two of these—youthful inexperience among his players and a woeful lack of pitching—had a predictable effect on the team's fortunes. Neither Gordon Slade nor Mickey Finn, for example, two fine infielders who were both headed for the Brooklyn Dodgers in 1930, had the kind of presence on the club or punch at the plate to serve as team leaders and replace the thirty-two home runs and 137 RBIs of Ike Boone, who went to the White Sox after the 1926 Missions season. Moreover, when Lefty Weinert, the Bells' best hurler, departed for the Chicago Cubs in midsummer, the club began a steady decline in the standings. It did not end until the Missions reached seventh place, only a notch above the Angels, whose championship roster of the previous season had been decimated with retirements and graduates to the Major Leagues.

Added to these roster problems was a more serious threat to Harry's managerial record. Despite McCarthy's initial assurances that he would not interfere with Harry's handling of the team, the owner reverted to his old habits and insisted on advising his manager on the use of the pitching staff. "McCarthy will go the limit for a man he likes," the press had reported, but it became increasingly clear that the price of rapport included deference to the owner's views on club conduct both on and off the field.[11] As injuries and miserable pitching hastened the Missions' slide, speculation mounted that Harry's hold on his job was no more secure than his immediate predecessors. "He bids to follow in [their] footsteps," observed one writer, who added that this was "a pity, for Hooper is a colorful individual and probably would make a pretty fair manager if he were under different conditions."[12]

Resenting the insinuation that he was simply a figurehead for McCarthy, Hooper wrote Paul Lowry, sports editor of the *Los Angeles Times*, to address particularly critical columns to this effect which had appeared in his paper. Labeling as false any impression that he did not have the full authority which his title implied, Harry insisted that "every move that has been made on the field since I took the club has been made on my own initiative." Furthermore, Harry wrote, "as long as I continue on the job I am going to run the club."[13] Hooper's explanation, however, underscored the double bind in which he found himself. If his management of the Missions was truly autonomous, then he could not escape criticism for the club's poor showing. If, on the other hand, he was subject to McCarthy's intrusiveness, then his position was just as untenable.

As the campaign wore on and the Missions' record worsened with it, Harry began to express his own doubts about the team's prospects and his chances of turning them around. "My boys are hustling and fighting," he told the press, but he confided to Esther that "the most disheartening circumstances" threatened to break their spirit.[14] The optimism of Hooper's initial weeks with the club had long since dissipated when the Bells ended their season on October 2. Their closing day split of a doubleheader with Portland left them with an 86–110 record, twenty fewer wins than the previous season.

McCarthy wasted little time in communicating his displeasure to his manager. On January 13, 1928, he announced that Hooper had been given his unconditional release from the club. Stating that Harry "had so many outside business interests that it was felt he was unable to devote the proper amount of time to the team," McCarthy fooled no one with this explanation.[15] Hooper hinted that he might sue McCarthy for a second year of wages on his two-year contract, but this was an empty gesture with no legal ground on which to stand. Managers, like players, served at the pleasure of the club to which they were contracted. Although Harry's initial contract with the Missions bound him to the club for two years, it lacked a reciprocal commitment of the club to him. Owners generally had full authority to release their employees whenever they desired. The principal check on this exercise was the fear that some other club would pick up the released man. Harry, however, no longer prized as a player and unproven as a manager, posed no such concern to McCarthy.

Back in Capitola after leaving organized baseball the second time, Harry settled into the routine of running his real estate agency and occasionally heading north to Marysville to check on his agricultural properties in the Sacramento Valley. With his orchards and fields still in the hands of foreman Bradley, Harry had no compelling reason to spend much time there. The holdings continued to turn a modest profit under Bradley's management, and this satisfied Hooper's minimal expectations for them. Lacking interest in devoting more of his own time to this enterprise, or, for that matter, any activity that dictated a conventional 9-to-5 commitment, Harry revealed that it was not simply the game that he missed, but the patterns of the season and the unique appeal of working at play.

Ironically, Hooper's Marysville acres afforded him a final opportunity to play professionally. Harry's visits to the town usually took him to the ballpark to watch the local minor leaguers play whenever they were at home. Finishing out their season in 1929, the Marysville Giants had an opening on their roster because of the illness of one of their starters. The club offered Harry a one-game contract to take the field. On forty-two-year-old legs, Hooper connected for a single and double in four trips to the plate and fielded his position in right flawlessly. But his performance merely stirred old memories; it did not tempt Harry or the Giants to try something more.

With baseball apparently behind him in any significant participatory manner, Harry devoted his sporting energies to hunting and fishing and the primary locus of these activities, his four-hundred-acre ranch on the edge of the Six Rivers Forest in the southeastern corner of Humboldt County, California. About two hundred miles north of San Francisco in rugged, pine-covered hill country, the first pieces of this tract had been purchased sight unseen by Hooper in 1921 for ninety dollars on the advice of Tom Murphy, a professional hunter who lived in the area. With his Capitola friends, Al Lent and Paul Johnson, Harry had hunted deer in Northern California with Murphy over the years. On these trips Harry had frequently mentioned his interest in acquiring some land in this challenging gaming country and had asked Murphy to keep him informed should something worthwhile come to his attention. Fed with several clear streams, some likely candidates for damming in order to create a trout pond or two, and featuring a somewhat dilapidated but sturdy five-room structure situated on level ground above a meadow which provided an open vista of the western valley between Blocksburg and Alderpoint, the property impressed Murphy as that for which Hooper had been looking.

It was exactly that. Devoting as much time as he could to the property—a commitment which elicited a reporter's observation that Harry's tanned and fit appearance suggested that "he did most of his real estating out of doors"—Hooper demonstrated the kind of dedication and skill for which he was noted when doing something he truly enjoyed.[16] Initially working with his hunting friends to repair and expand the land's single dwelling, develop an access road and trails, and dam one of the creeks, Harry soon brought Esther and the children to his mountain retreat. The boys loved the scene, Esther and Marie less so. But as the property and its amenities improved, particularly the arrival of indoor plumbing and electricity and the construction of a second dwelling in the 1940s, a ranch house that could accommodate a dozen guests, the annual expedition to Humboldt for the fall hunting season became a much anticipated family affair.

Three generations of Hoopers after him continue to attest to the appeal of Harry's other sporting passion and the place where he pursued it.

Despite Harry's disappointing season with the Missions, rumors continued to circulate that he would land a managerial position in the Majors. This was especially so in Boston, where, under new owner Bob Quinn and a parade of unsuccessful managers (Frank Chance 1923, Lee Fohl 1924–26, Bill Carrigan 1927–29, and Heinie Wagner 1930), the Red Sox had fallen on hard times. Six consecutive last-place finishes from 1925 through 1930 underscored the club's desperation to recapture some of the glory that had accompanied Hooper's playing career with it. Quinn had apparently given Harry some consideration for the job in 1930, but when he named Wagner, who suffered through a 52–102 season, his club finishing fifty games behind the pennant-winning Athletics, Quinn lost his last opportunity to bring Hooper back to Boston. For when he approached Harry again after the 1930 season, it was too late. Hooper had just agreed to a two-year contract to coach the baseball team at Princeton University.

Following his former teammates Joe Wood (Yale), Stuffy McInnis (Harvard), Jack Barry (Holy Cross), and Harry Wolter (Stanford) onto the collegiate diamond, Hooper reflected the improved image of professional ballplayers that merited their consideration for coaching positions at some of the nation's most prestigious institutions. Often former collegians themselves and sometimes alumni of the very institutions to which they returned to coach, these men seemed to offer an attractive combination of professional expertise and sensitivity to an academic environment. Although opposition to the hiring of former Major Leaguers came from members of the faculty who questioned the place of intercollegiate athletics at all and the institution's investment in big-name coaches, athletic directors did not hesitate to appoint former players they thought would be exemplary sportsmen and effective teachers of the game. Enjoying long collegiate coaching careers, Wood, Jack Coombs at Duke, Ray Fisher at Michigan, and later Larry Gardner at Vermont, for example, proved that they could make the transition from the big leagues to the ivy leagues with grace and success.

Hooper learned about the opening at Princeton from Gardner, who, while managing minor league ball in New England, was considering a return to his own alma mater to coach the Catamounts baseball team. Encouraged by Gardner and aware of the satisfaction that many of his former teammates were experiencing on their respective campuses, Harry decided to take a serious look at the Princeton situation. He liked what he saw. He discovered that the university had a rich baseball history that dated to the formation of the Nassau Base Ball Club in October 1860. Similar to the situation at Saint Mary's, baseball became the first intercollegiate sport at Princeton when the Nassau nine debuted on November 22, 1864, against Williams College. Although only three Princeton men had ever reached the Major Leagues—Woodie Wagonhurst, Class of 1888; Moe Berg, '23; and Charlie Caldwell, '25—several others had contributed to the development of the game. William Schenck, for example, an inventive member of the Class of 1880, draped several issues of the *Princetonian* on a cord around his neck and wore them inside his uniform shirt. Layered to the thickness of a telephone book, the papers constituted a primitive chest protector. Schenck probably had good use for it because the Princeton hurlers were beginning to experiment with a few new pitches that had been pioneered by former members of the team. Both Joseph Mann, '74, and William Smith, '77, had tossed breaking balls in competition, the former joining Charles Avery of Yale as an early curveballer, the latter one of the first to perfect a drop pitch.[17]

The baseball tradition at Princeton also was a winning one. Particularly under Bill Clarke, a veteran of thirteen Major League seasons, principally with the Baltimore Orioles of Hughie Jennings, Dan Brouthers, Willie Keeler, Joe Kelley, and John McGraw in the 1890s, Old Nassau fielded formidable teams after the turn of the century. Princeton's first paid baseball coach, Old Reliable Clarke, lived up to his nickname in guiding the Tigers to a .721 winning percentage from 1900 to 1916 before he left for France to do YMCA work in conjunction with the war effort. He returned for a second stint with the team in 1919 and notched another 116 victories against 75 losses before retiring in 1927. His successor, Byrd Douglas, Class of '16, however, had struggled through three consecutive losing seasons that had the baseball alumni and athletic administration looking to make a coaching change. They turned to another professional baseball man to restore a winning program at the University. "Tickled pink" to land Hooper, Charles M. Kennedy, chairman of the Princeton Board of Athletic Control, announced Harry's hiring on September 25, 1930, and indicated that the new coach would be traveling east immediately for fall practice sessions.[18]

Harry greeted twenty-eight candidates for the varsity and twenty-four first-year men for the freshman team on October 1. They had quite a surprise awaiting them when they took the field. For joining

Hooper to help with the off-season instruction and conditioning was the Grey Eagle himself, Tris Speaker. In Philadelphia for the World Series between the Athletics and the Saint Louis Cardinals, Spoke accepted Harry's invitation to spend a few days in nearby Princeton. Their reunion was the first time they had seen each other since the 1925 season and put to rest whatever notions that still existed about tensions between them stemming from the cliquish years with the Red Sox. Indeed, the brief time together in Princeton cemented their friendship and underscored a genuine regard and respect for one another that particularly would be evident in the years ahead whenever they participated in old-timers' games.

It would take more than his former outfield partner's help, however, to turn things around for Tiger baseball. "Coach Hooper will have quite a bit of difficulty in forming a winning combination from the remnants of last year's team," observed *The Daily Princetonian* about Harry's chances of rescuing Old Nassau from the bottom of the Eastern Intercollegiate League.[19] Inheriting few solid players, most notably center fielder Charlie Muldaur, first baseman George Morse, and pitcher Shorty Bowman, Hooper also faced the problem of competing with football for the best athletes on campus. It was a contest that he could not win. Those who lettered in both sports were, of course, not available for baseball practice in the fall and some of these, upon completing their collegiate eligibility on the gridiron, elected not to play ball in the spring because they no longer needed the sport in order to stay in shape for football. Although Harry's appointment as coach "aroused new interest in baseball" at Princeton, it never threatened to distract attention or resources from the game that mattered most on the nation's campuses.[20] With attendance figures and gate receipts growing even through the Great Depression years of the 1930s, college football was unrivaled in the support it drew and the popularity it achieved.[21]

Under such conditions, Harry focused his attention on restoring competitive respectability to the baseball program rather than raising expectations about imminent championships. Concentrating on developing in his players more teamwork and proficiency in the game's fundamentals, Hooper drilled them hard in the scientific game he knew best. The result was a squad that rarely suffered humiliating defeats but lacked sufficient experience and pitching talent to challenge the perennial powers in the league, Harvard and Yale, for a title. In the spring campaign of 1931, the Tigers went 10–17–1 overall, 3–5–1 in league play. The highlight of the season was a 3–1 victory over Smoky Joe's Yale team in Princeton's home finale that kept the Tigers out of the EIBL cellar. Showing "plenty of fight," the Nassau nine earned praise for their steady improvement over the course of the season under the "fine leadership" of the new coach.[22]

Harry continued to take the Tigers in the right direction during his second season. They approached their final games of the spring needing only a split with Yale to post their first nonlosing season since 1927. Led by Albie Booth, however, the Eli swept the series, winning 5–4 in New Haven and 6–3 in Princeton. The losses dropped Harry's boys to 11–13 overall, 3–6, and fifth place again in the league. The campus press kindly noted that the number of close decisions going against the team (nine of its losses were by three or fewer runs) made its record "considerably less disappointing," while a veteran observer of the collegiate baseball scene claimed that the Princeton nine "looked more like a real ball club . . . than any Nassau outfit the writer has seen for a long time."[23]

Despite the improved play of the team under Hooper, the university's athletic authorities identified the baseball program as a target for financial savings. The deepening economic crisis in the country compelled the university to undertake cuts throughout its budget, particularly in nonacademic areas which were neither revenue generating nor more clearly connected to community and alumni support. Princeton did not consider dropping intercollegiate baseball, only making its operation more economical.

A principal casualty of this decision was Harry's $5,000-a-year contract, which was now up for renewal. The university informed Hooper that he was welcome to stay on as coach, but at a 40 percent salary reduction. It was an offer that Harry did not hesitate to refuse. Citing his West Coast family and business interests but hinting at bitterness over a university decision which he regarded as wrongheaded, Hooper announced that he would not be returning to the Tiger diamond next year. His successor, Jack Jeffries, Class of '23, accepted the job at half Harry's salary. Princeton got what it paid for: Jeffries's team won only nine of twenty-eight games, dropping to last place in the EIBL with a 1–11 record.

If Harry had any regrets about leaving Princeton, he scarcely had time to dwell on them. Costing him more than his collegiate coaching job, the Depression played havoc with his California business interests as well. With transportation fees rising and market prices falling, Harry's peach orchards failed to produce enough revenue to cover the bank notes on the property and its equipment. Concentrating his resources on acreage closer to Capitola, Harry conceded all the Marysville land to foreclosure.

Conditions were hardly more favorable for his real estate agency. With sales falling off dramatically and the tentative steps of the Hoover administration inadequate to the task of addressing the money scarcity in the country, Harry staved off disaster for his family by borrowing on some of his holdings and dipping into a modest savings reserve. He refused, however, to sell any of his key coastal properties for any amount less than what he thought they were worth. Stubborn in his resolve, Hooper gambled that the economic crisis would run its course and that his patience would eventually yield high dividends. He was right on both accounts, although, like most in the country, he anticipated neither how long the recovery would take nor how prosperous its shape would be in California.

Not content merely to wait for recovery, Hooper played an active role locally in promoting the Democratic slate in the 1932 elections. His political leanings had been largely shaped through his friendly association with successive Democratic administrations in Boston during his playing days with the Red Sox. Responding to the kindness which Honey Fitz and his Irish Democratic cronies had consistently shown him over the years, Harry displayed a combination of personal loyalty and conviction in his political behavior. Prior to 1932, however, Hooper had generally exercised his support of the party through the votes he cast. This year, attracted to the magnetic personal appeal of Franklin Delano Roosevelt and his message of hope and promise of action, Harry decided to campaign for FDR and the state Democratic ticket. His efforts proved successful. The Capitola–Santa Cruz electoral district, like California as a whole, voted overwhelmingly for Roosevelt.

Hooper's efforts did not go unnoticed in the party's national headquarters. Shortly after the election, national party chairman James Farley wrote Harry to congratulate him for his role in the "glorious victory" and to thank him "from my heart for the support accorded me during the entire campaign." "I want you to know," added Farley, "that I am deeply grateful to you."[24] Several months later, with Farley installed as FDR's postmaster general, Hooper learned the measure of his gratitude. Dispensing patronage for the service that Harry and many others had rendered the party, Farley offered Hooper the position of postmaster of Capitola. Encouraged by Esther and assured that the responsibilities of running the third-class office would not interfere with his real estate activities and sporting interests, Harry accepted the appointment. Initially intending to serve only a few years until the economy improved enough to merit his full-time devotion to real estate, Harry sorted the mails in Capitola for twenty-four years until his retirement at age seventy in 1957.

Harry's passage from his middle to senior years looked very much like that which other middle-class professional men experienced in the United States between the 1930s and 1950s. His two sons went to college, then to war. All three of his children married and provided him and Esther with a growing lot of grandchildren. He became active in community affairs, particularly working for various environmental causes, including the protection of the coastal wetlands. His work provided him with the means to enjoy his leisure. And his baseball career receded ever further from relevance in his own life and ever fainter in the memory of those who had seen him play.

There were occasions, though, both private and public, for Harry to recall the distant days of his playing seasons. When son John briefly pursued a professional career of his own in the Yankee organization in the late 1940s, Harry maintained a steady correspondence with him in which the old veteran offered a combination of advice and encouragement. Constantly stressing hard work and fundamentals, Harry could not rescue John from "the clutches of old Joe Slump," however, and his son's baseball dreams faded on the baked fields of a Texas summer in 1948.[25]

In more dramatic and vivid fashion, though, Harry visited his past in several specially staged old-timers' games. The first of these occurred on September 8, 1930, when Hooper, Speaker, and Lewis, reunited for the first time in the outfield since 1915, joined a host of other Red Sox and Major League greats in a full nine-inning game benefiting Children's Hospital of Boston and needy baseball veterans. During a year when the regular Red Sox barely drew three thousand fans a game to Fenway, over twenty-two thousand turned out at Braves Field to catch a glimpse of their former heroes. The All-Bostons, also featuring Cy Young, Joe Wood, Candy LaChance, Jimmy Collins, and Dick Hoblitzell, defeated their All-Star opponents, led by Ty Cobb, Eddie Collins, Johnny Evers, Home Run Baker, Honus Wagner, Jack Coombs, and Chief Bender, 8–4. Affectionate applause greeted each of the players, but none more warmly or enthusiastically than Hooper. Collecting three hits, snagging a line drive with one of his "famous kneeling, sliding catches," and throwing the ball "with that rifle-like arm of his which seems to have gathered no rust with the marching years," Harry, "still the raven-haired darling of Boston fandom," paced his team's victory and "stole the show."[26]

Harry's subsequent appearances in similar games produced fewer heroics on the field but elicited no less an appreciative response from the fans in attendance. Participating with Spoke and Duffy, he donned his old uniform for a game sponsored by the Veterans of Foreign Wars in July 1938, an exhibition benefiting the Babe Ruth Foundation Fund in September 1947, a contest between Red Sox and Yankee old-timers in September 1949, and a day honoring Hall of Fame inductees in May 1955. Tris, however, was among the missing when Harry and Duffy joined eleven other surviving members of the 1912 championship team for a fiftieth-anniversary commemoration in 1962.

Each appearance in one of these games or at the testimonial dinners which usually accompanied them rescued Harry from the anonymity of his work for the postal service in Capitola. Locally, the press used Harry's participation in old-timers' events as the focal point for interviews with him about his playing career and times. Occasionally the larger papers in the Bay Area also ran profiles on Hooper and reminded their readers of his achievements on the diamonds of another era. Particularly when Speaker was alive, Hooper basked in the glow of his association with his former teammate, who did not hesitate to sing Harry's praises and to suggest that he should be similarly honored in the Baseball Hall of Fame.

The Hall of Fame, of course, was the centerpiece of a baseball museum established in Cooperstown, New York, to commemorate the one-hundredth anniversary of the alleged founding of the game there by Abner Doubleday in 1839. A special centennial committee had the task of selecting the initial inductees for the hall and it named five men—Ty Cobb, Walter Johnson, Christy Mathewson, Babe Ruth, and Honus Wagner—for enshrinement in 1936. Speaker was in the second class of inductees the following year. Thereafter, annual polls of the Baseball Writers Association of America and the periodic votes of various old-timers' committees, made permanent with the establishment of the Committee on Baseball Veterans in 1953, determined the hall's membership. Although the selection process has warranted charges of arbitrariness, capriciousness, and inconsistency over the years, it has neither prevented due recognition for those who have been elected nor dissuaded players from the dream of induction.

Hooper certainly shared this dream, although the prospects of its realization seemed ever more remote as he grew older. Receiving votes from several writers in the 1937 balloting, indeed, more than those gathered by such stars as Jack Chesbro, Sam Crawford, Red

Faber, Hughie Jennings, Eppa Rixey, and Zack Wheat, all of whom preceded him into the hall, Harry watched his vote totals steadily decline in subsequent elections. From 1940 to 1947, he failed to appear on any ballots and then drew only two or three votes in the elections between 1948 and 1951. The latter votes likely reflected the attention he received through his participation in well-publicized old-timers' games in the late 1940s.

The correlation between visibility and votes reflected the largely subjective basis on which the Hall of Famers are selected and against which most criticism of the process is directed. Particularly for players whose careers had not been observed by the voting members of the BBWAA, their chances for the hall primarily rested on the quality of the case that could be developed for them and the clout of their sponsors. Hooper's campaign for Cooperstown represented a lesson in this electoral reality.

An initial effort to boost Harry's argument for the Hall of Fame was launched in the early 1950s by Saint Mary's College alumnus Edward I. Fenlon. A regular contributor to *The Brickpile,* a newsletter for alumni who had attended the college when it was still in Oakland, Fenlon recalled how surprised and disappointed he was during a trip to Cooperstown in 1948 not to find Hooper enshrined. Concluding that this was the case because Harry "was not a show-off and he never learned the value of a press-agent," Fenlon decided to take up Hooper's cause himself.[27] Exhorting his fellow "Brickpile Seniors," graduates of the college prior to 1912, to write the Hall of Fame on Hooper's behalf, Fenlon produced a flurry of interest for Harry in the issues of *The Brickpile* and some attention from the San Francisco press, but little else.[28] "Let's all stand behind Harry," urged the newsletter's editor, "as we all know he surely deserves a place in the Hall of Fame."[29] Hooper expressed his appreciation of the efforts on his behalf but declined to take part in them.[30] The matter seemed closed at that point.

In 1966, however, the case was revived with George W. Poultney, one of the Brickpile Seniors whom Fenlon had enlisted to help in the first push for Harry. Poultney's interest in the case stemmed from his lifelong friendship with Hooper. A few years older than Harry, Poultney was a student at Saint Mary's and a member of the Phoenix when young Hooper arrived in 1902. Poultney played a few games with San Francisco and Oakland in the Pacific Coast League in 1904 and 1905 but lacked both interest and ability to pursue baseball professionally beyond that. He followed Harry's career closely, though, and now, serving as chairman of the Saint Mary's Alumni Baseball Committee, he organized a tribute for his friend.

The thrust of Poultney's effort was a ten-page document he sent to Paul Kerr, president of the National Baseball Hall of Fame, for distribution to the Veterans Committee.[31] Summarizing Harry's career and attaching letters of endorsement from Joe Wood, Larry Gardner, Marty McHale, and Bill Carrigan, Poultney attempted to address the shortcomings of the earlier effort on Hooper's behalf. His "case statement" focused on Harry's playing record and leadership role in both regular season and World Series competition and included a generous sampling of favorable evaluations of Hooper from Ruth, Cobb, McGraw, Barrow, and others. Particularly pointing out that sixteen men had already been inducted into the Hall of Fame who had batting averages under .300, "possibly the sole drawback to Hooper's recognition at Cooperstown," Poultney argued for Harry's achievements as a leadoff hitter in a dead-ball era dominated by outstanding pitching. "Under the circumstances," reasoned Poultney, Hooper's .281 average "is not alone commendable, but excellent." Unfortunately, however, as worthy as they, too, found Harry's record, the twelve members of the Veterans Committee failed to cast the necessary votes to induct Hooper at their January 1967 meeting.

Two years and two votes later, Harry still remained uninvited to the shrine. The campaign might have ended at this point had not the occasion of the greatest sadness in Hooper's life created the context for its renewal and, most important, his direct involvement in the effort. On March 19, 1969, Esther died of cancer. Heartbroken and inconsolable in his grief, Harry retreated within himself, causing his children deep worry about his well-being. Their efforts to lift his spirits were failing and they feared the worst from the depression that he seemed unwilling and unable to escape.

Back home in Baytown, Texas, after his mother's funeral and some time with Harry, John wondered whether the Cooperstown project might serve to get his father's mind off Esther's death. Staying up late at night, running old box scores and statistics through the computer at Sun Oil Company headquarters in Houston, where he worked, John began to formulate a better sense of his father's achievements in the game. Enlisting the help of Larry Gardner, who visited Harry and then sent him a copy of the *Baseball Encyclopedia*, John began to share his observations with his father, asking him for clarification on aspects of Harry's play, slowly engaging the old man in the research and restoring some purpose to his life.

With Harry guiding his work, John focused his attention on his father's defensive skills and, as Poultney had done, his record as a leadoff hitter. Liberally citing Hooper's contemporaries who attested to his greatness in these respects, John prepared an attractive brochure which he sent to Kerr in January 1970.[32] Still, Harry lacked the votes for induction. Undeterred, John revised the brochure, adding more testimony and presenting the data differently to emphasize Hooper's comparative strengths with other Hall of Famers.[33] The crux of the case lay in the figures demonstrating that Harry had performed his jobs as leadoff hitter and right fielder better than anyone else in the game to that point. Reaching base 3,602 times, stealing 375 bases, and scoring 1,429 runs, Hooper had compiled a record unmatched by any full-time leadoff hitter. Defensively, Harry had more assists (322) and double plays (79) than any right fielder, the latter still a Major League record, and his assists per chances ratio of 7.62 percent exceeded those of any outfielder in the Hall of Fame in 1970.

On Sunday morning, January 31, 1971, Harry received a conference call from Joe Cronin, Warren Giles, and Waite Hoyt, all members of the Veterans Committee. A few minutes later he telephoned John. "Son, we're in," he reported, "I made the Hall of Fame."[34]

For the induction ceremony on August 9, Harry gathered his children, grandchildren, and two old friends, Larry Gardner and Ed Daly, to share his joy. In a warm talk with a choking voice, Hooper recalled his passage from his parents' tenant farm in the Santa Clara Valley to his arrival in the Major Leagues. Mostly, though, he thanked those who had supported and encouraged him through the years—the fans in Boston and Chicago, the newspapermen who "kept my name before the public," his teachers, teammates, friends, and family. He particularly recognized John for "digging through the records and putting up a case for me." Harry then joined his fellow inductees and other members of the hall for a formal portrait on the lawn of the Otesaga Hotel overlooking Otsego Lake. At eighty-three the oldest living member of the Cooperstown gallery, Hooper posed with the greats of the game, younger men like Stan Musial, Bob Feller, Roy Campanella, and Joe DiMaggio, and others who harkened back to his own era, Sam Rice, Stan Coveleski, Jesse Haines, and Rube Marquard. Looking as tanned and fit as any of them, Harry shared the resounding applause of the onlookers for the distinguished company of which he was now a part, the most honored practitioners of the game of his youth.

Twice more, in the summers of 1972 and 1973, Hooper returned to Cooperstown for the annual induction ceremonies. The scene charmed the old veteran and he relished the attention he received. After waiting so many years for the recognition that a plaque in Cooperstown represented, though, he still found it difficult to put in perspective the meaning of his place among the game's immortals. Freely dispensing his autograph and posing for pictures for anyone who asked, he played the part of a celebrity but could not escape the modesty of his ways and the awkwardness of these moments to feel completely comfortable. "I've always thought I had the credentials and records to be voted into the Hall of Fame," he told an interviewer, "but now that it has happened, it's a little hard to believe."[35] What made the honor particularly bittersweet "is that it didn't come when Esther was still here. She was so much a part of it."[36]

In early 1974, Hooper suffered a stroke that curtailed his activity considerably and prevented a visit to Cooperstown that summer. However, it did not keep Harry at home for the deer season and he headed to the hills with his sons in September. For the first time in over fifty years of making this trip, though, he lacked the strength to participate fully in the chores and hunts and returned to Capitola before the season had ended. Moreover, the pains in his chest had returned and his doctors scheduled surgery to address an aneurysm. Walking alongside Harry's gurney as it was being wheeled toward the operating room on December 18, his son Harry, Jr. squeezed his father's hand. The old man opened his eyes toward him and said reassuringly, "Don't worry, son, I've had a good life."[37] Harry died in surgery. He was eighty-seven years old.

The announcement of Harry's death brought an outpouring of sympathy from around the country that reflected the wide circle of his associations and the deep respect he had earned in them. Contributions to his designated charity, the Santa Cruz County Association for the Mentally Retarded, and floral remembrances at the Mount Calvary Cemetery in Aptos, where he was laid to rest alongside Esther, bore the names of Saint Mary's College, Princeton University, the Boston Red Sox, the Chicago White Sox, the Baseball Hall of Fame, Duffy Lewis, Larry Gardner, and Rose Kennedy, the mother of President John F. Kennedy. Amid the glowing testimonials to his career appearing in the Bay Area newspapers, there were a few that captured the essence of his achievements in baseball particularly well. "In seventeen years as a Major League player," commented the *Santa Cruz Sentinel*, "the rock-bodied Hooper built performance statistics of excellence."[38] "Harry," added Larry Gardner, "was a class act."[39] Although his play often achieved the spectacular, it was always characterized by competitive steadiness and a craftsmanlike approach. These qualities underscored his claims on Cooperstown and forged the most lasting impressions about the character and conduct of his play. Baseball honored itself and its best professional traditions when it found a place in the pantheon for Harry the Cat.

Appendixes

Appendix A

Harry Hooper's Lifetime Record

Year	Club	League	G	AB	R	H	2B	3B	HR	RBI	BB	SB	BA	PO	A	E	DP	FA
1907	Alameda-Sac.	California	53	122	21	40	3	3	1	—	—	5	.328	—	—	—	—	—
1908	Sacramento	California	77	294	47	101	6	4	3	—	—	41	.344	116	17	4	3	.971
1909	Boston	American	81	255	29	72	3	4	0	16	16	15	.282	124	14	7	3	.952
1910	Boston	American	155	584	81	156	9	10	2	33	62	40	.267	241	30	18	7	.938
1911	Boston	American	130	524	93	163	20	6	4	43	73	38	.311	181	27	10	1	.954
1912	Boston	American	147	590	98	143	20	12	2	46	66	29	.242	220	22	9	6	.964
1913	Boston	American	148	586	100	169	29	12	4	40	60	26	.289	248	25	9	7	.968
1914	Boston	American	141	530	85	137	23	15	1	44	58	19	.258	231	23	7	5	.973
1915	Boston	American	149	566	90	133	20	13	2	48	89	22	.235	255	23	8	7	.972
1916	Boston	American	151	575	75	156	20	11	1	33	80	27	.271	266	19	10	5	.966
1917	Boston	American	151	559	89	143	21	11	3	43	80	21	.256	245	20	8	3	.971
1918	Boston	American	126	474	81	137	26	13	1	46	75	24	.289	221	16	9	8	.963
1919	Boston	American	128	491	76	131	25	6	3	48	79	23	.267	262	19	6	2	.979
1920	Boston	American	139	536	91	167	30	17	7	53	88	16	.312	263	22	11	2	.963
1921	Chicago	American	108	419	74	137	26	5	8	58	55	13	.327	182	12	5	2	.975
1922	Chicago	American	152	602	111	183	35	8	11	80	68	16	.304	288	19	12	7	.962
1923	Chicago	American	145	576	87	166	32	4	10	65	68	18	.288	272	15	12	5	.960
1924	Chicago	American	130	476	107	156	27	8	10	62	65	16	.328	251	22	4	8	.986
1925	Chicago	American	127	442	62	117	23	5	6	55	54	12	.265	231	16	6	4	.976
1926						(Out of organized baseball)												
1927	San Francisco Missions	Pacific Coast	78	218	35	62	9	0	1	19	—	4	.284	113	11	3	—	.976
	Major League Totals		2,308	8,785	1,429	2,466	389	160	75	817	1,136	375	.281	3,981	344	151	81	.966

World Series

Year	Club	League	G	AB	R	H	2B	3B	HR	RBI	BB	SB	BA	PO	A	E	DP	FA
1912	Boston	American	8	31	3	9	2	1	0	2	4	2	.290	16	3	0	1	1.000
1915	Boston	American	5	20	4	7	0	1	2	3	2	0	.350	8	0	1	0	.889
1916	Boston	American	5	21	6	7	1	1	0	1	3	1	.333	8	2	0	1	1.000
1918	Boston	American	6	20	0	4	0	0	0	0	2	0	.200	11	0	0	0	1.000
World Series Totals			24	92	13	27	3	3	2	6	11	3	.293	43	5	1	2	.980

Appendix B

Leading Colleges of Major League Players, 1871–1910

College/University	Type of institution	Location	Number of players
Notre Dame	Private/Catholic	Indiana	20
Holy Cross	Private/Catholic	Massachusetts	18
Georgetown	Private/Catholic	Washington, D.C.	17
Brown	Private/Nondenominational	Rhode Island	15
Saint Mary's	Private/Catholic	California	14
Pennsylvania	Private/Nondenominational	Pennsylvania	13
Fordham	Private/Catholic	New York	11
Manhattan	Private/Catholic	New York	11
Michigan	Public/State supported	Michigan	8
Bucknell	Private/Nondenominational	Pennsylvania	7
Dartmouth	Private/Nondenominational	New Hampshire	7
Illinois	Public/State supported	Illinois	7
St. Bonaventure	Private/Catholic	New York	7
Villanova	Private/Catholic	Pennsylvania	7
Princeton	Private/Nondenominational	New Jersey	6
Cornell	Private/Nondenominational	New York	5
Penn. State	Public/State supported	Pennsylvania	5
Pittsburgh	Public/State related	Pennsylvania	5
Santa Clara	Private/Catholic	California	5
Vermont	Public/State supported	Vermont	5
Washington	Private/Catholic	Missouri	5

Sources: Lee Allen "Notebooks," National Baseball Library; Player Files, NBL; College and University Alumni Directories; National Association of Professional Baseball Leagues, *The Story of Minor League Baseball* (Columbus, Ohio: Stoneman Press, 1952), "Outstanding Graduates of Colleges to Major Leagues," 661–66; Dave Anderson, Cappy Gagnon, Collegiate Baseball Committee *Newsletter*, Issue No. 1 (March 1989); and David L. Porter, ed. *Biographical Dictionary of American Sports: Baseball* (New York: Greenwood Press, 1987).

Appendix C

Proportion of Americans of College Age in College, 1870–1920

Academic Year	Population 18–21 years old	Higher education enrollments	% enrolled among 18–21 year-olds
1870	3,116,000	52,286	1.6
1880	4,253,000	115,817	2.7
1890	5,160,000	154,374	3.0
1900	5,931,000	231,761	3.9
1910	6,934,000	346,050	5.0
1920	7,386,000	582,268	7.9

Source: Seymour E. Harris, *A Statistical Portrait of Higher Education* (New York: McGraw-Hill, 1972), 412–13.

Appendix D

**Proportion of Major League Baseball Players
with Collegiate Experience, 1871–1920**

Decade	Players entering Major Leagues	Players with college experience	% players with college experience
1871–1880	489	20	4.1
1881–1890	1,068	30	2.8
1891–1900	647	52	8.1
1901–1910	1,218	269	22.1
1911–1920	1,532	427	27.9

Sources: Lee Allen "Notebooks," National Baseball Library, Baseball Hall of Fame, Cooperstown, N.Y.; Player Files, NBL; College and University Alumni Directories.

Appendix E

Former Collegiate Players on Selected Major League Rosters, 1876–1916

Year	Former collegians on ML rosters	Teams with greatest representation		Team record/finish
1876	5	Chicago (NL)	2	52–14/1st
1886	20	Chicago (NL)	3	90–34/1st
		Pittsburgh (AA)	3	80–57/2nd
		Cincinnati (AA)	3	65–73/5th
1896	23	Baltimore (NL)	5	90–39/1st
		Brooklyn (NL)	3	58–73/9th
1906	101	St. Louis (NL)	9	52–98/7th
		Chicago (NL)	7	116–36/1st
		Pittsburgh (NL)	7	93–60/3rd
		Brooklyn (NL)	7	66–86/5th
		Philadelphia (AL)	10	78–67/4th
		New York (AL)	8	90–61/2nd
		Boston (AL)	8	49–105/8th
1916	168	Chicago (NL)	13	67–86/5th
		Philadelphia (NL)	11	91–62/2nd
		Boston (NL)	11	89–63/3rd
		Pittsburgh (NL)	11	65–89/6th
		Philadelphia (AL)	19	36–117/8th
		Boston (AL)	16	91–63/1st
		Cleveland (AL)	16	77–77/6th

Legend: NL = National League; AA = American Association; AL = American League.

Sources: See appendix A. For rosters see also *The Baseball Encyclopedia,* 7th ed. (New York: MacMillan, 1988); John Thorn and Pete Palmer, eds., *Total Baseball* (New York: Warner, 1989).

Notes

Introduction

1. Other Hall of Fame inductees in 1971 were Jake Beckley, Dave Bancroft, Joe Kelley, and George Weiss. Only Weiss among these four was still living at the time, but his ill health prevented his attendance at the ceremony.

2. Eugene V. McCaffrey and Roger A. McCaffrey, *Players' Choice* (New York: Facts on File Publications, 1987), 22.

3. Bill James, *The Bill James Historical Baseball Abstract* (New York: Villard, 1986), 400.

4. Clipping of unattributed, undated Christy Walsh syndicated newspaper column in Hooper File, National Baseball Library, Cooperstown, N.Y.

5. John J. McGraw, *My Thirty Years in Baseball* (New York: Boni and Liveright, 1923), 234; interview between Ruth and Joe McGlone, 1947, quoted in John Hooper to Paul S. Kerr, president, National Baseball Hall of Fame, January 1, 1971, Hooper File, NBL.

6. See, for example, Harold Seymour, *Baseball: The Golden Age* (New York: Oxford University Press, 1971), 163; Robert W. Creamer, *Babe: The Legend Comes to Life* (New York: Simon and Schuster, 1974), 89, 114, 127, 150–51, 178–81, 184, 197; Charles C. Alexander, *Ty Cobb* (New York: Oxford University Press, 1984) and *John McGraw* (New York: Viking Penguin, 1988); Ed Linn, *The Great Rivalry: The Yankees and the Red Sox, 1901–1990* (New York: Ticknor & Fields, 1991), 47, 64, 73; Mike Sowell, *The Pitch That Killed: Carl Mays, Ray Chapman and the Pennant Race of 1920* (New York: Macmillan, 1989), 11–12, 23, 123, 231; Donald Honig, *Baseball America* (New York: Macmillan, 1985), 130–31.

7. On the social characteristics and geographic backgrounds of Major League players, see Steven A. Riess, *Touching Base: Professional Baseball and American Culture in the Progressive Era* (Westport, Conn.: Greenwood Press, 1980), 151–219; Carl F. Ojala and Michael T. Gadwood, "The Geography of Major League Baseball Player Production, 1876–1988," in Alvin L. Hall, ed., *Cooperstown Symposium on Baseball and the American Culture, 1989* (Westport, Conn.: Meckler, 1991), 165–85.

8. See, for example, Ellery H. Clark, Jr., *Boston Red Sox: 75th Anniversary History* (Hicksville, N.Y.: Exposition Press, 1975) and *Red Sox Forever* (Hicks-

ville, N.Y.: Exposition Press, 1977); Donald Honig, *The Boston Red Sox: An Illustrated Tribute* (New York: St. Martin's Press, 1984).

9. Although, as Jacques Barzun observed, "of all the books that no one can write, those about nations and national character are the most impossible," the effort has engaged observers of the American scene from John Winthrop to Jesse Jackson. Among the noteworthy in between have been Benjamin Franklin, *Autobiography* (1789), Michael-Guillaume-Jean de Crevecoeur, "Letters from an American Farmer" (1782), Alexis de Tocqueville, *Democracy in America* (1835), Frederick Jackson Turner, "The Significance of the Frontier in American History" (1893), David Riesman, *The Lonely Crowd* (1950), Henry Nash Smith, *Virgin Land: The American West as Symbol and Myth* (1950), David M. Potter, *People of Plenty* (1954), and Robert N. Bellah et al., *Habits of the Heart: Individualism and Commitment in American Life* (1985). An interesting essay on the futility of the search is Potter, "The Quest for the National Character," in John Higham, ed., *The Reconstruction of American History* (New York: Harper and Row, 1962), 197–220.

10. Kevin Starr, *Americans and the California Dream, 1850–1915* (New York: Oxford University Press, 1973), vii.

11. The all-star team was selected through the balloting of fans as part of a promotion to mark the one-hundredth anniversary of professional baseball, 1869–1969. The fans of each Major League team voted for their all-stars, the Baseball Writers Association of America then compiled an "ultimate" all-star team. Hooper shared the Chicago all-star outfield with Al Simmons and Johnny Mostil. Hooper finished second behind Carl Yastrzemski in the Boston balloting for the Red Sox right fielder. *The Sporting News*, July 5, 1969.

Chapter 1: Passage to California

1. As mentioned in the introduction, three generations of Hoopers have contributed to a rich and varied chronicle of the family's history. Harry was the first to undertake the effort, dating to a detailed diary he kept in 1909, his first season in the Major Leagues. He and his wife, Esther, meticulously saved his clippings and correspondence throughout his career and arranged them in scrapbooks and files. Years later, their two sons, Harry, Jr., and John, followed their parent's example, urging their father to record his memoirs in writing and on audiotape. They arranged for several taping sessions with Harry alone and with his old teammates and friends, notably Larry Gardner and Paul Johnson, and explored other aspects of the family's history through trips to Prince Edward Island and England. John, in particular, in conjunction with the effort to get his father into the Baseball Hall of Fame, began to organize Harry's papers in a more systematic fashion, placing some of them in computer files.

Among the papers in the possession of his sons are several first-person written narratives, six by Harry and one by his father, Joseph. They vary in length and detail, but they are remarkably consistent and complementary.

Although most are not specifically dated, I have been able to ascertain their approximate time of composition with the help of John and through marginal notes on them. These papers are as follows:

Narrative A: Joe Hooper on his early childhood, travels, many jobs, move to California, and early married years. Five typewritten pages. Approximate composition: early 1930s.

Narrative B: Harry Hooper on his parents' background and life on the San Luis ranch. Twelve handwritten pages. Approximate composition: 1964–66.

Narrative C: Condensed version of Narrative B. Two typewritten pages. Approximate composition: 1964–66.

Narrative D: Harry Hooper on selected highlights in his life, 1887–1957. Five handwritten pages. Approximate composition: 1964–66.

Narrative E: Harry Hooper on the family farms in the Santa Clara and San Joaquin valleys. Two typewritten pages. Composed 1966.

Narrative F: Harry Hooper on the background of his parents, early years in the Santa Clara and San Joaquin valleys, career at Saint Mary's. Eight typewritten pages. Approximate composition: 1966–68.

Narrative G: Detailed narrative of Harry Hooper's life beginning with his earliest recollections of the move to Volta in the San Joaquin Valley up to the 1915 World Series. Twelve typewritten pages. Composed 1968.

These papers will be referred to throughout the text as narratives A through G as appropriately cited. Other materials from the Hooper holdings will be cited generally as the Hooper Papers, Baytown, Texas, or Capitola, California, and more specifically as the citation warrants.

2. Anthony Hocking, *Prince Edward Island* (New York: McGraw-Hill Ryerson Ltd., 1978), 16–19. Sketches of William Hooper's commercial interests and political career are in *Hutchinson's Prince Edward Island Directory* (1864), 158; *The Canadian Parliamentary Companion and Annual Register* (1881), 374–75.

3. Patricia A. Thornton, "The Problem of Out-Migration from Atlantic Canada, 1871–1921: A New Look," in P. A. Buckner and David Frank, eds., *Atlantic Canada After Confederation: The Acadiensis Reader*, vol. 2 (Fredericton, New Brunswick: Acadiensis Press, 1988), 34–65.

4. Gilbert C. Fite and Jim E. Reese, *An Economic History of the United States*, 3d ed. (Boston: Houghton Mifflin, 1973), 291.

5. Bernard Bailyn, David Brion Davis, et al., *The Great Republic: A History of the American People*, vol. 2 (Lexington, Mass.: D. C. Heath, 1977), 780.

6. Leonard Dinnerstein and David M. Reimers, *Ethnic Americans: A History of Immigration and Assimilation* (New York: Dodd, Mead, 1975), 17, 162.

7. Starr, *Americans and the California Dream*, 68.

8. Leigh Irvine, *Santa Clara County, California* (San Jose: Board of Supervisors, 1915), 41.

9. E. W. Hilgard, *Report on the Physical and Agricultural Features of the State of California* (San Francisco: Pacific Rural Press, 1884), publisher's preface.

10. For accounts of the founding meeting of the National League, see David Q. Voigt, *American Baseball: From the Gentlemen's Sport to the Commissioner System,* vol. 1 (Norman: University of Oklahoma Press, 1966), 63–66; Harvey Frommer, *Primitive Baseball: The First Quarter Century of the National Pastime* (New York: Atheneum, 1988), 20–27; Harold Seymour, *Baseball: The Early Years* (New York: Oxford University Press, 1960), 80.

11. Andrew F. Rolle, *California: A History* (New York: Crowell, 1963), 367.

12. Two very different accounts of travel on a transcontinental train in the late 1870s are provided by Robert Louis Stevenson, "Across the Plains" in James D. Hart, ed., *From Scotland to Silverado* (Cambridge, Mass.: Belknap Press, 1966) and a series in *Frank Leslie's Illustrated Newspaper,* November 3, 1877, December 15, 1877, and February 9, 1878. Stevenson, a twenty-nine-year-old Scottish journalist at the time, traveled on an emigrant train in 1879 for the experience. He was shocked by the discomfort, boredom, humiliation, and unsanitary conditions which characterized his journey. In contrast, millionaire publisher Frank Leslie undertook a five-month western excursion from October 1877 to February 1878. Traveling in his own private hotel car (the kind that rented for fifty dollars a day), Leslie was accompanied by reporters, sketch artists, photographers, a few friends, his wife, and her dog. Said one of his well-heeled traveling companions: "The rarest and richest of all my journeying through life is this 3000 miles by rail."

13. Accounts of California in the 1870s include David S. Lavendar, *California: Land of New Beginnings* (New York: Harper and Row, 1972), 295–310, and Edward Staniford, *The Pattern of California History* (San Francisco: Canfield Press, 1975), 248–51. Specific studies of San Francisco during the decade include Oscar Lewis, *San Francisco: Mission to Metropolis,* 2d ed. (San Diego: Howell-North, 1980), 135–65, and Robert W. Cherny and William Issel, *San Francisco, 1865–1932: Politics, Power, and Urban Development* (Berkeley: University of California Press, 1986), 125–30.

14. Richly detailed descriptions of the Santa Clara Valley are presented in Eugene T. Sawyer, *History of Santa Clara County* (Los Angeles: Historic Record Company, 1922), 33–34, 85–86, and Yvonne Jacobson, *Passing Farms, Enduring Values: California's Santa Clara Valley* (Los Altos, Calif.: William Kaufman, 1984), 18, 20–22, 94–96.

15. Louis B. Wright, *The Cultural Life of the American Colonies* (New York: Harper and Row, 1957), 46, 58–62, 65–67.

16. Marcus Lee Hansen, *The Atlantic Migration, 1607–1860* (New York: Harper and Row, 1940), 244, 252–54, 274–76, 286–87, 293–94.

Chapter 2: The Game of His Youth

1. Narrative F, 2.

2. For descriptions of the San Joaquin Valley, land prices, and agricultural

conditions during the late nineteenth century, see Lavender, *California: Land of New Beginnings*, 292–93; Rolle, *California: A History*, 240; and Starr, *Americans and the California Dream*, 172–73.

3. Narrative F, 2–3; Narrative G, 1–3.

4. Narrative F, 2–3; Narrative G, 2–3.

5. Narrative G, 2.

6. Hooper ascribed Lulu's death in his memoirs to "brain fever." The symptoms he described—high fever, a steady loss of strength, and severe headache—suggest that she suffered from a viral infection known as cerebrospinal fever or meningitis. Narrative G, 2.

7. Narrative F, 4.

8. Darrow quoted in Harold Seymour, *Baseball: The People's Game* (New York: Oxford University Press, 1990), 19.

9. Hooper, Remarks at Induction Ceremony, Baseball Hall of Fame, Cooperstown, New York, August 9, 1971.

10. On the minor leagues in the late nineteenth century, see Neil J. Sullivan, *The Minors: The Struggles and the Triumph of Baseball's Poor Relation from 1876 to the Present* (New York: St. Martin's Press, 1990), 5–24; Bob Hoie, "The Minor Leagues," in John Thorn and Pete Palmer, eds., *Total Baseball* (New York: Warner, 1989), 581.

11. Narrative F, 6; Hall of Fame Induction Remarks.

12. Brooklyn was still an autonomous city in 1887. It would not lose this status until 1897, when it was consolidated into greater New York City as one of five boroughs. On this development, see Neil J. Sullivan, *The Dodgers Move West* (New York: Oxford University Press, 1987), 7. A general history of baseball in Brooklyn is Richard Goldstein, *Superstars and Screwballs: 100 Years of Brooklyn Baseball* (New York: Dutton, 1991).

13. The importance of the 1858 series in stimulating interest in baseball is discussed in Melvin L. Adelman, *A Sporting Time: New York City and the Rise of Modern Athletics, 1820–70* (Urbana: University of Illinois Press, 1986), 131–32; Warren Goldstein, *Playing for Keeps: A History of Early Baseball* (Ithaca, N.Y.: Cornell University Press, 1989), 70; Steven A. Riess, *City Games: The Evolution of American Urban Society and the Rise of Sports* (Urbana: University of Illinois Press, 1989), 40–41; Seymour, *Baseball: The Early Years*, 25–26; and Goldstein, *Superstars*, 5–6.

14. Quoted in Adelman, *A Sporting Time*, 132.

15. On the social and economic status of baseball players, 1845–65, see Adelman, *A Sporting Time*, 122–26, 138–42, 154–56, 175–83; Riess, *City Games*, 35–36; Goldstein, *Playing for Keeps*, 24–27; Donald J. Mrozek, *Sport and American Mentality, 1880–1910* (Knoxville: University of Tennessee Press, 1983), 104, 107–8. A brief biographical portrait of Creighton is provided by Mark D. Rucker in Robert L. Tiemann and Mark D. Rucker, eds., *Nineteenth Century Stars* (Cooperstown: Society for American Baseball Research, 1989), 32.

16. On baseball strategy in the 1890s, see Bill Felber, "The Changing

Game," in Thorn, *Total Baseball*, 270–74; James, *The Bill James Historical Baseball Abstract*, 38–40; Alexander, *John McGraw*, 25–26.

17. No one better exemplified this situation than Amos Rusie of the New York Giants. The big man from Indiana had earned his apt nickname, the Hoosier Thunderbolt, for the sheer velocity he generated with his pitches from only fifty feet away. Connie Mack, who observed the game for nearly sixty years, thought Rusie was the hardest thrower he had ever seen. Rusie's "heat" compelled his catcher to place a molded piece of lead, wrapped in a handkerchief and layered with sponges, in the palm of his hand to cushion the ball's impact. For the three seasons prior to the placement of the pitching rubber at the new, longer distance, Rusie won ninety-four games with an earned run average of 2.66. But he lost eighty-five. In 1890 he was 29–34 with a league-leading 345 strikeouts and an ERA of only 2.56, third lowest in the National League. Similarly, Wild Bill Hutchinson of Chicago hurled 627 innings and notched thirty-seven wins in 1892 with an earned run average of 2.74, well below the league ERA of 3.28. Yet the former star for Yale also lost thirty-six decisions. See David B. Merrell, "Amos Wilson Rusie," in David L. Porter, ed., *Biographical Dictionary of American Sports: Baseball* (Westport, Conn.: Greenwood Press, 1987), 493; Mike Shatzkin, ed., *The Ballplayers* (New York: William Morrow, 1990), 947–48.

18. Felber, "The Changing Game," 273.

19. Tyrus R. Cobb with Al Stump, *My Life in Baseball: The True Record* (Garden City, N.Y.: Doubleday, 1961), 41.

20. Sawyer, *History of Santa Clara County*, 630, 633.

21. Narrative B, 3; Narrative C, 1; Narrative F, 4.

22. Narrative F, 4–6; Narrative G, 2–3.

23. Narrative F, 6; Narrative G, 3–4.

24. Hooper, Hall of Fame Induction Remarks.

Chapter 3: College Days, Career Choices

1. Figures pertaining to enrollments are in Frederick Rudolph, *Curriculum: A History of the Undergraduate Course of Study Since 1636* (San Francisco: Jossey-Bass, 1977), 101; Edwin C. Rozwenc, *The Making of American Society*, vol. 2 (Boston: Allyn and Bacon, 1973), 155; Stanley Coben and Arthur S. Link, *The Democratic Heritage: A History of the United States* (Waltham, Mass.: Ginn and Company, 1971), 577; Bureau of the Census, United States Department of Commerce, *The Statistical Abstract of the United States*, 97th ed. (Washington: Government Printing Office, 1977), 5.

2. On the changing conditions of student life at American colleges and universities and the role of sport, see Ronald A. Smith, *Sports and Freedom: The Rise of Big-Time College Athletics* (New York: Oxford University Press, 1988), chap. 2, "Sport, the Extracurriculum, and the Idea of Freedom," 13–25; Joseph F. Kett, *Rites and Passages* (New York: Basic Books, 1977); Oscar Handlin and Mary F. Handlin, *The American College and American Culture*

(New York: McGraw-Hill, 1970); Frederick Rudolph, *The American College and University* (New York: Knopf, 1968); Lawrence A. Cremin, *American Education: The National Experience, 1783–1876* (New York: Harper and Row, 1980); David Henry, *Challenges Past, Challenges Present* (San Francisco: Jossey-Bass, 1975); Lawrence R. Veysey, *The Emergence of the American University* (Chicago: University of Chicago Press, 1965); Richard Hofstadter and Wilson Smith, eds., *American Higher Education* (Chicago: University of Chicago Press, 1961); Burton J. Bledstein, *The Culture of Professionalism: The Middle Class and the Development of Higher Education in America* (New York: Norton, 1976).

3. On the rise of intercollegiate athletics, see Smith, *Sports and Freedom;* Benjamin G. Rader, *American Sports: From the Age of Folk Games to the Age of Spectators* (Englewood Cliffs, N.J.: Prentice-Hall, 1983); John A. Lucas and Ronald A. Smith, *Saga of American Sport* (Philadelphia: Lea & Febiger, 1978); Betty Spears and R. Swanson, *History of Sport and Physical Activity in the United States* (Dubuque, Iowa: Brown, 1978); John R. Betts, *America's Sporting Heritage: 1850–1950* (Reading, Mass.: Addison-Wesley, 1974); C. W. Hackensmith, *History of Physical Education* (New York: Harper, 1966); Howard J. Savage et al., *American College Athletics* (New York: Carnegie Foundation, 1933); Donald Chu, *The Character of American Higher Education and Intercollegiate Sport* (Albany: State University of New York Press, 1989).

4. On the Harvard-Yale crew race of 1852 and other aspects of intercollegiate crew competitions in the nineteenth century, see Guy M. Lewis, "America's First Intercollegiate Sport: The Regattas from 1852 to 1875," *Research Quarterly* 38 (December 1967): 637 48, and "The Beginning of Organized Collegiate Sport" *American Quarterly* 22 (Summer 1970): 222–29; Joseph J. Matthews, "The First Harvard-Oxford Race," *New England Quarterly* 33 (March 1960): 74–82; Robert F. Kelley, *American Rowing: Its Background and Traditions* (New York: Putnam's, 1932).

5. *New York Herald,* June 26, 1897, 3, quoted in Smith, *Sports and Freedom,* 51.

6. The primary history of the San Francisco District of the Christian Brothers is Ronald E. Isetti, F.S.C., *Called to the Pacific: A History of the Christian Brothers of the San Francisco District, 1868–1944* (Winona, Minn.: Saint Mary's College Press, 1979). Historical accounts of Saint Mary's College include Matthew McDevitt, F.S.C., *The Early Years of Saint Mary's College, 1859–1879* (Moraga, Calif.: Saint Mary's College, 1970) and *The Late Years of Saint Mary's College, 1879–1969* (Moraga, Calif.: Saint Mary's College, 1970); William Beatie, F.S.C., "125 Years: An Educational Adventure," paper prepared for the Board of Regents, Saint Mary's College, 1988; and Mel Anderson, F.S.C., *The President's Report: 125th Anniversary Edition* (Moraga, Calif.: Saint Mary's College, 1988).

7. Saint Mary's College, *Catalogue, 1908–1909,* 126–53. This edition of the *Catalogue* provides a complete listing of graduates of the college since 1872. *The College Roll, 1883–1919* lists all matriculants in the collegiate programs.

8. Isetti, *Called to the Pacific*, 21–22. Also, editions of the college *Catalogue*, particularly for the 1870s and 1880s, provide details on the highly regimented schedule followed by the boarding students, who accounted for more than 90 percent of the school's enrollment.

9. Isetti, *Called to the Pacific*, 22–23. On Thomas Hughes's influence and the origins of the Muscular Christianity Movement, see William Blaikie, "American Bodies," *Harper's Weekly* 27 (December 1883): 770; Guy Lewis, "The Muscular Christianity Movement," *Journal of Health, Physical Education and Recreation* 37 (May 1966): 27–28, 62; John A. Lucas, "A Prelude to the Rise of Sport: Ante-Bellum America, 1850–1860," *Quest* 2 (December 1968): 50–57.

10. Although mainly a history of football at Saint Mary's during the Edward P. ("Slip") Madigan era of the 1920s and 1930s, Randy Andrada, *They Did It Everytime: Saga of the Saint Mary's Gaels* (Piedmont, Calif.: Randy Andrada, 1975, 1987), 5–7, 15–23, provides commentary on the beginnings of intercollegiate athletics at the college.

11. Ronald A. Smith, "The Rise of College Baseball," *Baseball History* 1, no. 1 (Spring 1986): 23–27. An exchange of correspondence between Col. A. M. Weyand and Maurice L. Ahern, Archivist of Fordham University (Ahern to Weyand, January 27, 1966; Weyand to Ahern, January 29, 1966) attributes an unspecified reference, "probably in the files of the old *New York Tribune*," to support the Fordham-Xavier contest as the first college game in the United States with nine men on a side. The letters are in the College Baseball File at the National Baseball Library in Cooperstown, New York.

12. Smith, *Sports and Freedom*, 56. For accounts of baseball play among the Civil War troops, see Jim Sumner, "Baseball at Salisbury Prison Camp," in Peter Levine, ed., *Baseball History* (Westport, Conn.: Meckler, 1989): 19–26; Bell I. Wiley, *The Life of Billy Yank: The Common Soldier of the Union* (Indianapolis: Bobbs-Merrill, 1952), 170, and *The Life of Johnny Reb: The Common Soldier of the Confederacy* (Baton Rouge: Lousiana State University Press, 1943), 159; Lawrence W. Fielding, "War and Trifles: The Meter Stick of the Civil War Soldier," *Journal of Sport History* 4, no. 2 (Summer 1977): 151–68

13. Goldstein, *Playing for Keeps*, 72; Jack Selzer, *Baseball in the Nineteenth Century: An Overview* (Cooperstown, N.Y.: Society for American Baseball Research, 1986), 5.

14. *Wilkes' Spirit of the Times* 19 (September 26, 1869): 89.

15. Smith, "College Baseball," 27.

16. Selzer, *Baseball*, 5.

17. Issel and Cherny, *San Francisco*, 14.

18. *Daily Alta California*, January 14, 1852, 2.

19. Baseball in 1860s San Francisco was only one recreational diversion among many. Enthusiasm for the game grew steadily but still paled in comparison with the city's fascination with gambling and racing, either horse or human. Trotters, quarter horses, and thoroughbreds attracted thousands of

spectators, while pedestrianism not only drew viewers to events but also encouraged many to take up vigorous exercise on their own. Sailing, cycling, and roller skating especially benefited from the interest in recreation for social and healthful purposes and engaged Bay Area residents in growing numbers. On early San Francisco sports and recreation, see Roger W. Lotchin, *San Francisco, 1846–1856: From Hamlet to City* (New York: Oxford University Press, 1974), 284–86; Roberta J. Park, "San Franciscans at Work and at Play, 1846–1869," *Journal of the West* 22, no. 1 (January 1983): 44–51; Joel Franks, "Sweeney of San Francisco: A Local Boy Makes Good, Then Not So Good," *Baseball History* 2, no. 4 (Winter 1987–88), 53. On the origins of San Francisco baseball, see Fred Lange, *History of Baseball in California and Pacific Coast Leagues, 1847–1938* (San Francisco: 1938); David Nemec, "A History of Baseball in the San Francisco Bay Area," *San Francisco Giants Official 1985 Yearbook* (San Francisco: Woodford Associates, 1985), 1–14; Robert K. Barney, "Of Rails and Red Stockings: Episodes in the Expansion of the National Pastime in the American West," *Journal of the West* 17, no. 3 (July 1978): 61–70; Natalie Vermilyea and Jim Moore, "A Ballad of the Republic," *The Californians* 6 (May-June 1988): 42–49; Joel Franks, "The California League of 1886–1893: The Last Refuge of Disorganized Baseball," *The Californians* 6 (May-June 1988): 50–56.

20. Adelman, *A Sporting Time,* 121.

21. Lange, *Baseball in California,* 6–7; Nemec, "Baseball in San Francisco," 3; *San Francisco Morning Call,* April 7, 1890, which provided biographical sketches "of the men who have aided in bringing the national sport to its present prosperous condition" in San Francisco.

22. Lange, *Baseball in California,* 6–7.

23. Issel and Cherny, *San Francisco,* 65.

24. *Daily Alta California,* April 23, 1867.

25. Accounts of the Cincinnati Red Stockings' 1869 season and tour include Barney, "Of Rails and Redstockings"; Joseph S. Stern, Sr., "The Team That Couldn't Be Beat: The Red Stockings of 1869," *Cincinnati Historical Society Bulletin* 27 (1969): 25–41; David Q. Voigt, "America's First Red Scare— The Cincinnati Reds of 1869," *Ohio History* 73 (1969): 13–24.

26. *Daily Alta California,* June 16, 1870, 1; *Oakland Daily News,* December 2, 1872, 3.

27. The travels of the Centennials can be traced in the pages of the *New York Clipper,* one of the major sporting journals of the nineteenth century.

28. *New York Clipper,* July 22, 1876, 133.

29. Ibid., August 12, 1876, 139.

30. Ibid., 155; August 19, 1876, 139.

31. Nemec, "Baseball in San Francisco," 3.

32. *San Francisco Chronicle,* June 21, 1880, 3; June 27, 1880, 5; March 28, 1881, 5.

33. Dick Dobbins, "Oakland's Long Baseball Heritage," *Official Magazine of the Oakland Athletics* 8 (1988): 39-43.

34. Charles N. Weber to George Poultney, September 1, 1904, Saint Mary's College Archives.

35. Franks, "Sweeney of San Francisco," 54.

36. On the play-for-pay controversy, see Smith, "Rise of College Baseball," 34–38, and *Sports and Freedom*, 62–66.

37. *Boston Post*, November 25, 1889, in "1899 Football Controversy" File, HUD 10889.1, Harvard University Archives.

38. Samuel L. Clemens, *Mark Twain's Speeches* (New York: Harper and Brothers, 1923), 145.

39. Gerald P. Beaumont, "A Training School for Baseball Stars," *Baseball Magazine* 18 (November 1916): 74.

40. A useful source for information and anecdotes on the Phoenix is the *Brickpile Seniors Newsletter*. Published from 1952 to 1955, it was the short-lived effort of several Saint Mary's College alumni to maintain contact among students who had attended the college when it was located in Oakland from 1889 to 1928. The one-square-block, five-story red brick building which housed the college during those years was affectionately called "the brick-pile." Entries in the issues of September 19, 1952, October 15, 1952, February 17, 1953, and June 15, 1953, provide some detail on the playing arrangements between members of the Phoenix and local semipro outfits.

41. Rick Wolff, editorial director, *The Baseball Encyclopedia*, 8th ed., rev. (New York: Macmillan, 1990), 901.

42. James, *Baseball Abstract*, 51.

43. Wolff, *Baseball Encyclopedia*, 959, 1742, 1819.

44. Other western institutions sending a representative number of players to the Major Leagues between 1871 and 1910 included the University of California-Berkeley (4) and Iowa State University (3). See appendix B for a listing of the colleges and universities that sent the most players on to the Major Leagues from 1871 to 1910.

45. On the development of intercollegiate sport at Catholic colleges and universities, see Chu, *American Higher Education and Intercollegiate Sport*, 34; Rudolph, *American College and University*, 385; and Savage et al., *American College Athletics*, 263–65.

46. *Brickpile Seniors Newsletter*, August 15, 1953, 6.

47. Beaumont, "Training School for Stars," 74.

48. Isetti, *Called to the Pacific*, 171-74; Andrada, *They Did It Everytime*, 7. Sports coverage in the college's student newspaper, the *Collegian*, amply documents the ever-present figure of Brother Agnon in the baseball program. From designing uniforms, testing equipment, and groundskeeping to recruiting players and coaching and mentoring them, the unofficial "dean of athletics" assumed something of a proprietary interest in the game. Both Isetti and Andrada suggest that the intensity of his commitment to baseball reflected his frustration at not having the opportunity to play professionally himself. Bay Area newspaper articles on Agnon include George T. Davis, "Big League Stars," *San Francisco Bulletin*, February 4, 1926, and Gene

Cohn, "Many Big League Stars Turned Out by Little California College," *Oakland Tribune*, April 8, 1923.

49. Hooper's career at Saint Mary's can be traced through newspaper clippings and press releases in the Saint Mary's College Archives and the National Sports Library Archives, San Jose, California. A particularly worthwhile piece is the brochure "Phoenix Guide," published by the Saint Mary's College Athletic Association in 1907.

50. "Phoenix Guide," 6.

51. On the California League, see Al H. Martin, "The Pacific Coast League," *Baseball Magazine* 3, no. 5 (September 1909): 39; Lange, *Baseball in California*, 3–4; Dobbins, "Oakland's Baseball Heritage," 39–40.

52. For discussions of the National Agreement and the reserve clause, see Seymour, *Baseball: The Early Years*, 104–15, 145–48, and Voigt, *American Baseball* 1:127–28.

53. Sullivan, *The Minors*, 54–55.

54. Hooper interview in Lawrence Ritter, *The Glory of Their Times* (New York: William Morrow, 1984), 139.

55. Mary Katherine Hooper to Harry, November 22, 1908, Hooper Papers, Baytown, Texas.

Chapter 4: A Season in the Majors

1. The letter from McBreen to Hooper, dated February 15, 1909, is in the Hooper Papers, Baytown, Texas, as is the Harry Hooper Diary. See the diary entry for February 27, 1909. Hooper purchased the diary at his mother's suggestion before leaving Capitola. By all indications, he intended to keep a detailed record of his entire first season with the Red Sox. In the early going he did, for the diary contains a richly detailed account of his first few months as a Major Leaguer. By June, however, the entries were less frequent, less expansive. By July they had stopped altogether. But for the brief time Hooper applied himself to his diary, he left a warm and informative account of a rookie's life in professional baseball.

2. John Milton Cutter, ed. and comp., *Cutter's Official Guide to Hot Springs, Arkansas,* 61st ed. (Hot Springs: Charles Cutter & Son, 1917), 7.

3. Seymour, *Baseball: The Early Years*, 184; Shatzkin, *The Ballplayers*, 26; Jim Charlton, *The Baseball Fan's Guide to Spring Training* (Reading, Mass.: Addison-Wesley, 1988), 7; Ray Robinson, *Iron Horse: Lou Gehrig in His Time* (New York: Norton, 1990), 77–78.

4. Quoted in Ross Newhan, "Spring Training Still One of the Great American Traditions," *Albany Times Union*, March 1, 1987, C–12.

5. *Brooklyn Daily Eagle*, February 24, 1907.

6. Dee Brown, *The American Spa: Hot Springs, Arkansas* (Little Rock: Rose Publishing Co., 1982), 92.

7. In 1911 the Red Sox traveled to Redondo Beach, California, for spring training. In 1919 they chose Tampa, Florida.

8. *Boston Globe,* March 6, 1909.

9. Ibid., March 1, 1909.

10. Ibid., March 5, 1909.

11. James, *Historical Baseball Abstract,* 49–51; James D. Smith, "Bowing Out on Top," *The National Pastime* (Fall 1982): 75. In addition, Albert Spalding picked Lange for his all-time all-star team in the outfield, and Al Spink of *The Sporting News* considered him the equal of the young Ty Cobb.

12. *Boston Globe,* March 6, 1909.

13. Hooper interview in Ritter, *Glory of Their Times,* 142; original transcript of interview with additional notes of Hooper, Hooper Papers. See also Robinson, *Iron Horse,* 81, for Lou Gehrig's similar treatment as a newcomer with the Yankees in 1924.

14. Hooper Diary, March 9, 1909.

15. *Boston Globe,* March 10, 1909.

16. Hooper Diary, March 10–16, 1909.

17. *Boston Globe,* March 10, 11, 1909.

18. Ibid., March 14, 1909.

19. Hooper Diary, March 21, 1909.

20. Ibid., March 21, 25, 1909.

21. Ibid., March 21, 1909.

22. *Boston Globe,* March 15, 1909.

23. Hooper Diary, April 10–12, 1909.

24. Ibid., April 12, 1909; *Boston Globe,* April 13, 1909.

25. Hooper Diary, April 13, 1909; original manuscript of Hooper-Ritter interview.

26. Hooper-Ritter interview; *Boston Globe,* April 14, 1909.

27. Hooper Diary, April 16, 1909.

28. Hooper-Ritter interview, original manuscript.

29. Hooper Diary, April 16, 1909.

30. Hooper-Ritter interview, original manuscript.

31. "Harry Hooper Fooled Training Camp Critics," *Boston Globe,* April 19, 1909.

32. Hooper Diary, April 17–19, 1909.

33. Philip J. Lowry, *Green Cathedrals* (Cooperstown, N.Y.: Society for American Baseball Research, 1986), 36–37; Michael Benson, *Ballparks of North America: A Comprehensive Historical Reference to Baseball Grounds, Yards, and Stadiums, 1845 to the Present* (Jefferson, N.C.: McFarland and Co., 1989), 40–41.

34. Richard Cohen and David S. Neft, *The World Series* (New York: St. Martin's Press, 1990), 3–4.

35. Hooper Diary, April 21, 1909.

36. Hooper engaged in a lengthy correspondence with his son John when John briefly pursued a professional baseball career of his own from 1945 to 1948. Sharing his knowledge and observations of the game, Harry keenly followed his son's play in the New York Yankee organization with Bingham-

ton, New York, in the Eastern League, Victoria, British Columbia, in the Western International League, and, finally, the AA club at Beaumont in the Texas League. For Harry's views on slumps, see Harry Hooper to John Hooper, July 18, 1947, April 28, 1948, and May 12, 1948, Hooper Papers, Baytown, Texas.

37. Harry Hooper to John Hooper, March 30, 1947.

38. Ibid., May 12, 1948.

39. Ibid., July 18, 1947.

40. Hooper to Ellery Clark, April 8, 1974, Clark Papers, Annapolis, Md.

Chapter 5: Trial and Triumph

1. Hooper to Committee on Veterans, National Baseball Hall of Fame, January 24, 1972, and January 17, 1973. Hooper recalled Lewis's career in these letters as part of a campaign to get Duffy elected to the Hall of Fame. Lewis has not yet been so honored.

2. John J. Evers with Hugh Fullerton, *Touching Second: The Science of Baseball* (Chicago: Reilly and Britton, 1910), 73, 79.

3. David Falkner, *Nine Sides of the Diamond: Baseball's Great Glove Men on the Fine Art of Defense* (New York: Random House, 1990), 256–57.

4. Babe Ruth with Bob Considine, *The Babe Ruth Story* (New York: Dutton, 1948), 223.

5. Harry Hooper to John Hooper, August 19, 1970, Hooper Papers, Baytown, Texas. Harry's addendum to this letter, a brief paper entitled "The Art of Hitting in Lead Off Position," contributed to his son's analysis of Harry's place among the best leadoff hitters in Major League baseball.

6. Ibid.

7. *Boston Herald*, April 27, 1909; *Cincinnati Enquirer*, April 27, 1909.

8. Mack to August Herrmann, June 9, 1910, Powers File, NBL.

9. Harry Hooper to John Hooper, December 10, 1970, Hooper Papers, Baytown.

10. Francis Richter, "The 1910 American League Teams," in *The Reach Official American League Baseball Guide* (Philadelphia: Reach, 1911), 60–61.

11. Frederick G. Lieb, *The Boston Red Sox* (New York: Putnam's, 1947), 83.

12. Walter Judge, "Bosox Finally Return for Series with SF," *San Francisco Examiner*, January 15, 1957, 7. Other accounts of the game are in the *Brickpile Seniors Newsletter*, Saint Mary's College, October 15, 1952, 2–3, and June 15, 1953, 4–5. Harry Simpson, Saint Mary's Class of 1912, contributed additional details on the game in a letter to the editor of the *Oakland Tribune*, April 21, 1953.

13. Quoted in Simpson's letter to the editor.

14. Connie Mack, *My 66 Years in the Big Leagues* (Philadelphia: John C. Winston Co., 1950), 43. Leonard saw action for Philadelphia in September

1911, splitting four decisions in five games with a 2.84 ERA. He did not make the club the following year. Cann never made it to the Majors.

15. Richter, "The American League 1911 Teams," *Reach Guide* (1912), 51.

16. Interview with Bob Wood, son of Joe Wood, June 6, 1991.

17. Comment attributed to Hall in an unspecified interview in 1911 and included in a compendium of remarks about his father assembled by Bob Wood.

18. Gardner interview in Henry Berry, *Boston Red Sox* (New York: Rutledge, 1975), 134.

19. Ibid. Cobb, however, remembered differently. Testing Gardner's skills during a game in May 1913, Ty challenged the Boston third baseman by telling him that he would be bunting the next pitch. He then laid down a perfect bunt and beat Larry's throw to first. See Alexander, *Cobb*, 113.

20. Bruce Kuklick, *To Every Thing a Season: Shibe Park and Urban Philadelphia, 1909–1976* (Princeton, N.J.: Princeton University Press, 1991), 15–17.

21. Linn, *The Great Rivalry*, 31.

22. Ibid., 34; Lieb, *Red Sox*, 91.

23. For descriptions of Fenway Park, see Craig Carter, ed., *Take Me Out to the Ballpark* (Saint Louis: Sporting News Publishing Co., 1983), 48–52; Lowry, *Green Cathedrals*, 37; Benson, *Ballparks of North America*, 41–49; "Fenway Park," in Ed Dalton, *Red Sox Triumphs and Tragedies* (New York: Stein and Day, 1980).

24. See, for example, the resolution adopted by the National League at its Saint Louis meeting on March 2, 1898, "to perpetuate base ball as the national game of the United States." Its preamble reads: "A measure for the suppression of obscene, indecent and vulgar language upon the ball field by players engaged in playing a game of ball during the championship season, while under contract to a club member of the National League and American Association of professional ball clubs, to the end that the game may retain its high position as respectable and worthy of the confidence and support of the refined and cultured classes of American citizenship" (*Reach Guide* [1899], 111–14).

25. *Boston Globe*, May 17, 1912.

26. Richter, "The 1912 American League Teams," *Reach Guide* (1913), 37.

27. Lewis to Ellery H. Clark, Jr., February 1, 1976, Clark Papers, Annapolis, Md.

28. Bill Deane, *Award Voting* (Kansas City, Mo.: Society for American Baseball Research, 1988), 6.

29. Walter Johnson interview, 1912, quoted in Ritter, *Glory of Their Times*, 154.

30. Excerpt from one of Runyon's columns, "Th' Mornin's Mornin," 1917, in Bob Wood's compendium of comments about his father.

31. Interview with Ritter, *Glory of Their Times*, 159.

32. Ibid.

33. For accounts of the Brush-Johnson relationship and its effect on post-

season play in 1904, see Benton Stark, *The Year They Called Off the World Series: A True Story* (Garden City Park, N.Y.: Avery, 1991), 45–46, 190–91; Linn, *The Great Rivalry,* 43–45; Alexander, *John McGraw,* 99–100, 108–9; Voigt, *American Baseball,* 1:312–13; Seymour, *Baseball: Early Years,* 254–55, 323.

34. Alexander, *McGraw,* 76–80, 88–90, 92–93.

35. Quoted in Lieb, *Red Sox,* 84.

36. Griffith interview, *Boston Globe,* October 6, 1912.

37. Jennings interview, *Boston Globe,* January 2, 1913.

38. Wood interview with David H. Lippman quoted in his article "Royal Rooters and Dropped Flies," *Baseball History* 2, no. 3 (Fall 1987): 34.

39. Quoted in Donald Honig, *The October Heroes: Great World Series Games Remembered by the Men Who Played Them* (New York: Simon & Schuster, 1979), 175.

40. William A. Phelon, "How the World's Series Was Lost and Won," *Baseball Magazine* 10, no. 2 (December 1912): 23.

41. *New York Times,* October 15, 1912.

42. *Boston Globe,* October 16, 1912.

43. Phelon, "Series Lost and Won," 22.

44. Lippman, "Royal Rooters," 38.

45. Richter, "The World Series of 1912," *Reach Guide* (1913), 149.

46. Wood interview, *Glory of Their Times,* 165.

47. List drawn up by Hooper, June 11, 1970, Hooper Papers, Baytown, Texas.

48. This incident is recounted in a letter from Hooper to Ellery H. Clark, Jr., reprinted in Clark's *Red Sox: 75th Anniversary History,* 29–30.

49. Interview with Lippman, "Royal Rooters," 38.

50. Hooper interview in Ritter, *Glory of Their Times,* 149.

51. Quoted in Mick Uhl, "The 1912 World Series," *All Star Replay* 2 (1979).

52. *Boston Globe,* October 18, 1912.

53. Phelon, "Series Lost and Won," 22.

54. McGraw, *My Thirty Years in Baseball,* 234.

Chapter 6: Dearest Esther

1. Alexander, *Ty Cobb,* 89.

2. Harry Hooper to John Hooper, April 10, 1947, Hooper Papers, Baytown, Texas.

3. Harry Hooper to John Hooper, June 24, 1947.

4. Harry to Esther, March 23, 1913.

5. Series of undated Easter greetings, Harry to Esther, 1913–15.

6. McGraw, *My Thirty Years in Baseball,* 257, 259.

7. Interview with Stan Musial in Anthony J. Connor, *Baseball for the Love Of It: Hall of Famers Tell It Like It Was* (New York: Macmillan, 1982), 125.

8. Harry to Esther, May 16, 1913, Hooper Papers, Baytown, Texas.

9. Harry to Esther, July 18, 1913.

10. Lewis interview with Joe Cashman, *Daily Record*, undated clipping in Hooper Scrapbook, Hooper Papers.

11. Program of the First Grand Concert and Dance of the Hooper Outing Club, April 26, 1915 (Charlestown, Boston: Bunker Hill Press).

12. Similar accounts of this incident are in the Lewis interview with Cashman, *Daily Record*, and Linn, *Great Rivalry*, 66.

13. Lewis interview with Cashman, *Daily Record*.

14. Carrigan interview with Joe Cashman, *Boston Advertiser*, January 17, 1943.

15. Ibid.

16. Speaker interview with John Drohan, *Cleveland Plain Dealer*, undated 1956 clipping, Hooper Scrapbook, Hooper Papers, Baytown, Texas.

17. Quoted in brochure prepared by John Hooper and submitted to the Committee on Veterans, National Baseball Hall of Fame, January 1, 1971, 7, Hooper Collection, NBL.

18. Interview between Ruth and Joe McGlone, 1947, quoted in John Hooper to Paul S. Kerr, President, National Baseball Hall of Fame, January 1, 1971.

19. Lewis interview with Cashman, *Daily Record*.

20. J. C. Kofoed, "Baseball as a Profession," *Baseball Magazine* 17, no. 5 (September 1916), 61.

21. On the efforts of Spalding and Chadwick in this regard, see Peter Levine, *A. G. Spalding and the Rise of Baseball: The Promise of American Sport* (New York: Oxford University Press, 1985), 103, 109–10, 118–19.

22. *Spalding Guide* (1889), 58.

23. Crawford interview in Ritter, *Glory of Their Times*, 51.

24. Voigt, *American Baseball*, 1:282–83.

25. Riess, *Touching Base*, 163.

26. See appendix C.

27. See appendix D.

28. Seymour, *Baseball: Early Years*, 332.

29. Mack, *My Years in Big Leagues*, 33.

30. See appendix E.

31. Harry to Esther, July 19, 1913, Hooper Papers, Baytown, Texas.

32. Honig, *Boston Red Sox*, 22; Lieb, *Boston Red Sox*, 116.

33. The principal Boston players who jumped to the Federal League in 1914 were Steve Yerkes and Clyde Engle, although both had been released from the club before joining the new league. Yerkes signed with the Pittsburgh Stogies, where he converted his .218 batting average with Boston to a .338 performance against the weaker pitching of the third league. Engle went to the Buffalo Blues and batted .255 for them. Other Red Sox leaving for the Federals were Esty Chaney and Adam Johnson. Only Johnson, a rookie in 1914, may have been missed. He appeared in sixteen games for Boston,

recording a 4–9 record and a 3.10 ERA, before departing for the Chicago Whales, where he was 9–5 with an ERA of 1.72. Chaney had pitched one inning for the Red Sox in 1913, allowing a run on a hit and two walks. He fared no better for the Brooklyn Tip-Tops in 1914, appearing in one game and surrendering three runs on seven hits and two walks in four innings pitched. For a brief history of the Federal League, see Marc Okkonen, *The Federal League of 1914–1915: Baseball's Third Major League* (Garret Park, Md.: Society for American Baseball Research, 1989).

34. Beaumont, "Training School for Stars," 73.

35. *The Sporting News,* October 27, 1915.

Chapter 7: The Phoenix at Fenway

1. Hooper to Clark, quoted in Clark, *Red Sox Forever,* 40.

2. John A. Mercurio, *A Chronology of Major League Baseball Records* (New York: Harper and Row, 1989), 96–97, and *Record Profiles of Baseball's Hall of Famers* (New York: Harper and Row, 1990), 97–99, 129–30, 178–79.

3. John B. Ward, "Harry Hooper of the Red Sox," *Baseball Magazine* 16, no. 7 (1915): 52.

4. Editorial, *Baseball Magazine* 16, no. 5 (August 1915): 7.

5. J. C. Kofoed, "The Star of World's Series Outfielders," *Baseball Magazine* 18, no. 2 (December 1916): 36.

6. Jim Nasium, "Harry Hooper First Man to Bat in World's Series," *Philadelphia Enquirer,* September 30, 1912.

7. Hugh Fullerton, "Hooper the Best Right Fielder in the Game," *Boston Evening Record,* March 24, 1916.

8. Johnson interview provided by the Christy Walsh Syndicate, 1923.

9. Hooper to Committee on Veterans, National Baseball Hall of Fame, January 24, 1972, Lewis File, NBL.

10. Martin Quigley, *The Crooked Pitch: The Curveball in American Baseball History* (Chapel Hill, N.C.: Algonquin Books, 1988), 176.

11. Sowell, *The Pitch That Killed,* 4, 22.

12. A. H. C. Mitchell, "Boston Red Sox," *The Sporting News,* June 5, 1915.

13. Kuklick, *To Every Thing a Season,* 49.

14. Quoted in Linn, *The Great Rivalry,* 65. The characteristics of the 1915 Red Sox that Cobb identified were among those that earned the club a spot on a list of "Baseball's 20 Greatest Teams of All Time," selected by *Sports Illustrated* in 1991. Labeling them the "savvy Sox," *SI* praised their pitching and "rock-solid defense," headed by the Speaker-Hooper-Lewis outfield, "the best defensively in the history of the game."

15. Irving E. Sanborn, "American League," *Spalding Guide* (1916), 173.

16. Rice, *New York Tribune,* 1921, quoted in a compilation of comments on Wood prepared by Bob Wood, 1991.

17. Cobb interview, Hotel Savoy Hilton, New York, 1958, in Bob Wood's collection of comments.

18. Hooper interview in Ritter, *Glory of Their Times*, 145.

19. Quoted in Creamer, *Babe*, 108.

20. *New York American*, May 7, 1915.

21. *New York Press*, May 7, 1915.

22. *New York Evening Journal*, May 7, 1915.

23. *New York American*, ibid.

24. Hooper interview in Ritter, *Glory of Their Times*, 145.

25. Patsy Dougherty of the Boston Pilgrims had done it first, hitting two home runs in the second game of the 1903 Series. Both were solo shots, the first an inside-the-park drive to deep right center, the other clearing the fence in left field.

26. Lieb, *Red Sox*, 134, 136.

27. Benson, *Ballparks of North America*, 49–50.

28. *Boston Globe*, October 14, 1915.

29. *North American*, October 9, 1915.

30. *Oakland Tribune*, October, 1, 1915, 2.

31. Bert Randolph Sugar, *Rain Delays: An Anecdotal History of Baseball Under One Umbrella* (New York: St. Martin's Press, 1990), 27–28.

32. Harry B. Smith, "Duffy Lewis Is a Modest Hero," *San Francisco Chronicle*, November 13, 1915, 5.

33. Joe Hooper to Harry, May 11, 1915, June 16, 1915, Hooper Papers, Baytown, Texas.

Chapter 8: Captain Harry

1. *Spalding Guide* (1917), 99.

2. David Q. Voigt, *America Through Baseball* (Chicago: Nelson-Hall, 1976), 135.

3. Fultz had earned an undergraduate degree at Brown and a law degree at Columbia.

4. Okkonen, *Federal League*, 25.

5. Lieb, *Boston Red Sox*, 139.

6. *Boston Globe*, April 13, 1916, 1.

7. Sanborn, "American League Season of 1916," *Spalding Guide* (1917), 101.

8. Frank Lane, "How the World's Championship Was Won," *Baseball Magazine* 18, no. 2 (December 1916): 12.

9. Interview quoted in *Boston Evening Record*, October 13, 1916.

10. "What the Players Thought of the Series," *Baseball Magazine* (December 1916): 79–80.

11. Original transcript, Hooper interview with Ritter, *Glory of Their Times*, with Hooper's marginal notes, Hooper Papers, Baytown, Texas.

12. "The Murnane Benefit Game," *Reach Guide* (1918), 22.

13. Sanborn, "American League Season of 1917," *Spalding Guide* (1918), 105, 109.

14. Ibid., 109; Seymour, *Baseball: The Golden Years*, 245–46.

15. Ad copy, *Baseball Magazine* 17, no. 1 (1915): 105.

16. Harry to Esther, May 16, 1913; Harry to Joe and Mary Hooper, May 7, 1913, Hooper Papers, Baytown.

Chapter 9: Bitter Victory

1. William A. Phelon, "How the Draft Has Upset the Pennant Race," *Baseball Magazine* 20, no. 9 (January 1918): 333; John B. Foster, "The World Series of 1918, *Spalding Guide* (1919), 55.

2. Burt Whitman column, *Boston Herald*, January 12, 1918.

3. Original manuscript of Ritter-Hooper interview, Hooper Papers, Baytown, Texas.

4. Ibid.

5. Quoted in Creamer, *Babe*, 109.

6. Hooper to Lee Allen, May 10, 1963, Hooper Papers, Baytown, Texas. Similarly quoted in Bill Libby, *Sports Today* (August 1971), 32.

7. Original manuscript, Ritter-Hooper interview, Hooper Papers, Baytown, Texas.

8. Ibid.

9. Johnson, "American League Race," *Reach Guide* (1919), 66.

10. Quoted in Sowell, *The Pitch That Killed*, 23.

11. John J. Ward, "Dividing the Big Money Right!" *Baseball Magazine* 20, no. 0 (January 1018): 333; John B. Foster, "The World Series of 1918," *Spalding's Guide* (1919), 55.

12. National Commission, "Financial Report, World's Series, 1918: Receipts."

13. Accounts of the players' reactions to the new revenue distribution plan and the strike threat are in Seymour, *Baseball: The Golden Age*, 254–55; Creamer, *Babe*, 178–81; J. G. Taylor Spink, *Judge Landis and 25 Years of Baseball* (New York: Crowell, 1947), 44–45; Eugene C. Murdock, *Ban Johnson: Czar of Baseball* (Westport, Conn.: Greenwood Press, 1982), 165–66; newspaper articles in the Hooper File, NBL; correspondence and memoirs in the Hooper Papers, Baytown, Texas, and Capitola, California.

14. Bill Gavin to John Hooper, December 19, 1982, and December 22, 1982, Hooper Papers, Baytown, Texas.

15. Thomas to John Hooper, January 18, 1983, and Spink to Harry Hooper, November 1, 1951.

16. Hooper to Bowie Kuhn, September 19, 1972; Hooper to Kuhn, June 4, 1973; Hooper to Kuhn, May 10, 1973.

17. *Boston Globe*, September 11, 1918.

18. Quoted in Frederick G. Lieb, "Commentary," *The Great World Series Program Collection: Volume 43* (Santa Clara, Calif.: RDO/Publications, 1984), 13.

19. Spink, *Landis,* 45.

20. Foster, *Spalding Guide* (1919), 55.

21. Phelon, "Series Lost and Won," 15.

22. Richter, *Reach Guide* (1919), 165.

23. Foster, *Spalding Guide,* 55–56.

24. *Boston Globe,* September 11, 1918.

25. Spink to Hooper, November 1, 1951, Hooper Papers, Baytown, Texas.

26. Spink to Hooper, May 17, 1961.

27. *Boston Globe,* September 13, 1910.

28. Heydler to Hooper, December 20, 1918, Hooper Papers, Baytown, Texas.

29. Hooper to Kuhn, June 4, 1973.

30. Hooper to Kuhn, May 10, 1973.

31. Kuhn to Hooper, May 29, 1973.

32. Bob McGarigle to John Hooper, May 16, 1980.

33. In summer 1990 the author renewed Hooper's effort to obtain the winners' emblems for the families of the Red Sox players who had been members of the 1918 World Series champions. He had been encouraged through his personal acquaintance with Commissioner Bart Giamatti that a fresh and fair hearing would be given the case. Giamatti's death, however, dashed hopes that this would happen. Finally, in December 1990, he received news from the commissioner's office of a decision in the matter. It reaffirmed the old line. The championship pins would not be awarded because the commissioner does "not as a matter of policy look to overturn decisions by previous commissioners especially from so long ago." Writing for the commissioner, David Alworth, director of publishing, explained that "we do not feel it is our place to change the manner in which the team members of the 1918 Red Sox were or were not recognized as champions." Alworth to Zingg, December 6, 1990, author's files.

34. Hooper to John Hooper, December 10, 1970, Hooper Papers, Baytown, Texas.

35. Richter, *Reach Guide, 1919,* 168.

36. Heydler quoted in Murdock, *Ban Johnson,* 165–66.

37. Bill Gavin to John Hooper, December 22, 1982, Hooper Papers.

38. Ibid. Compare, for example, with the reminiscences of Sam Crawford in Ritter, *Glory of Their Times,* 139.

Chapter 10: Changing Sox

1. Accounts of conditions in the United States during the war years and just after include William E. Leuchtenburg, *The Perils of Prosperity, 1914–1932* (Chicago: University of Chicago Press, 1958); David Brody, *Labor in Crisis: The Steel Strike of 1919* (Philadelphia: Lippincott, 1962); Francis Russell, *A City in Terror: 1919, The Boston Police Strike* (New York: Viking, 1975); David M. Kennedy, *Over Here: The First World War and American Society*

(New York: Oxford University Press, 1980); Christopher Lasch, *The American Liberals and the Russian Revolution* (New York: McGraw-Hill, 1962); Frederick Lewis Allen, *Only Yesterday* (New York: Harper and Row, 1931).

2. On the Red Scare, see Robert K. Murray, *Red Scare: A Study in National Hysteria, 1919–1920* (New York: McGraw-Hill, 1955); William Preston, *Aliens and Dissenters: Federal Suppression of Radicals, 1903–1933* (New York: Harper, 1963); Stanley Coben, *A Mitchell Palmer: Politician* (New York: Columbia University Press, 1963).

3. Quoted in Keith Ian Polakoff, Norman Rosenberg, et al., *Generations of Americans: A History of the United States* (New York: St. Martin's Press, 1976), 602.

4. Quoted in Richard C. Crepeau, *Baseball: America's Diamond Mind, 1919–1941* (Orlando: University of Central Florida, 1980), 6.

5. *Spalding Guide* (1920), 161.

6. Benjamin G. Rader, "Compensatory Sport Heroes: Ruth, Grange and Dempsey," *Journal of Popular Culture* 16, no. 4 (Spring 1983): 11–22, and *American Sports*, 176–77.

7. Tristam Coffin, *The Old Ball Game: Baseball in Folklore and Fiction* (New York: Harder and Harder, 1971), 13.

8. Stephen S. Hall, "Scandals and Controversies," in Thorn and Palmer, *Total Baseball*, 435.

9. Hooper interview with John Lindbloom, *San Jose Mercury-News*, July 23, 1972.

10. Ibid.

11. Quoted in Sowell, *The Pitch That Killed*, 40.

12. Other accounts of the Mays episode include Linn, *The Great Rivalry*, 80–83; Crepeau, *Baseball: America's Diamond Mind*, 6–7; Creamer, *Babe*, 198–200; Honig, *Boston Red Sox*, 45; and Murdock, *Ban Johnson*, 167–71, 206–7.

13. Hooper interview, *San Jose Mercury-News*.

14. Quoted in Creamer, *Babe*, 212.

15. Quoted in Lieb, *Boston Red Sox*, 183.

16. Hooper interview in Ritter, *Glory of Their Times*, 151.

17. Hooper interview, *San Jose Mercury-News*.

18. On labor-management relations in baseball, 1915–22, see Lee Lowenfish, *The Imperfect Diamond: A History of Baseball's Labor Wars*, rev. ed. (New York: Da Capo Press, 1991), 85–107.

19. District of Columbia Court of Appeals, 1921 (269 Fed. 681); United States Supreme Court, 1922 (259 U.S. 200).

20. Traded with Hoyt were Harry Harper, Wally Schang, and Mike McNally. Boston acquired Muddy Ruel, Del Pratt, Sammy Vick, and Hank Thormahlen. None of the new additions to the Red Sox lasted more than two seasons with the club.

21. Quoted in Eliot Asinof, *Eight Men Out: The Black Sox and the 1919 World Series* (New York: Holt, Rinehart and Winston, 1963), 172–73.

22. Quoted in Joseph Durso, *Baseball and the American Dream* (Saint Louis: The Sporting News, 1986), 130.

23. The others included first baseman Chick Gandil, shortstop Swede Risberg, third baseman Buck Weaver, center fielder Happy Felsch, pitcher Lefty Williams, and reserve infielder Fred McMullin.

24. *Chicago Tribune*, September 29, 1920.

25. Quoted in Asinof, *Eight Men Out*, 77.

26. Original transcript of Hooper interview in Ritter, *Glory of Their Times*, Hooper Papers, Baytown, Texas.

27. Ibid.

28. Ibid.

29. Hooper's observations of Chase's play in the California League are in Hooper Narrative G, 6, Hooper Papers, Baytown, Texas.

30. Hooper-Ritter interview, Hooper Papers, Baytown, Texas.

31. Only seven of the original eight players were reindicted. The case against McMullin, who demanded to be cut in on the action after he had overheard a conversation between Gandil and Risberg about the proposed fix, was dismissed by the second grand jury for lack of evidence.

32. *Chicago Tribune*, August 3, 1921.

33. Seymour, *Baseball: The Golden Age*, 335.

34. *The Sporting News,* March 10, 1921.

35. James C. O'Leary, "Hooper Has Not Signed, But Will, Duffy Says," *Boston Globe*, March 2, 1921.

36. Telegram, Frazee to Hooper, March 4, 1921, Hooper Papers, Baytown, Texas.

37. *The Sporting News,* March 10, 1921.

38. Quoted in Lieb, *Boston Red Sox*, 186.

39. Melville E. Webb, Jr., "Harry Hooper Traded to the White Sox," *Boston Evening Globe*, March 4, 1921.

40. Ibid.

41. *The Sporting News,* March 10, 1921.

42. I. E. Sanborn, "Sox Get Hooper For Leibold and Shanno Collins," *Chicago Daily Tribune*, March 5, 1921.

43. "Gleason Tickled Over Landing Boston Star," *Boston Globe*, March 5, 1921.

44. *Chicago Daily Tribune*, March 12, 1921.

45. Hooper-Ritter interview manuscript, Hooper Papers, Baytown, Texas.

46. *Chicago Daily Tribune*, March 22, 1921.

47. James Crusinberry, "Tip Top Team Rises From Sox Ruins," *Chicago Daily Tribune*, March 27, 1921.

48. Ibid.

49. Sanborn, "American League Season of 1921," *Spalding Guide* (1922), 155; Johnson, "American League 1921 Race," *Reach Guide* (1922), 59.

50. *Boston Globe*, June 11, 1921.

51. Burt Whitman, "Red Sox Stage Big Eighth Inning and Wring Rival Sox, 4–2," *Boston Herald*, June 12, 1921.

52. *Boston Globe*, June 12, 1921.

53. Ban Johnson, "The American League 1922 Championship Race," *Reach Guide* (1923), 65.

54. In 1922, Collins batted .271 with four home runs, thirty-three runs scored, and fifty-two RBIs. In his second, and last, full season with the Red Sox, Leibold hit only .258 with one home run, forty-two runs, and eighteen RBIs.

55. Johnson, "1922 Race," *Reach Guide*, 65.

56. Hooper to Bob Wood, February 9, 1974, Joe Wood Papers, Keene, New Hampshire.

57. Interview with Ted Lyons, May 24, 1978, in Eugene C. Murdock, *Baseball Players and Their Times: Oral Histories of the Game, 1920–1940* (Westport, Conn.: Meckler, 1991), 229.

58. Hooper interview with John Lindbloom, "The Rape of the Red Sox," *San Jose Mercury-News*, July 23, 1972.

59. Interview with Bucky Crouse, November 1, 1974, in Murdock, *Baseball Players and Their Times*, 81–82.

60. Esther to Harry, March 29, 1925, Hooper Papers, Baytown, Texas.

61. Esther to Harry, April 12, 1925.

62. Harry to Esther, April 16, 1925.

63. Esther to Harry, April 21, 1925.

64. Esther to Harry, April 18, April 21, April 24, 1925.

65. Esther to Harry, April 24, April 29, 1925.

66. Esther to Harry, May 6, 1925.

67. Esther to Harry, May 5, 1925.

68. Harry to Esther, Harry to Joe and Mary Hooper, May 4, 1925.

69. Joe Hooper to Harry, May 8, 1925.

70. Esther to Harry, May 7, 1925.

71. *Chicago Tribune*, August 12, 1925.

72. Walsh, "Big League Yarns" cartoon feature, *San Francisco Chronicle*, June 26, 1923.

73. John C. Hoffman, "Hooper May Manage Boston Red Sox Club," *Chicago Daily News*, September 25, 1925.

74. *Boston Evening News*, October 14, 1925.

75. Stephens to Johnson, July 17, 1925, Hooper Papers, Baytown, Texas.

76. Johnson to Stephens, July 31, 1925.

77. Stephens to Hooper, August 4, 1925.

78. Hooper to Stephens, August 15, 1925.

79. Hooper-Ritter interview, *Glory of Their Times*, 152.

80. *Chicago Daily News*, September 25, 1925.

Epilogue

1. Wood to Hooper, March 5, 1962, Hooper Papers, Baytown, Texas.

2. Riess, *Touching Base*, 198.

3. Riess, *City Games*, 91.

4. *San Francisco Daily Call*, May 4, 1927.

5. *Los Angeles Evening Herald*, May 4, 1927.

6. *San Francisco Daily Call*, May 4, 1927.

7. *San Francisco Examiner*, May 4, 1927.

8. *Los Angeles Times*, June 25, 1927.

9. *The Sporting News*, May 19, 1927.

10. *San Francisco Chronicle*, May 5, 1927.

11. *Los Angeles Evening Herald*, May 20, 1927.

12. *Los Angeles Times*, June 25, 1927.

13. Hooper to Lowry, June 29, 1927, reprinted in the *Los Angeles Times*, July 1, 1927.

14. Ibid.; Harry to Esther, July 23, 1927, Hooper Papers, Baytown, Texas.

15. *San Francisco Examiner*, January 13, 1928.

16. *San Francisco Chronicle*, May 5, 1927.

17. *Baseball Guide* (Princeton, N.J.: Princeton University, 1991), 2; Quigley, *The Crooked Pitch*, 40.

18. *New York Times*, September 26, 1930.

19. *The Daily Princetonian*, February 27, 1931.

20. *New York Times*, February 28, 1931.

21. Rader, *American Sports*, 209.

22. *The Princeton Bric-A-Brac* (1933), 170.

23. *The Princeton Bric-A-Brac* (1934), 191; Lawrence Perry, "For the Game's Sake," unattributed clipping (1932) in Hooper File, NBL.

24. Farley to Hooper, November 14, 1932, Hooper Papers, Baytown, Texas.

25. Harry Hooper to John Hooper, May 12, 1948.

26. *Boston Herald*, September 9, 1930.

27. Fenlon, Statement on Hooper's credentials for the Hall of Fame, undated, *Brickpile* File, Saint Mary's College Archives.

28. *San Francisco Call Bulletin*, February 9, 1953; *San Francisco News*, March 18, 1953.

29. *Brickpile Seniors Newsletter*, April 15, 1953.

30. Hooper letter to the editor, *Brickpile Seniors Newsletter*, quoted in the issue of April 15, 1953.

31. Poultney to Kerr, September 25, 1966, Hooper File, NBL.

32. John Hooper to Kerr, January 1, 1970.

33. John Hooper to Kerr, January 1, 1971.

34. Interview with John Hooper, September 26, 1990.

35. Hooper interview, *Santa Cruz Sentinel*, February 1, 1971.

36. Quoted in *Cabrillo Times and Green Sheet*, December 19, 1974.

37. Interview with Harry, Jr., September 6, 1989.

38. *Santa Cruz Sentinel*, December 19, 1974.

39. Quoted in *Oneonta Times*, December 20, 1974.

Bibliography

Primary Sources

Archives

Lee Allen "Notebooks," National Baseball Library, Cooperstown, New York.
Ellery Clark Papers, Annapolis, Maryland.
College Baseball File, National Baseball Library, Cooperstown, New York.
1899 Football Controversy File, Harvard University Archives, Cambridge, Massachusetts.
Larry Gardner Collection, National Baseball Library, Cooperstown, New York.
Harry Hooper Collection, National Baseball Library, Cooperstown, New York.
Harry Hooper Papers, Capitola, California, and Baytown, Texas.
Duffy Lewis Collection, National Baseball Library, Cooperstown, New York.
Clippings Files and Programs, National Sports Library, San Jose, California.
Michael ("Doc") Powers File, National Baseball Library, Cooperstown, New York.
Baseball Files, Princeton University Archives, Princeton, New Jersey.
Clippings Files and Scrapbooks, Saint Mary's College Archives, Moraga, California.
Tris Speaker Collection, National Baseball Library, Cooperstown, New York.
Joe Wood Collection, National Baseball Library, Cooperstown, New York.
Joe Wood Papers, Keene, New Hampshire.
World Series Files, National Baseball Library, Cooperstown, New York.

Interviews

Ellery Clark, Jr., telephone interview, January 9, 1991.
Lew Fonseca, Jr., Moraga, California, July 12, 1990.
Lou Guisto, Napa, California, August 21, 1989.
Christine Hooper, Capitola, California, February 17 and October 25, 1989.
Harry Hooper, Jr., Capitola, California, February 17 and October 25, 1989.
John Hooper, Baytown, Texas, September 15, 1989, September 14, 1990, Au-

gust 9, 1991; Hooper Ranch, Humboldt County, California, October 4, 1991.

Vincent Stanich, Moraga, California, June 24, 1989.

Marie Hooper Strain, Capitola, California, October 25, 1989; Burlingame, California, July 27, 1991.

Bob Wood, Keene, New Hampshire, June 5, 1991.

Memoirs and Autobiographies

Barrow, Edward G., with James M. Kahn. *My Fifty Years in Baseball.* New York: Coward-McCann, 1951.

Cobb, Tyrus R., with Al Stump. *My Life in Baseball: The True Record.* Garden City, N.Y.: Doubleday, 1961.

Evers, John J., with Hugh Fullerton. *Touching Second: The Science of Baseball.* Chicago: Reilly and Britton, 1910.

Mack, Connie. *My 66 Years in the Big Leagues.* Philadelphia: John C. Winston Co., 1950.

McGraw, Blanche, and Arthur Mann. *The Real McGraw.* New York: Putnam's, 1974.

McGraw, John J. *My Thirty Years in Baseball.* New York: Boni & Liveright, 1923.

Ruth, Babe, with Bob Considine. *The Babe Ruth Story.* New York: Dutton, 1948.

Ruth, Claire Hodgson, and Bill Slocum. *The Babe and I.* Englewood Cliffs, N.J.: Prentice-Hall, 1959.

Newspapers

Boston Globe, 1907–74
Boston Herald, 1907–19
Boston Journal, 1909–20
Boston Post, 1880–88
Boston Record American, 1919–62
Chicago Tribune, 1919–26
Daily Alta California, 1852–76
The Daily Princetonian, Princeton University, 1931–33
Frank Leslie's Illustrated Newspaper, 1877–78
Los Angeles Evening Herald, 1927–28
Los Angeles Times, 1927–28
New York Clipper, 1876–1900
New York Times, 1907–74
Oakland Daily News, 1872–76
Oakland Tribune, 1907–74
Saint Mary's College *Brickpile Seniors Newsletter,* 1952–56
Saint Mary's College *Collegian,* 1880–1974
Santa Cruz Sentinel, 1950–74
San Francisco Bulletin, 1907–26

San Francisco Chronicle, 1880–1974
The Sporting News, 1907–74

Government Documents

Bureau of the Census, United States Department of Commerce. *The Statistical Abstract of the United States*. 97th ed. Washington: Government Printing Office, 1977.

United States Congress. House of Representatives. *Hearings before the Subcommittee on the Study of Monopoly Power of the Committee of the Judiciary*, 82d Cong., 1st sess. (1951), Part 6: *Organized Baseball*.

Miscellaneous

Clemens, Samuel L. *Mark Twain's Speeches*. New York: Harper and Brothers, 1923.

Hilgard, E. W. *Report on the Physical and Agricultural Features of the State of California*. San Francisco: Pacific Rural Press, 1884.

Irvine, Leigh. *Santa Clara County, California*. San Jose: Board of Supervisors, 1915.

The Princeton Bric-A-Brac, 1931–1934.

The Reach Official American League Baseball Guide, 1903–1927.

Saint Mary's College, *Catalogue, 1908–1909*.

Saint Mary's College, *The College Roll, 1883–1919*.

Spalding's Official Base Ball Guide, 1903–1927.

Secondary Sources

Books

Adelman, Melvin L. *A Sporting Time: New York City and the Rise of Modern Athletics, 1820–70*. Urbana: University of Illinois Press, 1986.

Alexander, Charles C. *John McGraw*. New York: Viking Penguin, 1988.

———. *Ty Cobb*. New York: Oxford University Press, 1984.

Allen, Frederick Lewis. *Only Yesterday*. New York: Harper and Row, 1931.

Anderson, Mel, F.S.C. *The President's Report: 125th Anniversary Edition*. Moraga, Calif.: Saint Mary's College, 1988.

Andrada, Randy. *They Did It Everytime: Saga of the Saint Mary's Gaels*. Piedmont, Calif.: Randy Andrada, 1975, 1987.

Asinof, Eliot. *Eight Men Out: The Black Sox and the 1919 World Series*. New York: Holt, Rinehart and Winston, 1963.

Axelson, Gustave. *"Commy": The Life Story of Charles A. Comiskey*. Chicago: Reilly and Lee, 1919.

Bailyn, Bernard, David Brion Davis, et al. *The Great Republic: A History of the American People*. Vol. 2. Lexington, Mass.: D. C. Heath, 1977.

Benson, Michael. *Ballparks of North America: A Comprehensive Historical Reference to Baseball Grounds, Yards, and Stadiums, 1845 to the Present*. Jefferson, N.C.: McFarland and Co., 1989.

Berry, Henry. *Boston Red Sox.* New York: Routledge, 1975.

Betts, John R. *America's Sporting Heritage: 1850–1950.* Reading, Mass.: Addison-Wesley, 1974.

Bledstein, Burton J. *The Culture of Professionalism: The Middle Class and the Development of Higher Education in America.* New York: Norton, 1976.

Brody, David. *Labor in Crisis: The Steel Strike of 1919.* Philadelphia: Lippincott, 1962.

Brown, Dee. *The American Spa: Hot Springs, Arkansas.* Little Rock: Rose Publishing Co., 1982.

Carter, Craig, ed. *Take Me Out to the Ballpark.* Saint Louis: Sporting News Publishing Co., 1983.

Charlton, Jim. *The Baseball Fan's Guide to Spring Training.* Reading, Mass.: Addison-Wesley, 1988.

Cherny, Robert W., and William Issel. *San Francisco, 1865–1932: Politics, Power, and Urban Development.* Berkeley: University of California Press, 1986.

Chu, Donald. *The Character of American Higher Education and Intercollegiate Sport.* Albany: State University of New York Press, 1989.

Clark, Ellery H., Jr. *Boston Red Sox: 75th Anniversary History.* Hicksville, N.Y.: Exposition Press, 1975.

———. *Red Sox Forever.* Hicksville, N.Y.: Exposition Press, 1977.

Coben, Stanley. *A. Mitchell Palmer: Politician.* New York: Columbia University Press, 1963.

———, and Arthur S. Link. *The Democratic Heritage: A History of the United States.* Waltham, Mass.: Ginn and Company, 1971.

Coffin, Tristam. *The Old Ball Game: Baseball in Folklore and Fiction.* New York: Harder and Harder, 1971.

Connor, Anthony J. *Baseball for the Love Of It: Hall of Famers Tell It Like It Was.* New York: Macmillan, 1982.

Creamer, Robert W. *Babe: The Legend Comes to Life.* New York: Simon and Schuster, 1974.

Cremin, Lawrence A. *American Education: The National Experience, 1783–1876.* New York: Harper and Row, 1980.

Crepeau, Richard C. *Baseball: America's Diamond Mind, 1919–1941.* Orlando: University of Central Florida, 1980.

Curran, William. *Big Sticks: The Phenomenal Decade of Ruth, Gehrig, Cobb, and Hornsby.* New York: William Morrow, 1990.

Cutter, John Milton, ed. and comp. *Cutter's Official Guide to Hot Springs, Arkansas.* 61st ed. Hot Springs: Charles Cutter & Son, 1917.

Dalton, Ed. *Red Sox Triumphs and Tragedies.* New York: Stein and Day, 1980.

Deane, Bill. *Award Voting.* Kansas City, Mo.: Society for American Baseball Research, 1988.

Dinnerstein, Leonard, and David M. Reimers. *Ethnic Americans: A History of Immigration and Assimilation.* New York: Dodd, Mead, 1975.

Durso, Joseph. *Baseball and the American Dream*. Saint Louis: The Sporting News, 1986.

——. *The Days of Mr. McGraw*. Englewood Cliffs, N.J.: Prentice-Hall, 1969.

Falkner, David. *Nine Sides of the Diamond: Baseball's Great Glove Men on the Fine Art of Defense*. New York: Random House, 1990.

Fite, Gilbert C., and Jim E. Reese. *An Economic History of the United States*. 3d ed. Boston: Houghton Mifflin, 1973.

Frommer, Harvey. *Primitive Baseball: The First Quarter Century of the National Pastime*. New York: Atheneum, 1988.

——. *Shoeless Joe and Ragtime Baseball*. Dallas: Taylor Publishing, 1992.

Goldstein, Richard. *Superstars and Screwballs: 100 Years of Brooklyn Baseball*. New York: Dutton, 1991.

Goldstein, Warren. *Playing for Keeps: A History of Early Baseball*. Ithaca, N.Y.: Cornell University Press, 1989.

Golenbock, Peter. *Fenway: An Unexpurgated History of the Boston Red Sox*. New York: Putnam's, 1992.

Gropman, Donald. *Say It Ain't So, Joe! The Story of Shoeless Joe Jackson*. Boston: Little, Brown, 1979.

Hackensmith, C. W. *History of Physical Education*. New York: Harper, 1966.

Handlin, Oscar, and Mary F. Handlin. *The American College and American Culture*. New York: McGraw-Hill, 1970.

——. *The American College and University*. New York: Knopf, 1968.

Hansen, Marcus Lee. *The Atlantic Migration, 1607–1860*. New York: Harper and Row, 1940.

Harris, Seymour E. *A Statistical Portrait of Higher Education*. New York: McGraw-Hill, 1972.

Hart, James D., ed. *From Scotland to Silverado*. Cambridge, Mass.: Belknap Press, 1966.

Henry, David. *Challenges Past, Challenges Present*. San Francisco: Jossey-Bass, 1975.

Hocking, Anthony. *Prince Edward Island*. New York: McGraw-Hill Ryerson Ltd., 1978.

Hofstadter, Richard, and Wilson Smith, eds. *American Higher Education*. Chicago: University of Chicago Press, 1961.

Honig, Donald. *Baseball America*. New York: Macmillan, 1985.

——. *The Boston Red Sox: An Illustrated Tribute*. New York: St. Martin's Press, 1984.

——. *The October Heroes: Great World Series Games Remembered by the Men Who Played Them*. New York: Simon & Schuster, 1979.

Isetti, Ronald E., F.S.C. *Called to the Pacific: A History of the Christian Brothers of the San Francisco District, 1868–1944*. Winona, Minn.: Saint Mary's College Press, 1979.

Jacobson, Yvonne. *Passing Farms, Enduring Values: California's Santa Clara Valley*. Los Altos, Calif.: William Kaufman, 1984.

James, Bill. *The Bill James Historical Abstract*. New York: Villard, 1986.

Kelley, Robert F. *American Rowing: Its Background and Traditions.* New York: Putnam's, 1932.

Kennedy, David M. *Over Here: The First World War and American Society.* New York: Oxford University Press, 1980.

Kett, Joseph F. *Rites and Passages.* New York: Basic Books, 1977.

Kuklick, Bruce. *To Every Thing a Season: Shibe Park and Urban Philadelphia, 1909–1976.* Princeton, N.J.: Princeton University Press, 1991.

Laird, A. W. *Ranking Baseball's Elite: An Analysis Derived from Player Statistics, 1893–1987.* Jefferson, N.C.: McFarland, 1990.

Lange, Fred. *History of Baseball in California and Pacific Coast Leagues, 1847–1938.* San Francisco: 1938.

Lasch, Christopher. *The American Liberals and the Russian Revolution.* New York: McGraw-Hill, 1962.

Lavender, David S. *California: Land of New Beginnings.* New York: Harper and Row, 1972.

Leuchtenburg, William E. *The Perils of Prosperity, 1914–1932.* Chicago: University of Chicago Press, 1958.

Levine, Peter. *A. G. Spalding and the Rise of Baseball: The Promise of American Sport.* New York: Oxford University Press, 1985.

Lewis, Oscar. *San Francisco: Mission to Metropolis.* 2d ed. San Diego: Howell-North, 1980.

Lieb, Frederick G. *Baseball As I Have Known It.* New York: Coward, McCann, 1977.

————. *The Boston Red Sox.* New York: Putnam's, 1947.

Lindberg, Richard. *Sox.* New York: Macmillan, 1984.

Linn, Ed. *The Great Rivalry: The Yankees and the Red Sox, 1901–1990.* New York: Ticknor & Fields, 1991.

Lotchin, Roger W. *San Francisco, 1846–1856: From Hamlet to City.* New York: Oxford University Press, 1974.

Lowenfish, Lee. *The Imperfect Diamond: A History of Baseball's Labor Wars.* Rev. ed. New York: Da Capo Press, 1991.

Lowry, Philip J. *Green Cathedrals.* Cooperstown: Society for American Baseball Research, 1986.

Lucas, John A., and Ronald A. Smith. *Saga of American Sport.* Philadelphia: Lea & Febiger, 1978.

McCaffrey, Eugene V., and Roger A. McCaffrey. *Players' Choice.* New York: Facts on File Publications, 1987.

McDevitt, Matthew, F.S.C. *The Early Years of Saint Mary's College, 1859–1879.* Moraga, Calif.: Saint Mary's College, 1970.

————.*The Late Years of Saint Mary's College, 1879–1969.* Moraga, Calif.: Saint Mary's College, 1970.

Mercurio, John A. *A Chronology of Major League Baseball Records.* New York: Harper and Row, 1989.

————. *Record Profiles of Baseball's Hall of Famers.* New York: Harper and Row, 1990.

Mrozek, Donald J. *Sport and American Mentality, 1880–1910*. Knoxville: University of Tennessee Press, 1983.

Murdock, Eugene C. *Ban Johnson: Czar of Baseball*. Westport, Conn.: Greenwood Press, 1982.

———. *Baseball Players and Their Times: Oral Histories of the Game, 1920–1940*. Westport, Conn.: Meckler, 1991.

Murray, Robert K. *Red Scare: A Study in National Hysteria, 1919–1920*. New York: McGraw-Hill, 1955.

Okkonen, Marc. *The Federal League of 1914–1915: Baseball's Third Major League*. Harret Park, Md.: Society for American Baseball Research, 1989.

Palmer, Pete, and John Thorn, ed. *Total Baseball*. New York: Warner, 1989.

Porter, David L., ed. *Biographical Dictionary of American Sports: Baseball*. Westport, Conn.: Greenwood Press, 1987.

Preston, William. *Aliens and Dissenters: Federal Suppression of Radicals, 1903–1933*. New York: Harper, 1963.

Quigley, Martin. *The Crooked Pitch: The Curveball in American Baseball History*. Chapel Hill, N.C.: Algonquin Books, 1988.

Rader, Benjamin G. *American Sports: From the Age of Folk Games to the Age of Spectators*. Englewood Cliffs, N.J.: Prentice-Hall, 1983.

Riess, Steven A. *City Games: The Evolution of American Urban Society and the Rise of Sports*. Urbana: University of Illinois Press, 1989.

———. *Touching Base: Professional Baseball and American Culture in the Progressive Era*. Westport, Conn.: Greenwood Press, 1980.

Ritter, Lawrence. *The Glory of Their Times*. Rev. ed. New York: William Morrow, 1984.

Robinson, Ray. *Iron Horse: Lou Gehrig in His Time*. New York: Norton, 1990.

Rolle, Andrew F. *California: A History*. New York: Crowell, 1963.

Rozwenc, Edwin C. *The Making of American Society*. Vol. 2. Boston: Allyn and Bacon, 1973.

Rucker, Mark, and Robert L. Tiemann, eds. *Nineteenth Century Stars*. Cooperstown, N.Y.: Society for American Baseball Research, 1989.

Rudolph, Frederick. *Curriculum: A History of the Undergraduate Course of Study Since 1636*. San Francisco: Jossey-Bass, 1977.

Russell, Francis. *A City in Terror: 1919, The Boston Police Strike*. New York: Viking, 1975.

Savage, Howard J., et al. *American College Athletics*. New York: Carnegie Foundation, 1933.

Sawyer, Eugene T. *History of Santa Clara County*. Los Angeles: Historic Record Company, 1922.

Seymour, Harold. *Baseball: The Early Years*. New York: Oxford University Press, 1960.

———. *Baseball: The Golden Age*. New York: Oxford University Press, 1971.

———. *Baseball: The People's Game*. New York: Oxford University Press, 1990.

Shatzkin, Mike, ed. *The Ballplayers.* New York: William Morrow, 1990.

Smith, Robert. *Babe Ruth's America.* New York: Crowell, 1974.

Smith, Ronald A. *Sports and Freedom: The Rise of Big-Time College Athletics.* New York: Oxford University Press, 1988.

Sobol, Ken. *Babe Ruth and the American Dream.* New York: Ballantine, 1974.

Sowell, Mike. *The Pitch That Killed: Carl Mays, Ray Chapman and the Pennant Race of 1920.* New York: Macmillan, 1989.

Spears, Betty, and R. Swanson. *History of Sport and Physical Activity in the United States.* Dubuque, Iowa: Brown, 1978.

Spink, J. G. Taylor. *Judge Landis and 25 Years of Baseball.* New York: Crowell, 1947.

Staniford, Edward. *The Pattern of California History.* San Francisco: Canfield Press, 1975.

Stark, Benton. *The Year They Called Off the World Series: A True Story.* Garden City Park, N.Y.: Avery, 1991.

Starr, Kevin. *Americans and the California Dream, 1850–1915.* New York: Oxford University Press, 1973.

Sugar, Bert Randolph. *Rain Delays: An Anecdotal History of Baseball Under One Umbrella.* New York: St. Martin's Press, 1990.

Sullivan, Neil J. *The Dodgers Move West.* New York: Oxford University Press, 1987.

———. *The Minors: The Struggles and the Triumph of Baseball's Poor Relation from 1876 to the Present.* New York: St. Martin's Press, 1990.

Veysey, Lawrence R. *The Emergence of the American University.* Chicago: University of Chicago Press, 1965.

Voigt, David Q. *America Through Baseball.* Chicago: Nelson-Hall, 1976.

———. *American Baseball: From the Gentlemen's Sport to the Commissioner System.* Norman: University of Oklahoma Press, 1966.

Wagenheim, Ken. *Babe Ruth: His Life and Legend.* New York: Praeger, 1974.

Wiley, Bell I. *The Life of Billy Yank: The Common Soldier of the Union.* Indianapolis: Bobbs-Merrill, 1952.

———. *The Life of Johnny Reb: The Common Soldier of the Confederacy.* Baton Rouge: Louisiana State University Press, 1943.

Wolff, Rick, editorial director. *The Baseball Encyclopedia.* 8th ed., rev. New York: Macmillan, 1990.

Wright, Louis B. *The Cultural Life of the American Colonies.* New York: Harper and Row, 1957.

Articles

Barney, Robert K. "Of Rails and Red Stockings: Episodes in the Expansion of the National Pastime in the American West," *Journal of the West* 17, no. 3 (July 1978).

Beatie, William, F.S.C. "125 Years: An Educational Adventure," paper prepared for the Board of Regents, Saint Mary's College, 1988.

Beaumont, Gerald P. "A Training School for Baseball Stars," *Baseball Magazine* 18 (November 1916).

Blaikie, William. "American Bodies," *Harper's Weekly* 27 (December 1883).

Dobbins, Dick. "Oakland's Long Baseball Heritage," *Official Magazine of the Oakland Athletics* 8 (1988).

Fielding, Lawrence W. "War and Trifles: The Meter Stick of the Civil War Soldier," *Journal of Sport History* 4, no. 2 (Summer 1977).

Franks, Joel. "The California League of 1886–1893: The Last Refuge of Disorganized Baseball," *The Californians* 6 (May-June 1988).

———. "Sweeney of San Francisco: A Local Boy Makes Good, Then Not So Good," *Baseball History* 2, no. 4 (Winter 1987–88).

Kofoed, J. C. "Baseball as a Profession," *Baseball Magazine* 17, no. 5 (September 1916).

Lane, Frank. "How the World's Championship Was Won," *Baseball Magazine* 18, no. 2 (December 1916).

Lewis, Guy M. "America's First Intercollegiate Sport: The Regattas from 1852 to 1875," *Research Quarterly* 38 (December 1967).

———. "The Beginning of Organized Collegiate Sport," *American Quarterly* 22 (Summer 1970).

———. "The Muscular Christianity Movement," *Journal of Health, Physical Education and Recreation* 37 (May 1966).

Lippman, David H. "Royal Rooters and Dropped Flies," *Baseball History* 2, no. 3 (Fall 1987).

Lucas, John A. "A Prelude to the Rise of Sport: Ante-Bellum America, 1850–1860," *Quest* 2 (December 1968).

Martin, Al H. "The Pacific Coast League," *Baseball Magazine* 3, no. 5 (September 1909).

Matthews, Joseph J. "The First Harvard-Oxford Race," *New England Quarterly* 33 (March 1960).

McGuire, Bonnie. "Babe Ruth," *New York Folklore Quarterly* 1, nos. 1 and 2 (1975).

Moore, Jim, and Natalie Vermilyea. "A Ballad of the Republic," *The Californians* 6 (May-June 1988).

Murdock, Eugene. "The Tragedy of Ban Johnson," *Journal of Sport History* 1, no. 1 (Spring 1974).

Nemec, David. "A History of Baseball in the San Francisco Bay Area," *San Francisco Giants Official 1985 Yearbook* (San Francisco: Woodford Associates, 1985).

Ojala, Carl F., and Michael T. Gadwood. "The Geography of Major League Baseball Player Production, 1876–1988" in Alvin L. Hill, ed., *Cooperstown Symposium on Baseball and the American Culture, 1989* (Westport, Conn.: Meckler, 1991).

Park, Roberta J. "San Franciscans at Work and at Play, 1846–1869," *Journal of the West* 22, no. 1 (January 1983).

Phelon, William A. "How the World's Series Was Lost and Won," *Baseball Magazine* 10, no. 2 (December 1912).

Rader, Benjamin G. "Compensatory Sport Heroes: Ruth, Grange and Dempsey," *Journal of Popular Culture* 16, no. 4 (Spring 1983).

Smith, James D. "Bowing Out on Top," *The National Pastime* (Fall 1982).

Smith, Leverett T., Jr. "The Babe in '74," *Journal of Sport History* 6, no. 2 (Summer 1979).

Smith, Ronald A. "The Rise of College Baseball," *Baseball History* 1, no. 1 (Spring 1986).

Stern, Joseph S., Sr. "The Team That Couldn't Be Beat: The Red Stockings of 1869," *Cincinnati Historical Society Bulletin* 27 (1969).

Sumner, Jim. "Baseball at Salisbury Prison Camp" in Peter Levine, ed., *Baseball History* (Westport, Conn.: Meckler, 1989).

Uhl, Mick. "The 1912 World Series," *All Star Replay* 2 (1979).

Voigt, David Q. "America's First Red Scare—The Cincinnati Reds of 1869," *Ohio History* 73 (1969).

Ward, John J. "Dividing the Big Money Right!" *Baseball Magazine* 20, no. 9 (January 1918).

———. "Harry Hooper of the Red Sox," *Baseball Magazine* 16, no. 7 (1915).

Zingg, Paul J. "Bitter Victory: The World Series of 1918—A Case Study in Major League Labor-Management Relations," *NINE: A Journal of Baseball History and Social Policy Perspectives* 1, no. 2 (March 1993).

———. "Diamond in the Rough: Baseball and the Study of American Sports History," *The History Teacher* 19, no. 3 (May 1986).

———. "Myth and Metaphor: Baseball in the History and Literature of American Sport," in Paul J. Zingg, *The Sporting Image: Readings in American Sport History* (Lanham, Md.: University Press of America, 1988).

———. "The Phoenix at Fenway: The 1915 World Series and the Collegiate Connection to the Major Leagues," *Journal of Sport History* 17, no. 1 (Spring 1990).

Index

PAUL J. ZINGG, a professor of history and provost and senior vice-president for academic affairs at California Polytechnic State University, San Luis Obispo, is the author of five other books on American sport history including *Runs, Hits, and an Era: The Pacific Coast League, 1903–1958; A Good Round: A Journey through the Landscapes and Memory of Golf; The Sporting Image: Readings in American Sport History;* and *Pride of the Palestra.*

Sport and Society

Making the American Team: Sport, Culture, and the Olympic Experience
  Mark Dyreson
Viva Baseball! Latin Major Leaguers and Their Special Hunger
  Samuel O. Regalado
Touching Base: Professional Baseball and American Culture in the Progressive
  Era (rev. ed.)   *Steven A. Riess*
Red Grange and the Rise of Modern Football   *John M. Carroll*
Golf and the American Country Club   *Richard J. Moss*
Extra Innings: Writing on Baseball   *Richard Peterson*
Global Games   *Maarten Van Bottenburg*
The Sporting World of the Modern South   *Edited by Patrick B. Miller*
The End of Baseball As We Knew It: The Players Union, 1960–81
  Charles P. Korr
Rocky Marciano: The Rock of His Times   *Russell Sullivan*
Saying It's So: A Cultural History of the Black Sox Scandal   *Daniel A. Nathan*
The Nazi Olympics: Sport, Politics, and Appeasement in the 1930s   *Edited by
  Arnd Krüger and William Murray*
The Unlevel Playing Field: A Documentary History of the African American
  Experience in Sport   *David K. Wiggins and Patrick B. Miller*
Sports in Zion: Mormon Recreation, 1890–1940   *Richard Ian Kimball*

REPRINT EDITIONS
The Nazi Olympics   *Richard D. Mandell*
Sports in the Western World (2d ed.)   *William J. Baker*